So You Want to Move to Florida

*How to Save Time and Money in Becoming a Resident
and Exploring Florida's Treasures*

Your Guide to Securing Your Dreams in Florida

by

Stan Farnham

authorHOUSE

*1663 LIBERTY DRIVE, SUITE 200
BLOOMINGTON, INDIANA 47403
(800) 839-8640
www.authorhouse.com*

First published by AuthorHouse 08/13/04

ISBN: 1-4184-5142-8 (sc)

Library of Congress Control Number: 2004094307

Printed in the United States of America
Bloomington, Indiana

This book is printed on acid-free paper.

Here's What People are Saying About
So You Want to Move to Florida

The chapter on Friendly Florida Flora is "pretty comprehensive for a non-gardening book. It should give newcomers a good 'feel' for what it's like to garden and keep up a yard in Florida."

> Kathy Nelson, Editor
> *Florida Gardening* Magazine

"I wish we had this book before we moved to Florida. Even after we moved here, we picked up cost and timesaving tips. The book is chock full of powerful information and practical advice."

> Maureen and Jerry Fischler
> Retired Customer Service Representative and Computer
> Supervisor, Moved to Florida, 2002

"Farnham's book captures the lure of the Florida lighthouses and should inspire new visitors to these treasures. The chapter on lighthouses is great!"

> Tom Taylor
> Author, Former President, Florida Lighthouse Association
> Editor, The Lighthouse Trail

"Wow. Well written and thought out chapter on 'Choosing and Living in a Florida Home.' All the necessary steps are included. All you need to do is read it and follow it. I wish I would have had such a book earlier to pass out to my clients."

> Laura Faustino, Realtor, South Bay Realty.
> Moved to Naples 2002

"We followed the chapter on 'Key West Mini Vacation' to the letter, had a great time and saved money. We were able to pinpoint and visit the attractions we wanted to see based on this book. We also enjoyed the restaurants."

> Sondra and Tom Greer
> Teacher and Basketball Coach
> Moved to Florida 2002

" We would have avoided some missteps when we moved to Florida, especially in buying our house with the features and upgrades, such as a three-car garage and tile floors, if this book had been available then. Even so, the book helped us. So we sold our first house, and bought one with these and other features we wanted later."

> Carole and Gary Neff
> Nurse and Optometrist
> Moved to Florida in 1999

"This book will give newcomers a good overview in three chapters of wildlife, birding and refuges to see and enjoy the wonders of natural Florida."

> Phil Nye, Master Naturalist

Dedication

*This book is dedicated to our Baby Boomer children
and their 77 million cohorts, born 1946 –1964,
for whom this book was especially written.*

*Steve and Sherry Farnham
Linda and Mike Colby
Tim and Pam Farnham
Marlene and Steve Bysted
Mike and Sue Farnham
Greg Farnham*

*In Memoriam
Tom Taylor (1949-2004)*

Website

For errata, web links and other information about moving to, and living in, Florida, see the supporting web site for this book. http://soyouwanttomovetoflorida.com. Throughout the book, and at the web site, we provide you helpful URLs (Uniform Resource Locator), which make it easier to check details. These can change. Those in the book were accurate at the time of writing.

Warning-Disclaimer

This book is designed to provide information on Florida residency. It is sold with the understanding the publisher and author are not engaged in providing legal, accounting or other professional services. If legal or other expert assistance is required, the services of a professional should be sought. Books do not, and cannot, substitute for competent legal help. Laws change and rules may vary from county to county. Sometimes general situations may not address your specific situation.

Further, our purpose is not to cover material already available, but complement and amplify other texts in simple English. Every effort has been made to make this book as complete and accurate as possible. There may, however, be mistakes, or information that is current only up to the publishing date.

In journalism school, the professors taught that reporters should not get emotionally involved in a story. "Check to be sure your own bias isn't creeping in," they admonished. Bias has crept in because we do like Florida, so we aren't entirely objective. When I use "we" in this book, this usually refers to wife Mary, who has been a partner in the adventures described in the book.

The author and publisher shall have neither liability nor responsibility to any person or entity with respect to any loss or damage caused, or alleged to have been caused, directly or indirectly, by the information contained in this book.

If you do not wish to be bound by the above, you may return this book to the publisher for a full refund.

Acknowledgements

This book has taken four years to research (including all our visits to Florida locations) and write. I appreciate the many people who offered encouragement or shared their experiences with us during our travels in Florida.

I am indebted to the people on the reader's panel, who helped by reviewing parts of the manuscript and making suggestions and noting corrections. These included Steve Bookbinder, Steve Farnham, Gregory Farnham, Mike Farnham, Laura Faustino, Sondra and Tom Greer, Carole and Gary Neff, and Natalie and Dennis Tracy.

Thank you to Tom Taylor for his encouragement, support and review of the chapter on lighthouses. Thank you to Phil Nye for sharing his expertise on birds and wildlife. Thank you to Kathy Nelson, who reviewed the chapter on Florida flora. Also, thanks to Ron Drake, Randy Essig, Chrissy Bianchi, and others for reviewing parts of the manuscript. A special thank you to Natalie Tracy and Linda Colby for manuscript proofreading.

I'm grateful to the people who have shared our adventures, too numerous to list, but including: Ray Caplis, Bob and Joan Cloward, Bob and Jane Corning, Curly (Walter) and Carolyn Draheim, Bea Foulks, Don and Sandy Glenton, Joe and Sue Greco, Werner and Betty Grimberg, Bob and Barbara Hamill, Hank and JoAnne Henricksen, Dennis and Lee James, Carol Licata, Theresa Oliva, Dave and Jane Pontius, Joan Potts, Charlie and Joan Siciliano, Helen Sjoblad, Joan and Pete Toole and Carol and Howard Walker.

Also: Ron and Chris Barette, Wally and Pearl David, Al and Norma Diamant, Jerry and Maureen Fischler, Al and Lucy Gonsalves, Al and Maggie Goodall, Tom and Sondra Greer, Bruno and Militta Kern, John and Chris Lozinak, Joe and Natalie Mandarano, Jim and Sandee Moore, Dave and Ginny Murray, John and Peggy Olney, Sue and Walter Pfeiffer, Ed and Diana Regnier, Tom and Marlene Sexton, Ray and Carole Shaw, Arleen and David Sivakoff, Dan and Carol Stoffel, Janet and John Stoffel, Gordon and Nieves Thompson, Joel and Karen Wagner.

Thanks to the association presidents (and alternates) who served on a master board with me, and shared their views and worked to improve the community, including Sherrill Booker, Dave Calimici, Lou Darovic, Ed Dionne, Jr., Carolyn Draheim, Robert Hughes, Jack Kingston, Helen Krieger, Bob Liston, Ed Makosh, Frank Meridith, Judy O'Donnell, Maury Olsen, Sheldon Reisman, George Riordan, Paul Rodewald, Bob Sempsey, Larry Shaw, Angelo Tiezzi and Howard Walker; and to association manager

Beatrice Diller, who competently juggled a number of associations, but always made the meetings and provided expertise.

Thanks to those who served with me on the Cinnamon Cove Single Family Association, including Bob Francess, Joe Licata, John Thurlow, Joan Toole, Paul Ripchik, and Roland Roy. Together we resolved some difficult issues and boosted the association performance for the benefit of all the homeowners.

Thank you to Waterways Ad Hoc Committee members who served with me during my time as chairman and helped develop the strategic plan: John DePrisco, Al Diamant, Rick Gamret, Paul Joyal, Joe Lofria, Cindy Mariconda, Sharon McCorkle, Lisa Saxton, Eddie Sharrett, Kevin Smith, John L. (Jake) Sullivan and Dave Sivakoff. Thanks also to the many volunteers, especially Nancy and Charlie Wright.

Thank you to those who granted permission to use their material in this book, including Paul Bradley, Tom Taylor, Chris Foster, Wae and Kathy Nelson (Florida Gardening Magazine), Dick Brewer of Corkscrew Swamp Sanctuary (bird photos), Bruno Kern (photo), Jack Canfield, Les Standiford, Buddy Taylor and others.

Contents

Introduction

" As a rule he who has the most information in life will have the greatest success in life. " Benjamin Disraeli

This book focuses sharply on not only living in Florida, but how and what to do to become a Florida resident. We learned the hard way. Our perspective comes from moving to Florida from the North, and not from being a native Floridian, or someone who has lived in Florida for years. Our experience has been earned from making lots of mistakes. You not only can learn from what we did, but save time and money by avoiding our mistakes.

We will provide you with some stories of our personal sights and sounds in the zoo that is Florida, a zoo without cages, fences or gates. Florida has a rich history and a vibrant future for you to enjoy. There are simple pleasures to living in Florida. Advertisements point to the lure of the outdoors, the unparalleled beauty of the sunset reflecting on the water, the feel on your toes as you stroll along the white powdery beaches, the smell of saltwater spray and the delight in watching pelicans and egrets perched on pilings waiting for a snack. Simply looking out the window and seeing palm trees evokes good feelings.

Over the years, we visited the Bahamas, Barbados, Cancun, Grand Cayman, and Hawaii, all of which have these pleasures. So, yes, you can enjoy those pleasures elsewhere, but not coupled with an easy-to-get-to location for children and grandchildren to visit, low-cost living (relatively speaking) and freedom from income, gift and inheritance taxes. People move to Florida for the climate, lifestyle and affordability. Job opportunities abound.

No place is perfect, however, and one person's progress can be another person's problem. That's life in fast growing Florida, where infrastructure hasn't always kept up with the population growth. The large numbers of new people coming to paradise tax resources. Traffic snarls during the season, over development, bugs, severe water restrictions because of dangerously low water tables during droughts, and the hurricane season can be more than irritating. Sun and surf, with balmy weather for outside leisure activities, make up for the irritants.

Florida, which is the most popular spot for America's tourists, has seven of the top ten attended theme parks in the United States. More than 43 million visitors come to Florida each year. Twenty million visitors a year travel just to Orlando with the theme parks an obvious big draw. So, tourists think of Florida as a land of theme parks for good reasons.

We will *not* talk in this book about the most visited destinations, however, which include Walt Disney World, Epcot Center, Disney-MGM Studios, Universal Studios, Sea World, Busch Gardens, Spaceport USA (Kennedy Space Center), Typhoon Lagoon, Lake Buena Vista, Church Street Station, and Miami Beach. Countless books, brochures and pamphlets already describe those popular attractions. We also will *not* describe all the entertainment, spectator and cultural activities, about which local newspapers keep you up-to-date.

Instead of theme parks and tourist attractions, we will share with you the resident lifestyle quest for happiness in tranquility, relaxation, and personal peace available in the paradise of Florida. From the Space Coast to the Gulf Coast, from the Panhandle to the Keys, Florida offers a wide variety of opportunities for this active lifestyle.

Tourists.

Most new residents came to Florida first as tourists, as we did. Our introduction to Florida was a business meeting on Marco Island, followed by a week of vacation. We wrote this book for tourists who fall in love with Florida as we did and plan to move to the sunshine state. Follow our tips to save time, money and hassle in fulfilling your dream.

The Purpose of This Book: What's In It For You?

The main purpose of this book is to help you avoid saying, "Had I known, I would have......." Or "I wish I had...."

- Had I known the need for storage, I would have added another garage.
- Had I known, I could have avoided some hassles in getting my license.
- Had I known, I would have specified tile, not carpet, in most of the house.
- Had I known, I would have gone on Wednesday for my license, not Monday.

- Had I known of the appreciation leverage, I would have bought a home in Florida sooner.
- Had I known about it, I would have filed for the homestead exemption.
- Had I known the value, I would have made our yard more Florida Friendly.

The book lays out straightforward questions and keen insights you need to shed light on a clear path to do a better job of moving to, and living in Florida. The book combines real-life experiences and learned lessons of Florida residents. Use our strategies for savings and for enjoying Florida, even if you already are a resident.

Learn How To:
- ✓ Establish Florida as your domicile.
- ✓ Save thousands of dollars, and avoid mistakes, in buying your new home.
- ✓ Avoid or minimize Florida intangible taxes.
- ✓ Lead vibrant, interesting lives in Florida.
- ✓ Protect your nest egg.
- ✓ Have a Florida friendly yard.
- ✓ Deal with the unique challenges and problems of Florida.
- ✓ Tap into 55 cost saving ideas.
- ✓ Do business in Florida.
- ✓ Identify birds and wildlife.
- ✓ Find the best places to visit as a resident.
- ✓ Find the best grouper sandwiches.

Are these things you can relate to? If so, this book can help you in a variety of ways to save money, time, hassles, avoid mistakes and to enhance your Florida living. And, of course, if you have already moved to Florida you can still benefit from reading this book and avoid some "Had I known about..." comments. If you follow the ideas I'm about to share with you, you could save yourself a bundle.

How to Get the Most Out of This Book.

Our goal was to make this book easy-to-read user-friendly. We have organized the book in a logical way to progress from learning the most compelling things you need to know as a newcomer in choosing a house, establishing residency, enhancing lifestyle and dealing with problems. After helping you understand the flora, fauna and wide variety of recreational activities available, chapters follow that will galvanize you to action in visiting the Florida treasures that will enrich your life. We have created new memories from experiences that give you a blueprint to do the same. We are confident the ideas will work for you because the ideas have already worked for us, and many of our family and friends.

Magic Threes.

Throughout the book we identify our favorite Top Three birds, animals, day trips, beaches, lighthouses, mini-vacations and activities. The "cool" factor weighed heavily with us in the ratings.

You'll also find three interest or expertise levels. You may want to think about taking the elevator to Level Three to get to a new level, because you'll meet and be with new people on a new playing field with new dreams and goals. If you don't know another person, clearly you need to look for people with a common interest. One of the best ways to do that is to go to the next level. This book will give you ideas about how to do that by participating at Level Three.

The local newspapers do a good job of briefly describing all the activities in the area each week, including churches, concerts, sports events and restaurants, which aren't a part of this book. The *Naples Daily News*, for example, has a section each Friday on all the local events and activities. Most newspapers have similar sections, including top circulation daily newspapers: *St. Petersburg Times, Miami Herald, Orlando Sentinel, South Florida Sentinel* (Fort Lauderdale) and *Tampa Tribune.*

See Florida magazine's 18 area free pamphlets (www.see-florida.com), such as *See South Florida,* provide you with all the attractions, local maps, restaurants, where to stay, advertisements and coupons. We recommend you use them as a resource. Our purpose differs by sharing with you our top three in each category and personal experiences. By focusing on the top three of things to do and see, you will be able to select the activities that best fit your unique needs and desires. These exciting experiences can unleash a new level of success for you and change your life profoundly. Moving to Florida should mean travel, recreation, having fun and eating out; not sitting around the house! Simply follow the plan in Chapter Nineteen after reading the first 18 chapters.

Chapter Overviews.

In Chapter One, we help you with some dos and don'ts for newcomers.

Chapter Two explains how to choose where to live with valuable money saving tips. This chapter can mean the difference to you of a happy choice or the later anxiety of second-guessing.

In Chapter Three, you'll find what you need to do to establish residency, get licenses and minimize taxes.

Chapter Four explains lifestyle after fifty, with some powerful guides to take life to a higher level; and valuable mental, physical and financial health hints.

In Chapter Five, you'll get a glimpse of the Calusa Indians and the best beaches. In Florida, because of the concentration of people near the coast, most people are minutes from world-famous beaches and islands. On the beach, with the sun reflecting on the water, you can find a personal inner peace, tranquility and calmness, while also achieving happiness in participating in beach activities.

Chapter Six tells you about Florida problems and how to best deal with them.

Chapter Seven tells you how to have a Florida friendly garden and lawn.

Chapters Eight, Nine, and Ten provide a basic primer for Florida wildlife, birds and wildlife refuges and parks to visit. You'll get a good non-technical overview in each of these chapters without eye-glazing details, but with the best reference resources to go to if you want to dig deeper. Get to know the birds and wildlife.

Chapter Eleven focuses on recreation in Florida (golfing, boating, fishing, shelling, swimming, and tennis) to give you a summary of differences as a resident, rather than a visitor; including how to save money.

Chapter Twelve describes some day trips. It starts the first of five chapters on enjoying Florida; places to go, things to see and learn. If these strike a cord within your heartstrings, decide now to take the trip or visit the area or attraction. We have picked ones we enjoyed, but also referenced guidebooks for detailed descriptions of state parks (157), lighthouses (30), national parks (3), beaches, cities, and other attractions. Finally, during our travels we started paying close attention to restaurants and started seeking out "the best grouper sandwich." The results of our culinary search are described in Chapter Seventeen.

Chapter Eighteen summarizes powerful cost busting and timesaving tips mentioned in the book you have in your hands that will put thousands of dollars in your pocket!

Use Chapter Nineteen to prioritize your activities for the next five years to enhance your lifestyle and boost your savings. Planning needs to be on the front burner. We'll tell you how.

Are we Happy in Florida?

The simple answer is yes: especially when the snow piles up and the temperature plummets up North. Despite the problems described in Chapter Six, we love it here. We have found our paradise. We've learned much about living in Florida, which we are delighted to share with you in this book. Are we living in paradise? You bet. And loving every minute of it.

Chapter One
Florida Lifestyle and Lingo

Brief Florida History.

"If God made a better place, he kept it to himself," a neighbor exclaimed. Although humans may have inhabited Florida for 10,000 years, there are fewer than 500 years of recorded history of this "best place." The extraordinary growth and momentous change in Florida, however, has been in the century and a half since statehood.

The cultural transition from a nomadic life to villages occurred during the years 500-900, according to most historians. The Spanish explorers then "discovered" the villages of the Indians in Florida 600 years later.

Juan Ponce de León, the sixteenth century Spanish explorer who visited here in 1513 and 1521, named Florida "Pasque Florida." In Spanish, it means festival of flowers at Easter. Many historians now dispute the oft repeated search for the Fountain of Youth as the reason for Ponce de Leon to travel April 8, 1513 to the peninsula he named "Florida." Whatever the reason for his adventure, it ended badly. The Spaniards fought the Calusa Indians. Juan died from an infection of a suppurating arrow wound in the thigh in 1521; perhaps why the Spaniards called the area near Sanibel Island, Matanzas (massacre). The native population at that time was 350,000.

Hernando de Soto (1497-1542) brought five large and four small ships with 600 soldiers in 1539 and marched north from Tampa as far as Arkansas. Pedro Menéndez de Avilés (1519-1574) brought ten ships and more than a thousand men in 1565 to St. Augustine. Spain then ruled Florida except for a couple of decades of British control after King George III victory in the Seven Years War in 1763. Earlier in 1702 and 1740, Castillo de San

1

Marcos, the fort in St. Augustine, saved the city and Spanish Florida from British conquest.

The Europeans brought diseases, slaving raids, and war that effectively wiped out the Calusa Indians by the late eighteenth century. Only the small populations of Seminole and Miccosukee Indians remain, although some archeologists believe some Calusa Indians survived and went to Cuba.

More than 300 years passed before Spain ceded Florida to the United States in a treaty February 22, 1819. General Andrew Jackson "received" Florida from Spain in 1821. Florida became the twenty-seventh state March 3, 1845. In 1861, with the outbreak of the Civil War, the population of Florida was just 140,000, the least populous of the Confederate States. Now more than 17 million call Florida home.

As a newcomer, knowing the names of major developers, and what they did, will give you an insight into Florida history during the late nineteenth and early twentieth centuries: Henry Flagler (1830-1913), Henry B. Plant (1819-1899), Hamilton Disston (1844-1896), Barron G. Collier (1873-1939) and George Merrick (1886-1942).

Henry Flagler, called the "father of modern Florida," developed the Florida east coast starting in 1885, reached Key West with his railroad in 1912. You'll learn more about him later.

Henry B. Plant developed the Gulf Coast with railroads, steamships and eight hotels. Plant's opulent Moorish Tampa Bay Hotel, built in 1891, is now Plant Hall of the University of Tampa. The Hall also houses The Henry B. Plant museum. During the Spanish American War (1898), Colonel Teddy Roosevelt and the Rough Riders trained nearby. Roosevelt, the generals and officers stayed at the hotel, before embarking with the troops to Cuba from Tampa.

Although Henry S. Sanford (1823-1891) wasn't a major developer, he did found Sanford in Seminole County in 1870 and led the way for rail lines that extended to the interior of central Florida. So, three Henry's played the major roles in the railroads: east (Flagler), central (Sanford) and west (Plant).

Hamilton Disston (1844-1896) at age 36, in 1881, presciently bought four million acres from the state of Florida for one million dollars, and became the largest single landowner in the U.S. at the time. He bailed Florida out of debt. Later he ran into cash flow problems, so he did not have the impact of the other developers, but imagine what his land in and around Walt Disney World would be worth today.

Barron G. Collier, who had made his fortune selling advertising card franchises for train and subway lines, visited Florida from New York in 1911. He became "mesmerized by its beauty" and "captivated by the warm climate and golden sunshine," which have lured so many to Florida before and after him. He bought Useppa Island for $100,000 in 1911 and built a luxury hotel. He amassed 1.3 million acres during 1921-1923, to become the largest landowner in the state at the time of his death (1939). He helped build the Tamiami Trail and provided funds to complete it, but he also drilled for oil in Sunniland and drained some of the Everglades for development. He turned over to the state the land that became the 6,430-acre Collier Seminole State Park.

Collier County, Barron Collier High School, and Collier Seminole State Park honor his name. The Barron Collier Company he founded continues with third and fourth generation family members.

Merrick envisioned and built the "City Beautiful," Coral Gables in 1922, one of the first planned communities in the United States. The Biltmore Hotel, the Venetian Pool, city hall and broad tree-lined boulevards attest to his vision.

These visionary developers impacted the ecosystems in both positive and negative ways. During the Depression, the CCC (Civilian Conservation Corps) also had an impact by employing 50,000 Floridians, ages 18 to 25 years old, to plant millions of trees and work on numerous state parks.

Among women born in the nineteenth century, several had a major influence on Florida in the twentieth century: Dr. Mary McLeod Bethune (1875-1955), Marjory Stoneman Douglas (1890-1998), Marjorie Kinnan Rawlings (1896-1953) and Anna Brenner Meyers (1896-1983).

Bethune founded Bethune-Cookman College in 1904, served as president until 1942. She said, "From the first, I made my learning, what little it was, useful every way I could." That she did! She received the Great Floridian award in 2002. Douglas, of course, wrote *The Everglades-River of Grass* and worked to preserve and restore the Everglades. Rawlings wrote the 1939 Pulitzer prize-winning *The Yearling.* The 1948 movie starred Gregory Peck, Jane Wyman and Claude Jarman, Jr. The book, a compelling story of a boy growing up in the hard times of frontier life in the swamps, also provides a perspective on the Florida interior before the turn of the nineteenth century. She also authored *Cross Creek.* She lived in Cross Creek, Florida. Meyers pioneered efforts to desegregate schools and established Miami-Dade Community College. She received the Great Floridian award in 2000.

My top three Floridians from this era: Flagler, Douglas and Collier, followed closely by Bethune, Merrick and Plant. As Ralph Waldo Emerson said: "All history resolves itself very easily into the biography of a few stout and earnest persons." Flagler and Plant received the Great Floridian award in 2003.

That gives you a quick outline of Florida history with a look at important Floridians and some key milestones. You will find more historical information throughout this book. History will come alive when you visit the places described, but let's skip along to focus on the here and now. You can find plenty of books on the history of Florida, and biographies of the important Floridians, but we want to help you enjoy Florida today! Come along and share our experiences. If you want to soak up Florida's history in detail, read *The New History of Florida* edited by Michael Gannon.

Florida Today.

Today a busy weekend at Disney World attracts more people than lived in Florida a century and a half ago! Traffic during the season resembles the long lines at Disney's Space Mountain.

Fast growing Florida ranks among the most livable areas in the United States. Air conditioning and mosquito control made Florida habitable for humans. When you think of it, people flock to Florida for one primary reason—the weather. To paraphrase a politician: It's the weather, stupid. But, no income taxes and no inheritance taxes help as reasons. So does the lifestyle. Cloudy, dull days and long cold nights make life dull and can lead to depression; all of which improves with Sunshine State light!

In a Lou Harris poll in 1997, Florida was the first choice of Americans as the place they'd like to live other than their current state. (Arizona was runner-up, followed by California and Colorado)

Crunch the numbers.

The numbers do tell a story. In just forty years, Florida jumped from twentieth to fourth place in population in the United States with a dazzling growth pace. The population added more than three million newcomers in the 1990s, growing 23 percent to 15.9 million persons (U.S. Census Bureau estimated 17 million in 2003), although Southwest Florida grew an even faster 39 percent. Only California and Texas added more people. Nine of the nation's fastest growing metropolitan areas are in Florida: Ocala, Bradenton, Ft. Myers, Naples, Daytona Beach, Orlando, Melbourne, Ft. Pierce and West Palm Beach. The state estimates 2010 population will grow to more than 19 million. Perhaps that's too optimistic. Another estimate shows reaching that level in 2024. Clearly, fast-track growth continues.

In Southwest Florida, Lee County (Ft. Myers) has more than doubled in just 20 years. Nearby Collier County (Naples) jumped 65.3 percent in the 1990s to more than 251,000, then to more than 291,000 by 2003. Fast growing Lee County has been adding 1,500 persons a month and Collier County 1,000 a month. Cape Coral had a population of 5,000 in 1970; now the population has soared past 100,000. Miami-Dade County shot up from 1.9 million in 1990 to more than 2.25 million persons in 2000.

The graying of the 77-million Baby Boom generation (born 1946-1964), and the longer life expectancies, will boost market growth for retirement homes. Experts see this already fast-growing market on the verge of another boom because of baby boomers.

Just over half the Florida population lives in the largest cities of Tampa-St. Petersburg-Clearwater, Miami, Orlando, Fort Lauderdale and Jacksonville. Two-thirds of the population lives along the coasts. Not surprising, when you realize Florida has 8,246 miles of tidal coastline. The tourism departments identify lots of "coasts:" The Space Coast (Brevard County); the Gold Coast (Palm Beach County), Nature Coast (west coast of Florida from Wakulla County south through Pesco County), the Paradise Coast (Collier County, changed from "Classic Florida"), Emerald Coast (Pensacola), Forgotten Coast (Port St. Joe east of Panama City) and Lee Island Coast (changed in 2003 to Beaches of Fort Myers and Sanibel).

The largest counties: Miami-Dade (Miami) and Broward (Fort Lauderdale) in the southeast, Palm Beach on the Treasure Coast, Orange (Orlando) in central Florida, Hillsborough (Tampa) on the Gulf Coast, Duval (Jacksonville) in the northeast and Lee (Fort Myers) in the southwest.

You can find a plethora of statistics and information for Florida's 67 counties at the official portal of the state at www.myflorida.com and Florida Enterprise site at www.eflorida.com.

Florida Seasons.

Some of the people who don't live here say we have no seasons in the Sunshine State. After all, the average year-round temperature is above 70 degrees Fahrenheit. The sun, on more than 300 paradise days, "kisses the soft white sand beaches and washes across the sea." We are just minutes from beaches and Gulf waters. Unlike the North, where changing color of leaves, temperature and snow can define seasons, Florida does have seasons, but of a different kind. The sign of a change in season starts in the spring with the migration of Northerners returning home. The tourist season has ended.

The northern lands of Florida have more distinct seasons and climate changes with hard freezes and even snow. In the southern lands, anything other than warm weather is unusual. No snow has fallen in the south.

If the northern United States has two seasons of winter and road construction, Florida has two seasons: with, and without, tourists and snowbirds. The tourist season peaks in the months after Christmas and before Easter. Many snowbirds live in Florida from November to April or May, then live in the North the rest of the year. These two seasons make a big difference in the ease or difficulty for you in everything from getting licenses to dining in a restaurant. In the tourist season, count on long lines. So, the first tip is to get licenses and move during the slow season!

To put the population change in perspective, Ft. Myers Beach, with 7,000 year-round residents, swells to 40,000 persons in season. The population of Sanibel and Captiva Islands soars from 6,000 to 25,000. Collier County blossoms by more than a third from 291,000 (2003) to more than 405,000 at season peak. That guarantees heavy traffic!

Most locations in Florida face the dilemma of a desire to welcome tourists and their dollars to support the economy, and perhaps, some resentment over their effect on lifestyle. Residents may be a bit ambivalent about tourists, because they affect the fragility of the ecology, but their absence affects the fragility of the economy! Residents know Florida's economy depends primarily on a three-legged stool of tourism, construction and agriculture, but tourism and construction are the top two and interrelated. People not only flock here for vacation, but many then move here in increasing numbers. For those who live in Florida, the explosive growth happens best when schools, roads and other basics are in place concurrently with the added population.

When the tourist season ends, the traffic thins and full-time residents don't have to wait an hour to get in their favorite restaurant. Bargains exist that haven't been available for five months as lower off-season prices apply. The stores have more sales events to help boost their business. Restaurants offer discount coupons to attract patrons. You can find deserted beaches.

One morning in July, we had breakfast outdoors at a beach café after walking a mile up the beach. We saw only four people during our walk on what during the season would be a crowded beach. The temperature was 72, the cloudless cerulean sky brightened with the rising sun. Gorgeous day. Only one other table was occupied!

During our beach walk, we saw an osprey perched in a tree. We saw a swallow-tailed kite, a black-and-white bird of prey, swooping. Pelicans soared along as we walked. The migratory birds leave, along with people. We stay. So do the bald eagle, sand hill crane, belted kingfisher and many egrets. An old saying declares, "people who live at the seashore eventually stop hearing the waves." No. Who could tire of the sound of waves, palm fronds rustling in the ocean breeze, powder-white beaches, vibrant colors of the setting sun and a year-round average temperature of 74 degrees? Most visitors miss the best "seasons" of April/May and then later, October/November.

With the departure of the tourists and snowbirds, many Floridians take vacations within the state. Summer can be a good time to visit now less-crowded places like the Everglades, Key West and other attractions described in this book. Of course, there's yet another season of summer downpours and hurricanes, along with pesky mosquitoes and no-se-ums.

Year-Round Swimming.

One of the great things about living in Florida is the chance to swim year-round. Florida leads the nation in swimming pools with 89.4 per 1,000 people (Arizona is second with 73.7 per 1,000 people).

Citrus, Boats and Golf Courses.

Florida is first in the nation in citrus production, but you knew that!

For golfers, Florida has more than 1,370 golf courses of nine holes or more, with total holes approaching 19,000! Southwest Florida claims more golf holes per capita than any region in the United States, with, at last count, 155 golf courses.

Florida has a large registered boat population. Lee County alone has more than 40,000 registered boats, for one of the highest boat ownership per capita rates in the United States, although smaller Collier County with more than 21,000 registered boats is a close second with one boat for every 12 residents, according to the Florida Department of Highway Safety and Motor Vehicles. More than 22,000 boats are registered in the Florida Keys. Clearly, boating is a major pastime.

So, you have some outstanding reasons to pick Florida for your new residence, whether full-time, part-time or for vacations. Ten retirees move to Florida every hour. If you are one of them, or plan to be, then this book will help you.

Good News/Bad News: Healthy Lifestyle/Unhealthy Lifestyle.

Organic Style Magazine named Fort Myers the number one healthiest city in the southeast, and fifth out of the 125 cities ranked (Santa Fe, New Mexico ranked first overall). Living in Florida, whether Fort Myers, or elsewhere, is a healthy lifestyle.

"People live longer," neighbor Bob said. "I think it's because you are able to get outside all year and be active. Sunshine means a happier outlook, than cold, dark and dreary where we came from."

On the other hand, Florida can be hazardous to your health. Chapter Six explains some of the problems in paradise, and what you can do to avoid them or prepare for them.

Dos and Don'ts for Newcomers

Florida led the nation with the fewest number of native-born residents in 2000. According to a U.S. Census Bureau report, less than a third of Floridians are native born. In Southwest Florida, more than three-fourths of the population came from another state! So as a newcomer, you are in good company. Most of those who moved to Florida, pulled like the tides to white sandy beaches, didn't know another person. It's not always easy to meet new people, but knowing some of the Dos and Don'ts and Florida lingo will help you. Having a positive Florida attitude also helps.

Top Three Dos and Don'ts.

1. Don't jump in the pool at night without turning on the pool light.
2. Stingray Shuffle. Shuffling your feet in the water can help you avoid a painful sting, during May into September. If you do get stung, put your foot in hot water (as hot as you can stand). The pain will go away because hot water kills the enzymes in the stingray's venom. Then, get an x-ray to check if pieces of the stingray's spine were left in the wound (which is rare). Stingrays mate in spring, with young ones staying close to shore after being born. They later head for deeper water as they mature.
3. Leave your lawnmower up north if the deck does not allow you to cut grass at least four inches height.

Other Dos and Don'ts.

4. Don't feed the alligators. DON'T FEED THE ALLIGATORS. If you do they'll lose their natural fear of people and become a problem.
5. Don't walk your small dog near a lake.
6. Know the difference between an anhinga and a cormorant, an ibis and an egret so you can impress your northern visitors. See Chapter Nine.
7. Cockroaches here are bigger than up North; and are called palmetto bugs.
8. Anything wet will mildew. Mold can be a very big problem.
9. Having two refrigerators can be a good idea. We have a second one in the garage.
10. Realize in Florida you measure distance in minutes. For example: How far is the mall? Twenty minutes.
11. Sand spurs grow in lawns, sandy areas and beach dunes. These sharp-spine spurs cling to clothes and can be painful to touch. The solution: moisten two fingertips, and then gently pull straight out.
12. Don't kick at mounds of dirt in the yard. They could hold thousands of red fire ants. Walking barefoot in the "grass" can also be dangerous because of fire ants.

Helpful Florida Things to Know and to Show you Aren't a Newcomer (or for Trivia games).

Top Three Things to Know!

1. No city in Florida is more than 75 miles from either the Atlantic Ocean or the Gulf of Mexico

2. Why do you see so many cars parked a long way from the mall? To park in the shade. The best parking spot is determined by shade, not distance.

3. Swamp Cabbage. The more genteel up-north term is heart of palm; it comes from the state tree, the Sable Palm.

26 More Helpful Things to Know.

4. The state reptile is the alligator and the state marine mammal is the Manatee.

5. The state tree is the Sabal Palm (also called Cabbage Palm). The sabal has a majesty that sets it apart, it grows in almost any soil, and it has uses in food and medicine.

6. Florida is the only state with two state fish: Largemouth Bass and Atlantic Sailfish.   \

7. Lanai. What is a lanai? Lanai (pronounced luh-NYE) is a Hawaiian word that means "a veranda or patio."

8. Chickee Hut. Thatched roof shelter or small building.

9. When judging the ripeness of oranges and grapefruits, color is not the important factor; weight is. The heaviest you find will generally be the sweetest and juiciest.

10. Gatorade, the popular sports drink, was first developed at the University of Florida, and named for the Florida "Gators" football team.

11. The phrase "cool as a cucumber" originated in Florida. On a hot day, the pulp of a cucumber can be up to 10 degrees Fahrenheit cooler than the surrounding air.

12. Here's a "Who-is-buried-in-Grant's-tomb?" easy kind of question for you. What is the state beverage? Orange juice became the official Florida state beverage in 1967.

13. Florida has 4,510 islands that are 10 acres or more in size, second only to Alaska in the United States

14. Orlando has 110,000 hotel rooms, second only to Las Vegas with 126,000.

15. In July, farmers feed their chicken's crushed ice to keep them from laying boiled eggs. Hey, just a joke, folks.

16. The first grapefruit tree was planted near Tampa in 1823. Christopher Columbus brought the first orange trees. The

first one planted in Florida was in 1565 and planted in St. Augustine.

17. Florida has the second-most loggerhead turtle nests in the world.

18. Florida is one of the few places where you may switch from "heat" to "A/C" in the same day.

19. All the Florida festivals seem to be named after a fruit, vegetable, grain, insect or animal.

20. Although California and Texas lead the way in total number of horses (678,000 and 642,000, respectively), Florida ranks third with 299,000 according to the American Horse Council. The Ocala area has trademarked the claim: "Horse Capital of the World."

21. Naples, Florida has more CEOs per capita living in the community than anywhere else in the world.

22. Florida's Ten Thousand Islands comprise the world's largest mangrove forest.

23. The National Marine Manufacturers Association statistics show that Florida, with 4,917 boat-related businesses, has more than twice as many as second-place Michigan with 2,212.

24. Florida has 1,700 lakes of 10 acres or more (7,700 total).

25. The Florida geology boasts 300 clear springs, more than anywhere in the world.

26. Florida has 21 military installations with the best known of these Cape Canaveral, Pensacola Naval Air Station, and MacDill Air Force Base.

27. The first scheduled airline service was between St. Petersburg and Tampa.

28. Florida has more spring water than is held in all the Great Lakes combined from hundreds of springs that bubble to the surface (all in the north of Florida), including some of the biggest and deepest on earth.

29. Florida is one of only two states with names that begin with double consonants. (The other is Rhode Island.)

Florida Attitude.

We have lived in 18 different homes. What is the key lesson learned? Don't compare. Life is too short to worry about what your new home or area doesn't have, compared to what you had before. Cherish the positives of your new area. Look for the new experiences, and the wow moments, to enrich your life. Life, which is truly a gift from God, should be savored every day in every way.

A Florida attitude comes out in the lyrics of a Chris Foster song: "This little piece of paradise has everything, you'll never want to leave after you come." He is singing about Cayo Hueso (Key West), but the thought applies to our little piece of paradise.

Experts say to seize every minute as opposed to simply living day-to-day, mourning the past and worrying about the future. Good advice. When you no longer talk wistfully about "up North," you will start making Floridians feel you are one of them. That usually happens when the snowbird becomes a full-time resident and sells the place up North, as we did. Bumper sticker wisdom says: "We Don't Care How You Did It Up North."

Sharply focus on keeping two things in particular in good shape; your health and your finances. See Chapter Four. According to an American Psychological Association study, people with positive attitudes about aging live more than seven years longer than those with negative attitudes. "Have easy-to-reach goals, visualize what you want, repeat affirmative statements, believe you are healthy and form positive habits." Easy to say, sometimes not so easy to do, but life can be short, so you need to do what you want to do. In this book we provide you with a lot of choices. Don't wait.

"How far you go in life depends on your being tender with the young, compassionate with the aged, sympathetic with the striving, and tolerant of the weak and strong, because someday in your life, you will have been all of these," said George Washington Carver.

Unique Florida Treats.

You'll look forward to January so you can enjoy Florida's gourmet fruit, the honey bell tangelo. It's colorful, uniquely shaped, sweet and easy to peel. It's so juicy you'll need to have a napkin handy. We love them, but there's one problem. They're available only in January!

Honey Tangerines, "sweet as honey" and "easy to peel" come in February and March. February is also National Grapefruit week with heart healthy choices of ruby red, star ruby or white. The succulent golden Valencia is the last orange of the Florida citrus season, available in March through May.

The Tree of Gold blooms in mid March to signal the peak of the tourist season and that spring is around the corner. You can walk out your door in March and smell the tangy essence of orange blossoms, saturating the air like dense fog. The striking blue flag iris adds blue and purple blossoms along wetland trails in March and into April.

The bell-shaped purple flowers of the Jacaranda tree add color to April.

May has to be Florida's best-kept secret with beautiful weather and quiet because the snowbirds and tourists have left.

Tarpon season brings sport fishermen to Florida, especially June/July to Boca Grande.

July and August provide our favorite fruit, mangoes.

September ushers in a month merchants dread with the low point in business. Even the barber wails, "no one gets a haircut in September." But September has opportunities for residents to get things done before the onrush of the season.

In October, we saw the wild coco and scented ladies tresses orchids near Corkscrew Swamp; and the endangered species clamshell orchid at the Fakahatchee Strand.

How about stone crabs? Terrific, but they're available only in season. We're ready to line up October 15 for the first day of stone crab season (October 15-May 15), which brings the delectable, and ecologically correct, stone crab claws. The meaty claws can be snapped off, while the rest of the crab gets returned to the water, where the claw will renew in a year or so. In Florida, Gulf Coast residents enjoy these crustacean's claws first. Stone crabs produce claws three times in two years. We like them chilled with a mustard sauce. Some purists, however, don't use anything except perhaps melted butter and some lemon to add zest.

Birds return, including snowbirds (the human kind), starting with a trickle in October then an increasing-stream in November and December. You see only a few out-of-state license plates in the summer, but by December they are everywhere.

What to do when you move to Florida.

The next two chapters will help you to know what to do when you move to Florida, how to do it, and how to save time and money doing it. Moving can be stressful, so getting key things done in advance as described in the two chapters, will reduce your stress of the transition.

List 99 things you want to do, in the next five years, based on this book.

If you follow the system I'm about to share with you, you could save thousands of dollars and enhance your lifestyle at the same time. Setting up the system is easy. It is simple and straightforward. As you go through the book, make a note of all the things you'd like to do. Then, after completing the book, list all of these in Chapter Nineteen and follow the instructions. Bingo, you have a plan! With challenging and exciting things to do you will avoid settling into boredom and get the most from living in Florida.

Chapter Two
Choosing and Living in a
Florida Home

Where to Live in Florida.

You can live in any one of many great places in Florida. To find your ideal place that fits what you want to do, check out www.fl.living.net/community/. This site gives you information on real estate, schools, major employers, climate and what's happening in 50 Florida locations.

When we first thought about a place to retire, we read several books on retirement locations. One of these was *"Fifty Fabulous Places to Retire in America,"* by Lee and Saralee Rosenberg. The authors asked many retirees where they were moving, along with asking realtors, long-distance movers, chamber of commerce people, AARP people, and others. They narrowed a list of more than 100 places to the 50 they selected for their book.

"Finally a pattern began to emerge," they wrote. "Predictably we heard about the three S's of relocation: St. Petersburg, Scottsdale and San Diego. And about the latest 'hot spots': Las Vegas, Santa Fe and Naples."

We visited all six of these and most of the 50 locations. We looked at houses in Scottsdale and Las Vegas. We subscribed to Sunday newspapers. But, we kept coming back to a preference for Florida. We vacationed on Marco Island, south of Naples, for several years. We rented condos and stayed on Marco Island and Fort Myers Beach several times. We also stayed in condos at New Smyrna Beach, St. Petersburg Beach and Orlando. We visited an adult community near Ocala. We vacationed in Panama City. So we visited both coasts and interior regions.

Additionally, I was fortunate to have flown to Florida on business a number of times. I traveled with our sales people, by car, to visit customers in Ocala, Orlando, Jacksonville, Daytona Beach, Fort Pierce, Melbourne, Miami, Fort Myers, Tampa, Polk City, and Gainesville. On two of the trips, we made a giant circle starting at Orlando and going down one coast and up the other.

Perhaps this gave me the best understanding of Florida living, because after the first trip in a January, all the other business trips were in the summer. My purpose was to visit customers to show we cared, to ask questions and listen, and to support our people in the field. The first customer we visited on the first trip in January said: "Yeah, yeah, you suits just want to get away from that frozen tundra in Wisconsin and come to sunny Florida in winter."

So, my trips after that were in June, July or August. I learned about heat, humidity and the four p.m. thunderstorms that pop up many summer afternoons. If you plan to live in Florida, visit at least once in summer! Based on our experience, your best first step is to pick areas you believe you'd like, and then visit them. You can narrow the search by using the Internet.

When we vacationed, we usually took a day or two to go look at condos and houses. We talked to people other than the realtors, including people who lived in the community, people we met in stores and restaurants. The locals know best! We also took a lot of photographs, picked up and saved brochures on homes and communities.

Visiting the regions in Florida also helps give you a feel for the weather. Below Sarasota, for example, the region is sub-tropical. Living in Naples, the temperature in winter often is 10 degrees, or more, warmer than living in the northern part of the state. It's also hotter and more humid in summer. Northern Florida is more affordable than southern Florida. Homes in Ocala or Pensacola cost less than homes in Naples or Fort Lauderdale, although, like politics, all real estate is local, so home prices vary.

When we decided to buy, we bought a single-family home in a gated community in Fort Myers, near but not on the beach.

Summary, Eight Tips For Picking a Location.

1. Visit several places in the state in the different regions.
2. Rent before buying.
3. Subscribe to local papers. You can track the building activity, real estate values and the community problems by subscribing to the Sunday paper.
4. Visit in the summer rather than just in the season.
5. Ask questions and listen. Ask the locals!

6. Take photographs, notes and pick up brochures to look at later.
7. Timing. Consider looking at homes in the off-season, when builders frequently offer incentives. You'll pay less by buying straw hats during December in the North and buying homes in Florida, June-September.
8. "Location, location, location" may be the first law of real estate but in Florida translate it to "water, water, water." A realtor told an incredulous potential buyer who couldn't believe a $1.3 million price for what appeared a modest home: "Yes, the home is a less than $300,000 home, but it is on a $1 million lot."

Buy Sooner or Later?

What would we do differently? Buy earlier. We didn't buy earlier than we did, because we enjoyed the places we visited on vacation, and the variety. We also traveled a great deal. Nearly all our vacations were either a week, or tied into a business trip of a week or less. If you can break away for longer times, then buy sooner. You'll have enough stress retiring and moving, so buying sooner will ready yourself for the move and adjustment. Looking back, the appreciation of real estate has made it a good investment. That is still true. *The Wall Street Journal,* October 29, 2003, noted that 68.4% of United States households own a home, the most ever. Some thought this the peak of a "bubble." Long term your home makes a good investment. Real estate values depend largely on the health of the *local* economy. Real estate value is *local*.

After a few years in Fort Myers, we later bought a larger home in Naples, on a lake, and with a swimming pool. If we were making a new pro/con list today for all the places we have been, we would choose Southwest Florida; even using 20-20 hindsight; and buy sooner rather than later had we known what we are sharing with you in this book.

Friends told us: "We went up and down both coasts of Florida, and Naples was far and away the best place." Other friends picked Largo. Other friends picked the Orlando area. Each of us has different wants and needs.

Although baby-boomers Larry and Ann, for example, don't plan to retire for another five years or more, they've been thinking for some time about buying a second home in Florida. That home can serve as a vacation residence and provide some rental income until the couple can use it on a more permanent basis. They'll join thousands of others taking this approach. You can do the same. Using these steps in identifying where to

15

relocate will help them, and you, save time and money and make the best decisions.

If you buy a $200,000 home with 20 percent down, and it appreciates just five percent a year, you would have a 100 percent return (approximately) in less than four years. What if you pay just 10 percent down ($20,000)? If it appreciates five percent the first year, you will have a 50 percent return in just one year! If you are 55 years old, and plan to retire at 60, buying a home at 55 rather than at 60 could be the best use of your investment money. If in five years, or later, you want to buy a new home, you undoubtedly will turn a tidy profit on the one you bought ahead of the next boom.

In summary, if you buy now, you know you have purchased a solid asset, because property values continue to appreciate. If you want to move later, the increased value will help you with the purchase of a new property.

What Can You Afford?

Financial advisers say the rule of thumb for a house payment (principal, interest, taxes and hazard insurance) should add up to no more than 28 percent of take-home pay. Others recommend a maximum home value of 2-1/2 times your income. Planners don't want you to have more than 36 percent of total debt payments, so if you spend 28 percent on the house, that means eight percent or less on car payments and other monthly payments. You can increase the amount for a home by not having other payments.

Don't forget the cost of maintenance, taxes and repairs, which can average more than the cost of principal and interest of a house payment. Remember, too, closing costs, which can be two percent or more of the purchase price, pre-paid (insurance, taxes) and moving expenses. Take into account your lifestyle change with a move. The bottom line: be sure the mortgage payment fits comfortably in you finances.

Condos, Villas, Coach Homes, Carriage Homes, Garden Condos, Pool Villas, Courtyard Villas, Townhouses, Single-Family Homes.

Some definitions are in order because the terms can be confusing, even when you think you know what the term means, like the obvious one of "single-family home." This does mean a detached home, as you would expect, but in a condominium association, you may not own the land or the exterior of the house. The idea of a single-family home as a "condominium" confuses some people. Further, homes come in a vast array of architectural styles. A single-family home in a condominium association is treated differently than a single-family home in a homeowners association. There is a big difference and one you should understand before you buy. We'll tell you why in this chapter.

16

Villas generally mean attached units of one story. Some are essentially duplexes. Other builders will string three or four or five together.

Detached villas mean units that are not connected, but close to one another in a zero lot line approach. Typically these units will have very small front and back yards and be just 10 feet from the neighboring villa. Zero-lot line homes are sometimes marketed as garden homes or patio homes.

Builders distinguish villas by arranging them in a rectangle around a courtyard (*courtyard villas*) or a swimming pool (*pool villas*). Carriage houses, townhouses and coach homes usually mean attached units of two stories. Typically a building will have four or six units.

The word condominium refers to a legal form of ownership, not a particular type of property, but "condos" typically are apartments in a building, often a high rise. To add to the confusion, one builder might call a unit a villa, that others may call a condo. And vice versa.

One other category is assisted living facilities that have 24-hour nursing staff available. Costs are all-inclusive and vary depending on the level of care and amenities offered.

Square Feet.

In a middle-class mixed development of condos, villas and single-family homes, the condos are 850-1,050 square feet, two-bedroom, two-bath villas 1,000-1,200 square feet and single family homes 1,400-1,750 square feet.

In another more expensive community, "coach" homes are 1,480-1,850 square feet, villas 1,670-1,750 square feet and "estate" homes 1,825-2,845 square feet.

In a single-family home community, seven models range from a three-bedroom, two-bath model at 1,728 square feet to a four-bedroom, three-bath plus den at 3,014 square feet.

Size, and the community, are perhaps more important than what the unit is called. The other important thing to know about square feet is whether it is "total" (which includes garage, entry, lanai) or "living space under air." Don't compare "total" of one house with "under air" of another. For example a home with 3,300 square feet probably has "under air" 2,600 square feet.

What are Teardown and Move-Up Homes?

Teardown homes are old homes, usually on a valuable beachfront, waterfront or intracoastal lot, which are demolished to make way for a new luxury home. Move-up homes are luxury homes that homebuyers purchase to "move-up" from a smaller, less-expensive home. Sometimes, buyers fail to consider fully all the increased costs in trading up, including higher property taxes, insurance costs, utility bills, and maintenance. Furnishing a new home adds a lot of hidden expenses, too.

What are Luxury Homes?

Developer advertisements bandy words like magnificent, stunning, opulent, exceptional, gorgeous and luxurious with the abandon of a circus barker. Luxury and estate homes can be 3,000 square feet costing $300,000 and more, but most define luxury homes above $1 million. One community advertises "luxury homes" of "3,000 to 5,000 square feet, from $600,000 to over $1 million (not long ago the ad used "from $450,00 to the $700,000s").

Several enclaves in Florida of several hundred homes have median prices of $6.5 million, including Jupiter Island on the East Coast and Port Royal (Naples) on the Gulf Coast. One major Florida developer reported its homes averaged $625,000 with 45 percent above $1 million. Not even the best of these is "perfect" so look for your definition of luxury within what you can afford. No matter the price range, the hints and ideas in this chapter will save you money and later regrets.

What to Live In is Perhaps More Important than Where to Live in Florida.

Although buying a new home is exciting, it can also be stressful. Purchasing a home ranks high on the stress scale. Even though you have bought homes in the past, buying one in Florida, particularly for a retirement move, can cause feelings of buyer's remorse if you don't take care. The antidote for feeling sorry later is shopping around enough *before* you buy the home. You have a vast array of choices. The more information you gather, the better you will feel about your decision. Start with the guidelines in this chapter to avoid later second guessing yourself. You'll also save money.

Just as deciding on a Florida location can best be done by visiting a variety of places, deciding on a home, means looking at many different kinds of homes. Should it be a condo, villa, townhouse or single-family home? And, what is the difference between a condominium association and a homeowner's association? Should you buy new or existing? What is the warranty? How do we avoid problems in selection of colors, options? Where, within the city or area you chose, should you look, because location influences price, lifestyle and resale value (for example, close to the beach versus inland)? Even if you can afford a pricey palace, as we noted, you'll get some help from this chapter. No matter what your taste or budget, you have numerous housing choices to consider.

Buyer's Remorse.

The answers to these and other questions in this chapter may spell the difference between a happy choice and the anxiety and second-guessing of buyer's remorse. We'll help you with the two major reasons for buyer's remorse: not enough information to make the proper choice or don't have a clear idea of what you want.

You are the best judge of your wants and needs, so we'll help you with some insights and checklists you might not otherwise think of that pertain to living in Florida. This chapter will help you clarify your needs and wants and narrow your search.

Amenities and "For A While!"

Many newcomers to Florida suffer from the "for a while" syndrome. What seemed appealing early at first, lasted only "for a while."

From the literature of one upscale gated-community, here is an advertising gem that evokes a feeling and sells the sizzle not the steak: "It's a wonderful stroll down landscaped pathways to the scenic beach or to the adjacent deep-water marina. Join the ritual of toasting the sunset under the fronds of a chickee hut, take a last soak in the spa, or a dip in the heated swimming pool, and savor the pleasure of the Club, located nearby."

The problem is not with the sales hyperbole, but many of the amenities end up in the "for a while" category. For example, we rarely saw people using the chickee hut near the lake. Newcomers use the amenities frequently, but after a year, use begins to drop off. Jack, a gated community resident, said: "When we first came here we were at the Clubhouse all the time. Now we go to the Clubhouse only once in a while."

Avoid being oversold on the sizzle and look to the core values. Will this location be a "true oasis of serenity" after you've lived there a while? A golf-course community advertised: "Spectacular views of the (insert celebrity golfer name)-designed golf course, sparkling lakes and nature preserves." What is that really worth to you? And for how long? One of the "lakes" was five acres. A visitor from Minnesota derisively called it a pond. Many of the "lakes" are indeed retention ponds.

Listen to Bill: "I dreamed of the day I could retire, buy a place on the water and have a boat. One day the dream came true. I have to tell you, it was a nightmare. I hated it. I didn't know anything about sea walls, and ended up with a $10,000 repair bill. The boat frightened me because of the tides and not being a mechanic. What if the engine quits? Anyway we sold the boat, and the house and moved into a condominium. Now I can enjoy the lifestyle."

19

Friends Jan and Walt bought a home in a gated "country club" community. Although this was a non-golf community, it did have a large clubhouse with restaurant. Their fees included a monthly minimum cost in the restaurant, whether they used it or not. They liked to go out to a variety of restaurants, and tired of what they perceived as "country club" snobbery, sold their home and bought in a community that had a clubhouse but not a restaurant. In their new community, the residents had potluck dinners once or twice a month, which Jan and Walt found more to their liking. Is the "country club" important to you?

Golfer Charlie bought a beautiful home on a golf course, fully intending to play golf daily. Then, he injured his back and his golf days were over. He had not thought through what else there would be to do if he did not golf. The gated golf-community was far from shopping, grocery stores, and the hospital. Not only do homes in gated golf communities cost more than ones in gated non-golf communities, the monthly fees are higher. You can use the difference in assessments to afford a much larger home in a non-golf community, and then golf at public courses. Or golf at private courses that allow non-residents and non-members. How important is living on a golf course to you?

Amenities at a typical gated community include a clubhouse with kitchen, multi-purpose rooms, fitness equipment, heated pool, lighted tennis courts, tot lot (children's playground) and guest parking. Community lifestyle amenities include lakes, waterways, pedestrian walkways and quiet neighborhood streets. Which of these are important to you? Is the pool one you would use? Is it heated? Do you want to share the pool? How would you use it to swim laps?

All the costs of the amenities get built into the price of homes. All the maintenance costs of all the amenities get built into the homeowner's maintenance fee. As we noted, the most expensive amenity is a golf course, so you generally get a better value home and lower maintenance fees in a non-golf course community.

Some communities focus on boating. If boating is high on your to-do list, then a boating community with a marina and a slip for your boat can be an important consideration. In Florida, boat storage can be very expensive.

Golf, an active lifestyle and tennis remain the top three amenities most buyers look for in a country club community, but many buyers now look for walks and bicycle paths. Many of the communities are not "country club." Amenities can be a driving factor in a decision to buy, according to realtors, so thinking through the amenities most important to you will narrow your search. It will also save you money.

20

Here's a checklist of amenities.

- ✓ Clubhouse. Is there an activity director to plan programs? Kitchen? Restaurant?
- ✓ Golf
- ✓ Tennis (are the courts lighted? Har-Tru surface?)
- ✓ Fitness, Exercise Equipment
- ✓ Walking paths
- ✓ Tot lot; playground for youngsters
- ✓ Swimming Pool
- ✓ Basketball court
- ✓ Bocce Ball court
- ✓ Horseshoes
- ✓ Activities: Classes, Music, Hobby Clubs, Health & Support, Drama, Dance, Arts & Crafts, Annual Variety Show by Residents, Potluck Dinners.

Community Appearance and Convenience.

Does the neighborhood meet your needs for commuting, shopping, quality of schools, recreational activities, and church? In Florida, schools receive a rating. Check out the rating, because even if you don't have children, A-rated schools nearby help property values.

Are the grounds well kept and cared for? Some gated communities show wear and tear and the lack of maintenance. Some look tacky. They may be keeping their fees artificially low by skimping on maintenance. Not a good sign. We lived in a 20-year-old, gated-community that surprised even jaded realtors at the high level of appearance and upkeep. Not surprisingly, property values were significantly higher, than in a nearby and comparable community that had a lesser appearance and lower property values.

Are streets safe and devoid of speeding cars so you can feel safe riding your bike (or your children or grandchildren riding bikes? What health care facilities are nearby?

Community Density.

What is density and why is it important? The density of a community is the number of units per acre. In a community of a mix of condos, villas and single family homes, a density of four could mean 700 units in a half-mile square, or perhaps 2,000 people. In another community of single-family homes, in a half-mile square, a density of two would mean half as many people. The higher the density number, the more people, the more crowded, and the more stress on infrastructure.

Renting Before Buying.

One way to avoid unpleasant surprises is to rent a unit in the community before you buy one. Realtors, who sell in mature gated-communities, told us their best potential buyers are the renters. One renter-turned-buyer said: "We rented two seasons here, each for two months. We liked it so much we bought a unit here. We knew what we were getting. We actively used many of the amenities. We liked the people."

For undecided empty nesters, renting makes sense so they can take the time to gather all the information on making the important decision of what to buy and to get a good feel for the area. Don't forget, however, that just renting only during the season won't do it because summer differs greatly from winter.

After renting, Pete and Joan bought a condo in a building with 30 units. Later they sold it and bought a single-family home when they decided to live here full time. Why change? "We had a 1,000 square foot condo. It worked fine for short stays, and as a second getaway home for several months, but became too confining living in it full-time," Pete said. "I got tired of living in a tunnel. We had a door and window at the front and at the back but solid walls on both sides."

Over 55 Years Old Communities.

Age-restricted communities create a comfort level for people of similar background and age, and who have raised their kids. These require at least one member over 55 years old and no children under 18 as full-time residents. Many age-restricted communities have amenities designed to encourage neighbors to meet and interact. Because people are of similar age, they grew up through the same times and often have similar philosophies, so easing into a new community is smoother. Meeting new friends is easier.

Friends with a different view said they like "interacting with families of all ages, so we prefer a higher ratio of year-round residents in a mixed community. We enjoy the infusion of youth we get from all the children. The young can stretch our minds and we can relive our youth through them."

A community with all single-family homes, a mix of ages and diversity, and more than 90 percent full-time residents has a completely different atmosphere than a 55-year-old and over community with a mix of condos, villas and single-family homes and more than half part-time (snowbirds) residents. We have lived in both and prefer the former, but there are variations in between the extremes.

Living in a 20-year old community of people 55 years old, means many residents in their 70s and 80s. What is one thing the realtor won't tell you? Ambulances make frequent appearances, which can be depressing.

Homeowner's Association and Condominium Lifestyle.

Nationwide, an estimated 50 million people live in one of the nearly one quarter-million homeowner associations. The Community Association Institute says one in six Americans lives in an association-managed community. In Florida, nearly every new home involves a community association. By the year 2010, more than 40 percent of Floridians will be living in communities with a mandatory membership association. But association rules and regulations differ. Knowing what the regulations mean to you may spell the difference of being happy in a new environment or not. Despite many benefits, living in an association isn't for everyone. Community living is a lifestyle of trade-offs.

Most of us don't want to wade through all the fine print of lengthy documents, but if the documents are the covenants, bylaws, rules and regulations of the condominium in which you might live, not reading them can be a tragic mistake. Take the time to read the documents. How stringent are the rules and regulations? Can you live with them? Rules and regulations vary widely, depending on the community.

The deed restrictions are legally binding rules. They can control house colors, fences, building heights, building additions, what can be parked in a driveway (no trucks for example), pets (number, size; or none) and a myriad of dos and don'ts. You give up some rights and live with some restrictions, but at the same time the rules, regulations and architectural standards preserve home values.

Until the 1977 Condo Act was passed, there were many abuses in Florida. Chapter 718 of the Florida Statutes pertains to Condominium Associations. Chapter 720 pertains to Homeowners Associations. Understand the difference before you commit to living in the community.

The owner has an obligation to notify you of the association and provide association documents. Ask for the documents. Read them!

Maintenance fees vary widely in different communities depending on the scope. Know what the fees include and don't include when comparing fees. Also check the financial condition of the association, including the reserves, which should be roughly 25 percent of the annual income. Some buyers have been duped into believing an association with the lowest fees is the best run, when in fact fees were artificially low because they weren't setting aside enough reserves. That could result in an unwelcome large special assessment later. You don't want to buy and then soon after be stuck with a large special assessment because the under-funded reserves are inadequate to cover a major project.

Five Key Steps to Take Before Committing to Living in an Association.

1. Read the documents carefully beforehand. Don't wait until signing to read them. It's too late then to find out you can't have a pet, or can't have a boat, or can't add on to your home.

2. Ask for the financial statements. Review, especially the reserves and any pending assessments. Are the reserves fully funded?

3. Ask residents about the association. What do you like best? Least?

4. Get involved, by at least attending meetings.

5. Get elected. In one association we lived in, several ran for the board and were elected an officer with one motivation being to get rules changed to their liking. "If you don't like the rules, run for the board and quit whining."

More people should get involved. People who cause all the problems are rarely involved in running of the association. They love to complain but will not put forth the effort to help resolve the problems. Some people seem to have nothing better to do than nitpick minor problems. You have a choice. You signed on. If you don't like the rules, you can get involved and change them, or you can leave. Staying and making everyone else unhappy isn't a good option. Conflicts will develop until people see there is no "they" in the association (as in "they did this…"). Substitute "we" for "they," because the association consists of all the members.

Having been an association president a couple of times, the job is much like being the mayor of a small town, without the pay.

Enforcement.

Not following the rules and regulations in most associations will result in a violation letter. Failure to correct the problem can result in a fine. Before deciding to move into a community with an association, ask some residents if the rules are enforced.

Looking at some of the most frequent reasons for the rules tells a story. Clearly, the purpose is to assure an attractive-looking community, and homeowners not having to worry about an eyesore next door. Property values will only stay strong as long as community appearance stays fresh. As one association president exclaimed: "This requires everyone to do their part, and comply with the rules and regulations."

As a prospective buyer, however, you need to know about enforcement because rules that are not enforced become unenforceable. In one community, here are most frequent violations:

- Trashcans left in front of houses after trash pickup.
- Lack of fertilizer for grass, trees, shrubs.
- Yellow palm fronds (lack of fertilizer).
- Pet violations.
- For sale signs on property.
- House needs exterior cleaning (power wash).
- House needs painting.
- Removal of trees without permission.
- Chinch bugs damage necessitating sod replacement.

Even if you don't live in community association, Florida, which had one of the weakest property code enforcement laws of all the states, tightened the laws in 1999 to strengthen the enforcement codes. Now Florida ranks as one of the nation's toughest so communities can enforce against neglectful property owners.

Buying a New Home or an Existing One

There's no right or wrong answer as to buying a new home or an existing one. We have done both in Florida. An older one in an established neighborhood has a certainty that a new home does not as to how the neighborhood will develop. When you look at an existing home, look beyond the presentation and see the possibilities and problems. You need to be sure you not only see how it is, but how it will be. You need to look beyond the possible hyperbole of a realtor and owner doing their best to show the home the best. Cozy and charming, for example, are simply more pleasant words than "small." If you like the community, and it's built out, your only choice could be to buy an existing home.

Hiring an inspector may be a good investment. When are the appliances going kaput? Air conditioners have a much shorter lifespan than up North, sometimes as little as five years, simply because they operate much more. Inspect for termites and radon. Inspect for mold.

How old is the unit? If the house is a dozen years old, and the hot water heater has a life of twelve years, an early replacement probably will be needed! Bill, when he replaced a 13-year old water heater, commented: "My appliances are dying. I have outlived all of them." When we moved into an 11-year old unit, the water heater did in fact need replacing after we were there two years.

A new home will have the most up-to-date hurricane and energy-efficient construction, new energy-saving appliances and the latest in Florida-friendly architecture. Perhaps the biggest advantage to buying a new home is your opportunity to pick colors, options and upgrades that customize the home to your desires for your dream home.

25

Whether buying a new or existing home, get pre-approved for a mortgage.

Include a finance contingency clause so if the home does not appraise for at least the sales price, you can cancel the purchase and get your deposit refunded. A contingency clause on a satisfactory inspection also makes sense.

Condos.

The condominium association owns the structure, walls, hallways, elevators, grounds, parking areas, plumbing, wiring and everything outside each condo's inner wall, floor and ceiling surfaces. The association, as the owner, maintains these common areas. Condo owners own the airspace between the floor, ceiling and walls to the inner surface of their unit.

If you are buying a condominium, whether new or existing, there are some key things to know.

The number one complaint for condo owners is poor soundproofing. So, if you plan to buy a condo, checking for adequate soundproofing should be number one on your list, along with knowing who your prospective neighbors are, especially if they are noisy night owls who play the television or stereo loudly at all hours, or have some pet birds that squawk constantly.

How old is the unit? Although building maintenance may be done by your association appliance maintenance is your responsibility.

End units sell for more than inside units because they share fewer walls and generally have more windows. The view from higher floors is better, so the higher the units in a condo building, the more they will cost. Is the view important to you? And will it be important a year from now? How good is the elevator if you plan to live on a higher floor?

How many renters? What is the percentage of the units? If the percentage is above 20 percent, then the rental occupancies can have a negative effect on property values. If there are too many renters, maintenance often declines.

Keep in mind that condos, by and large, do not appreciate as well as a single-family home, although appreciation often depends on location, whether condo or home.

In many condos, association rules forbid having an outdoor grill, or barbeque, except at the clubhouse. You probably can't plant a garden. Are pets allowed? Is there a size limit on pets?

What is the financial condition of the association?

You may be saying you want to buy it and use it for short periods for a few years and avoid having to worry about maintenance, yard work and damage. You can buy a single-family home in a condominium association, where the single-family home is treated in the same way as a condo in terms of maintenance. Our first home was a single-family home in a condominium association that included condos, villas and homes. The homes appreciated more than the villas and condos. You have the advantage of more space. In this case, for example, condos were in the 850-1,050 square feet range, villas 1,000-1,200 square feet, and single-family homes 1,400-1,750 square feet. The monthly fees were the same; and included maintenance of all common areas plus for all units, including single-family homes, lawn maintenance (mowing, fertilizing, trimming), exterior of home (power washing, painting), and roof maintenance and replacement.

Henry and Joan bought a condo and lived in it for a few years. They bought a home after deciding they "really didn't like condo living." They noted: "We wanted a bigger place; now our guests can have their own place to relax, if they like."

Home Characteristics, New or Existing (Pre-Owned)

Whether you buy a new home, or an existing one, some characteristics apply to both. Here are some of the important factors to consider:

Orientation. When you shop, having a compass will help you to get a good sense of the site's orientation to the sun. Remember, too, the midday sun is high in the southern sky in summer and low in winter. A north-south exposure is best for the sun; an east-west orientation is best for breeze. A sunny garden needs southern light.

A pool on the south in full sun will reduce pool heating in winter. A pool on the west side also gets the afternoon sun. Don't buy a home with a shaded pool. Broad overhangs keep the sun and rain out.

In Florida, screened-in lanais are often furnished and used as a living room. Most Florida homes are built with a screened porch or patio at the rear to capitalize on the year-round weather. Most condos have balconies.

Cross Ventilation. Residents can also enjoy cross ventilation of opening a window or door on one side of their home and their patio doors on the other to allow cool breezes to blow through. No breeze will come into anything it can't exit, so you need two opposite openings of equal area.

Size. We have seen so many instances of people downsizing when they move to Florida, then regretting it and buying a larger home, that we recommend you buy larger rather than smaller.

Senior Friendly Homes. Plan ahead by making your home senior friendly. Look for "aging-friendly" features that can be of future help. Tempus fugit. (Time flies.)

Kathy, a neighbor pointed out an obvious, but sometimes overlooked feature: "We wanted to be sure everything was on one floor with no stairs of any kind with wheel chair-wide doors; just in case." The only steps in our home are steps in the swimming pool.

  ✓ Look for lever-type door handles instead of knobs, which might be difficult to grip for anyone with arthritis.
  ✓ Are light switches the rocker-arm type with easy touch on and off? They're a snap to operate!
  ✓ Check for grab bars in bathtubs and showers, wide doors (36 inches).
  ✓ Is there a large walk-in shower in addition to the bathtub?
  ✓ Look for more light by having plenty of windows. Some seniors look ahead to potential illness and install a flasher at the front door in case of emergency.
  ✓ Extra lighting in closets.
  ✓ Shelves easy to access?
  ✓ Lazy Susan in corner cabinets.
  ✓ Lower drawers that glide open (roll out).
  ✓ Rounded corner walls.

Volume (High) Ceilings. Lofty ceilings with high windows and ceiling fans are good choices in Florida. Our first house had standard height ceilings. Our new Florida house has ten-foot and 12-foot ceilings. What a pleasant difference. Does the house you are looking at have ten-foot ceilings?

Tile Roof. A tile roof not only looks better, but it will last much longer. This is a clear case of long-term value for an initial higher cost. A home with a tile roof has been built stronger to support the roof weight, which is another plus.

Find Out How to Save Thousands of Dollars in Buying Your New Home

You can save thousands of dollars in your home purchase, and be a savvy buyer, by:

  1. Buying your home in the off-season, May-September. Most developers say September is the slowest month. You'll see advertisements offering $4,000; $5,000; $7,000 and more in options and upgrades during the slow time. Headline from advertisement: "Single family homes from $300s. $10,000 free options for first five buyers."

2. Knowing ahead of time, for commitment of upgrades and options, which ones you should choose and those you can do later for less money. Examples: pool heater, garage door opener, some light fixtures.
3. Having a mortgage pre-approved.
4. Considering a "spec" or inventory home, if you can accept less customizing and can move in soon.
5. Checking on whether the developer will offer a discount for payment of cash. This could save you one or two percent.
6. Buying the new house during the year. You'll save on real estate taxes because the full amount, including the home, won't apply until the following year. We closed and moved in April, so owed for the first year approximately 25 percent of the next full year's taxes.
7. Considering a "leaseback" deal if you're not ready to move (buying a model home and leasing back to the developer for a year or two).
8. Making sure the developer/builder is financially strong.
9. Applying for Homestead Exemption of $25,000, soon after purchasing your new home.
10. Check to see if flood insurance, which is expensive, is required.

Let's assume you have done your homework, understand the homeowner association rules, like the community, and have fallen in love with a floor plan of one of the models. In most developments, you have a choice of a "spec" (built on speculation of sale) home or one that will be built for you. Typically, the "spec," or inventory, homes appeal to the buyer who is in a hurry and needs to move soon. The disadvantage is that you have a limited number of options, mostly interior paint and flooring. You're better off to plan ahead and allow the time needed to get the customized features that can make a big difference later. Adding them later simply costs more, whether it's a swimming pool, extra hose bibs, additional electrical outlets, cable TV outlets, and a host of other features big and small. See the checklist, which will help you with many often overlooked options. Some aren't on the developer's list, so unless you ask, you probably will later say: "Had I known....". We'll help you avoid this, by telling you some key things to consider.

Selecting New Home Options, Upgrades

When you have a home built based on one of the models in a development, most developers give you the opportunity to customize to some degree, especially with upgrades. These add to the total cost, so you need to know what is standard and included in the model, and what is extra and an upgrade. Yo! Not so fast. Slow down and take time to prepare carefully for the session to select paint colors, options, and upgrades.

"We came down from New Jersey," Carole said. "We had maybe an hour to go over these things. We didn't know about carpet, or a lot of things we learned later when it was too late. Had we known......."

Rarely will someone buy the advertised price for a home because it is a base price much like an automobile without all the extra accessories. A home that has a base price of, for example, $210,000 can reach $290,000 before you know it! For example, a premium charge for a tip lot on the lake ("expansive lake views") $25,000 and up; swimming pool $25,000 (and up) plus $5,000 for extended paver deck; upgrade floor tile and tile throughout, $10,000; three-car garage, $7,500; Corian® countertops, $3,000; lighting package, $2,000; French door $1,300; and miscellaneous options $800.

For every $1,000 of upgrades figure on six dollars added to the typical monthly payment. Upgrades like better insulation, energy-efficient appliances and systems, and higher quality windows have better payback than custom paint and carpeting. We skipped a fireplace upgrade because we never used it in our first Florida home and didn't select an intercom system for the same reason.

We'll include the things that can get overlooked, which can cost more money later; and some features you can do later for less. Either way, the following items will save you money, regardless of the home price. Ask the sales person for a list of "commonly requested upgrades and options" to study, before you make choices. More importantly, read the rest of this chapter!

Swimming Pool. With our new home, having the pool installed during construction saved money compared with neighbors who installed pools later. It also avoided a *big* mess. We did save by not having a pool heater installed at time of construction, but later. Just remember to make sure a separate 220-volt, 50-ampere power line exists for the heater. Putting the line in at construction is less costly than having an electrician do it later.

Tile Floors. In Florida, choose tile for floors, especially if you are close to the beach. Sand raises havoc with carpet. And Florida soil is sand! Tile has a longer life than carpet, less upkeep and cleaning. Tile may cost more at the outset, but will last many years longer, so the annual average cost is much lower. We prefer large tiles (13 to 16-inch). Use a neutral color. Install on the diagonal for better appearance. This could add $1,000-$3,000.

Extra Garage. If you have the choice, add an extra garage. Three is better than two, especially if you have two automobiles. The main reason is for storage. Many people move to Florida from the North, where basements are common and used for storage, and don't anticipate the storage need in homes built on slabs. In our first house, we had a double-car garage. In our next one, we had a three-car garage. By the way, check the garage depth and your car length!

Appliances. Which appliances come with the house? In our new house, the washer and dryer did not come with the house. Further, you may be able to save money, and get exactly what you want by buying appliances separately. Most new homes use standard appliances with additional costs to upgrade. "Standard" quality appliances seem to have a short life. Ask what the deduction would be to not include an appliance. In comparing the upgrade cost and the deduction, you may want to opt to buy your own higher-quality, energy-efficient appliances and save money. We did.

Microwave. Microwaves often are built into the cabinets and not vented to the outside. We specifically asked for the microwave to be vented. This added a modest charge ($100) during construction that would have been costly later. "Most people don't ask for this," the consultant said. "Who cooks that much?" If you use it much, vent it.

Countertops. If you want Corian® or granite, those choices may be an upgrade, depending on the developer. Ask what is standard. Corian® or granite helps sell the house later, so upgrade if necessary.

Outlets. Typically, a builder may offer five fan outlets, five TV cable outlets, five phone jacks and charge $50-$100 for additional ones. Make sure you add as many as you think you might use, because the cost is modest to do it during construction, and costly later. We didn't put a cable TV outlet in the office (den) because we didn't use a TV. The computer was on the phone line. Later we switched to broadband and wished we had put in the cable TV outlet. Don't overlook the lanai for outlets. Quite a few people put a TV on the lanai.

Electrical Outlets. Adding electrical outlets is inexpensive during construction; but can be costly later. Everyone we talked with wished they had more outlets. We have one outside on one side of the walk. One on the other side would have been a good idea for Christmas decoration lights. Other possible extra ones to consider: added outlets on lanai, added outlets above shelves in kitchen (to add ambiance lighting), outdoor lighting under soffets connected to a timer for Christmas lights, extra outlet in entry way (both sides instead of one side) and extra in garage (for refrigerator, for example). In short, don't forget to review and ask for additional electrical outlets.

31

Light Fixtures. The developer did not include outside coach lights at the garage, dining room fixture, or breakfast area. Good. Light fixture (and ceiling fan) stores abound. Buy and install or have them installed later.

Ceiling Fans. Ceiling fans are a must, but with so many competitive sources for these, you can buy and have installed later. Just make sure you have the developer put in the fan outlets. Don't forget the lanai. In a four-bedroom plus den house, you will need seven-nine fans (bedrooms, den, family room, living room, master bathroom, lanai). Choose a 50 to 60-inch fan for rooms up to 225 square feet, a 42- to 44-inch fan for rooms up to 144 square feet. For safe operation, fan blades need to be at least seven feet above the floor, so this is another reason to buy a house with 10-foot ceilings. For a fan to "disappear," make it the same color as the ceiling, which is why all our fans are white.

Air Conditioning. Check for vents in closets, which help prevent mildew. Check into the option of adding an ultra-violet light system in the air handler to kill mold.

Humidistat. Ask if the system includes a humidistat. If not, have it added (probably just $100)

Extra Insulation. Is insulation R30? If not, consider an upgrade.

Brick Paver Driveway and Walks. These look better and add "curb appeal" to your house. Some developers now have these as standard on some models. Others charge an upgrade cost.

Outside Hose Bibs. Whoops. We specified hose bibs on each side of the house. We should have also put one on the lanai. Doing it later cost more. Also have a showerhead put on the wall in lanai if you have a swimming pool. You need only cold water.

Cabinets. Neighbors wish they had upgraded the cabinet quality. Later is too late. With the higher ceilings, you can also use 42-inch cabinets to gain cabinet space. Check for rollout drawers. These were an upgrade. We added some later at more cost than if done at time of construction.

Crown Molding. Crown molding in some homes is an upgrade; in others crown molding is included. If it is an upgrade, most chose to do this later at less cost than the upgrade price.

Hurricane Shutters. New building codes help hurricane protection, but shutters still are an important part of a Florida home. Having them installed at the time of construction, especially if electrically operated roll-down shutters, may be a good idea. If you are inland, however, having ultraviolet protecting high-impact film installed on all the windows can be a good option. It also helps protect furniture and decorations from fading from the harsh sun and cuts air conditioning costs.

Recessed Lighting. The home may come with recessed lighting Hi-Hats but frequently not enough. Adding these during construction saves money. We added eight in the kitchen, two in the master bedroom and two in the living room.

Outside Lighting. You might easily overlook extra outside spotlights (security), especially at the corners of the house. If you want them, having the wiring done at construction saves money.

Garage Door Openers. If these are an upgrade cost, you can easily compare the cost with readily available installed opener costs and decide based on the cost and quality comparison. In one community, openers were an upgrade cost of $300.

Garage Pull-Down Stairs. Is there a pull-down stair system for access above the garage? Some builders offer the stairs as an extra cost option.

Whirlpool Tub. A developer may offer an upgrade of the Roman tub in the master bathroom to include a whirlpool feature. If this is something you want, doing it during construction is less costly than doing it later.

Systems. Builders offer central vacuum systems, security alarm systems and intercom systems. Each of these adds perhaps $1,000. Are they worth it to you? If so, these cost less to do during construction, than later.

Outside Kitchen/Bar Area. An outside kitchen with gas grill, sink and under-the-counter refrigerator makes a nice amenity for the lanai if you plan to entertain. Unless your new home is very large, this may be one of those "opulent" extras. Doing it later can cost a great deal because of the wiring and plumbing needed.

Pest Defense. Pest defense systems use small plastic tubing in the walls, into which small quantities of insecticide are injected periodically. Obviously if you choose to have a system, it's best done during construction.

Other Options and Upgrades. Pocket doors, French doors instead of sliding doors, and laundry tub and a variety of others options may be available, depending upon the builder.

To Do Later. When selecting upgrades and options and checking your budget: make sure you have planned for shelving in the garage, window treatments, extra shelving in closets and extra landscaping, even if just adding flowers. For window treatments, consider easy-to-maintain plantation shutters, which are very popular. Get plastic, not wood.

Your Perfect Luxury Home

As we said earlier, luxury is how you view and define it. Some say there's no such thing as a "perfect" home, but a home is really a work in progress; more like a journey than a destination. It's an ongoing, changing place that reflects your personality and changes in your life. Isn't a dream home high on your priority list?

No home ever gets "done." You have followed our lists and made your choices. You may have deferred some of the bells and whistles of upgrades for financial reasons, or because it made economic sense to do later. Further, even after selecting paint colors, you will later decide to change the paint color in a room, or add cabinets, or shelves.

Home Inspection, Walk Through

Let's do another, "Yo! Not so fast." Doing the walk through is not routine. The new home seller does it all the time, but you have just one chance to check out the house before closing. Take the opportunity to bring along a clipboard, paper and pen to jot down notes.

When we bought a new home, the customer service person, Pam, pointed out 17 items we probably would have missed, so she truly was "customer service." Most were small defects, but all were later fixed. We turned on all the faucets, flushed the toilets, checked the electrical switches, looked for gaps in woodwork (areas not caulked well), checked the sprinkler system, and checked out the landscaping.

The walk through also is important for learning where things are and how they work.

Warranty

Typically, new homes have a one-year builder's warranty on everything and customer service people to follow up on requests from residents. Ask your potential new neighbors how the developer has handled fixing the inevitable things that go wrong in the first year. All new homes have a myriad of problems that crop up. In looking at a one-year "fix everything" warranty, we noted some exceptions: shrubs were warranted for just 45 days, paint touch up for 30 days, chipped ceramic tile for just 10 days.

How financially strong is the developer? You don't want him to go bust halfway through your home construction, or immediately after it's built. What is his track record for fixing defects?

Most developers use a "Request for Service" form for you to fill out and submit for correction of defects. Make sure you fill these out in time! Here are some of the things that went wrong in our new house:

- o Water backed up into the bathtubs.
- o Carpet in master bedroom had a small stain we didn't even see. After a couple of months the small stain spread to the

size of a platter. After several visits, and discussions, the sub-contractor removed the carpet and installed new carpet in the room.

o Toilet "rocked." The plumbing sub-contractor promptly arrived to re-set the toilet.
o Crack in outside stucco wall.
o Three windows leaked. Two leaked after being fixed and required two more repair visits.
o Outside electrical outlet didn't work. We didn't realize this for more than six months.

Other homeowners could add to this list with problems, large and small. The point to underscore is to know the builder will fix them. In our case, every problem was resolved. That's what you want to hear when you ask residents about the warranty.

Living in and Maintaining Your New Home

Little Problems.

Make sure little problems don't grow up and become major problems. Two examples: Leaks and ants can wreak havoc with mold and damage.

Running the furnace fan alone can push moisture into the house with mold and mildew not far behind. Not doing this will avoid a little problem that can become a big one.

Mold needs to go, not grow because of the danger to health and home. The key is to avoid excess moisture. An excellent book about mold is *What Every Homeowner Needs to Know about Mold,* by Vicki Lankarge.

Bright sunshine causes problems, especially for your furnishings, paintings and photographs which can fade even those not in direct sunlight. Installing UV protection to windows cuts this problem. Window tinting with high-impact film strengthens the glass, blocks glare, protects discoloring of fabric and lowers power bills.

Replace heating/air conditioning filters monthly.

Pressure wash your stucco house annually to keep it clean and extend paint life.

Pressure wash roof; needed every few years to avoid mold (or to remove it).

Check your landscaping and lawn weekly and you'll save on costly treatments for insect infestation and fungus infection. Like so many things, these problems when small can be easily and inexpensively taken care of, but when this is not done, then the treatment can be expensive. Check Chapter Seven for information of Florida friendly lawns and landscaping.

If you aren't thrilled with doing all this "home-work" you have two major alternatives: buy a condo where nearly all this maintenance is done for you, or hire people to do it for you.

Find Someone Else To Do It

"I don't want to move to Florida and spend my time mowing the lawn and cleaning the pool. What is the cost to have someone do this?"

If you buy into a condominium community, nearly all the services will be in your maintenance fee, as mentioned. In homeowner associations, however, most provide cable TV but few of the home services. Go into any gated community and you'll see the service company vans and trucks at many of the homes. Here are some typical costs, but these vary depending on the area and the scope of the work.

Service	Frequency	Cost Per Month
Pool Service	Weekly	$50-80
Lawn Service	Weekly	$70-100
Pest Control	Quarterly	$25
Air Conditioner/	Bi-Annual	$175 annual cost
Power Wash House	Annually	$175 annual cost
Home Cleaning	Weekly	$80-300 ($10/hr.)
Cable TV	Monthly	$40

Typically, lawn-care consists of "mow, blow and go" with added costs for trimming and fertilizing.

Pool service cost can vary depending on what you want done. Most pool service companies will do all, including pool vacuuming, filter cleaning, and chemicals, or part of the task, such as chemicals only. Even if you don't mind doing the vacuuming, having a pool company check the chemicals weekly and adding as necessary saves a lot of mess and storing of acid and chlorine.

Eleven Tips for Home Energy Savings.

Energy saving not only puts money in your pocket but also helps save natural resources Realize also that appliances being manufactured now are more energy efficient than older ones. Check the energy efficiency rating on older appliances and consider investing in new ones, particularly refrigerators. Listen up! Here are money-saving tips, including some from Florida Power and Light:

1. Cool your home at 78 degrees, or warmer. For additional savings, raise the thermostat to 82 degrees as we do when we are away from home.

2. Although heat is not often used, set the thermostat on 68 degrees with the thermostat fan switch on "auto." Lower the thermostat at night or if away for more savings.

3. Install a programmable thermostat to adjust temperature automatically. Include a humidistat.

4. Clean or replace your air conditioner's filter every month. This not only saves cooling costs, but also helps your unit run more efficiently.

5. Turn off ceiling fans when you leave the room. Ceiling fans don't cool the room; they cool people in the room. A fan that runs constantly cost approximately $7 a month!

6. Avoid pre-rinsing dishes before putting in dishwasher. This can save up to $70 a year.

7. Limit the time you run your pool pump. We cut our run time to six hours; and turned the heater off in summer. In winter, we adjust the time for heater to maintain water temperature.

8. If you have a swimming pool, use a "solar blanket." It extends the pool season, cuts nighttime heat loss, cuts evaporation and chemical loss and increases water temperature. A good one with a warranty costs only $100.

9. Adjust the water level on your washing machine to match the load size, especially when using hot water. Use a cold water rinse.

10. Clean the lint filter in your dryer before every load to dry your clothes faster and save money. Clean the filter exhaust stack. If it becomes plugged, dryer operation is lengthened and therefore more costly; and it could be a fire hazard.

11. Use the auto sensor function on your dryer, if you have one, to conserve energy by not over-drying your clothes.

Leaving Town---Burglar Prevention and Protecting Your Assets.

Here are a baker's dozen tips for you to use when you leave town, with the first half-dozen related to burglar prevention:

1. Notify local law enforcement, neighbors or Neighborhood Watch before you leave. Provide them with an emergency phone number.

2. Leave a key with a friendly neighbor.

3. Stop your mail and newspapers.

4. Put any valuables and cash in your safe deposit box. Don't leave in the home.

5. Use timers on lights (and radio) to give the house a "lived-in" look (unless you have hurricane shutters).

6. If you have a security alarm, use it. Many burglaries are stopped simply by noise alone.

7. Keep your shrubs trimmed so there are not places for a burglar to hide.

8. Install movement sensor-lights outside, especially at the back of the home.

9. Close hurricane shutters; or close blinds enough to prevent a direct view into your home.

10. If you're going to be gone long, have someone mow your lawn, and maintain pool. Not having the lawn mowed destroys the "lived-in" look. Who wants to return to a green pool!

11. Unplug the water heater.

12. If you have an outside water shutoff valve, turn it off. If you have a valve at the street, turn it off. That will prevent your home being flooded from a water line break or other leak. You are liable for water from the main connection to the house, so if a leak occurs while you are away, you could end up with a huge water bill.

13. Unplug electrical and electronic devices, especially if you are away during the hurricane/lightning season. Florida Power & Light offers insurance on computer and appliances to protect against lightning and power surge problems. The $2,000 coverage typically is the deductible on homeowner's insurance so it is good "gap" protection for about $5 a month.

Common-Sense Business Practices for Associations

If you do get involved in your association, here are some common-sense business practices that will enhance the performance of your association. Board members can not only build a high-performance association by following some simple precepts, but can also avoid some of the horror stories of condo commandos and dictatorial boards who are unresponsive to members.

Great associations are based on feelings, attitudes and relationships, which means:

- *Ask Questions and listen.* Listen to the people. Collectively all the people know all the problems and solutions, even if few individually do.
- *Communication.* Climate of trust and open communication. Don't assume good news will trickle down, or that you communicate enough.
- *Team Attitude.* Cooperative effort makes winners.

- ***Cool heads in choppy waters.*** Three guides: get conflict on the table, disagree but don't be disagreeable and don't make it personal. Ask about any issue: Is it fair? Is it honest? Does it meet our goals?
- **Recognition**: Make sure volunteers who contribute get recognition for their efforts for the community.

Other key actions:

1. Avoid the "damned if we do, damned if we don't" dilemma of low bid and shoddy work, or higher bid and be criticized for not using the low bid. Use well-written specifications, and detailed "Requests For Quotes" to get apples-to-apples bids from qualified bidders.
2. Hold back a percentage on purchases, or contracts, until project approved.
3. Use Ben Franklin pro and con lists to analyze as a basis for decisions.
4. Have a cost reduction team. Attack waste. Simplify, combine, eliminate.
5. Use pilot projects. Try a pilot project first before expending money on a major project.
6. Benchmark other associations and developments to compare performance and gain new ideas.
7. Hire an attorney. Have an attorney on retainer, who specializes in association law. Don't hesitate to ask for counsel.
8. Have a strategic plan. This assures a future focus, a sense of common purpose based on the plan and proactive, not reactive actions. Change is an opportunity to improve residents' lifestyle and property values. Use the 80-20-focus rule (20 percent of the problems involve 80 percent of the dollars).
9. Invest in experts for major projects if none exists within. Select experts who are a "yard wide and a mile deep."
10. Minimize short-term cost mentality (versus life-cycle cost). Too often, we see associations try to save money in the short run, to avoid assessments or increasing fees, and end up paying large amounts later because they did not take into account life-cycle costs.
11. Confront and resolve issues quickly but don't over-promise and under-deliver.
12. Accrue reserves adequately by looking at the long-term needs first based on a strategy and plan and then anticipating by spreading costs.

Chapter Three
Establishing Florida Residency; Taxes, Licenses and Doing Business in Florida

General.

Florida residency for you means tax savings, including the fact that Florida does not have a personal state income tax, inheritance or gift tax. Doing all you can to avoid a claim by another state makes sense.

Several sources say there are six ways to establish Florida residence status: obtain a driver's license and automobile registration, register to vote, file your federal income tax return in Florida, file Florida intangible tax, redraft your will showing Florida residence and have it notarized and file a declaration of domicile.

Not so fast.

Doing one of these six probably will not suffice, especially if you live in two states.

One expert provided a common-sense answer: "The more proof you have, the better." This book tells you the key actions and how to save time and money doing them. This chapter will tell you how to register to vote (and cancel your previous one), how to register your vehicle(s), and obtain a driver's license. You will also learn about taxes and saving money by obtaining your Homestead Exemption. If you plan to move to Florida you face a lot of details to resolve. We'll help you make the adjustment easier.

For licenses and documents, here are five quick tips: know the office hours, avoid the lunch hour (and avoid in-season if possible), bring the needed documents and don't drive to the wrong office (the driver's license is obtained at a different place from the car registration). Read this chapter first to save time and money.

Residency

Declaration of Domicile.

You can obtain a Declaration of Domicile, which is an affidavit attesting to Florida residency, at the county courthouse, from the clerk of the circuit court. It is useful for having when three legal forms of Florida residency are required, such as filing for Homestead exemption. The declaration can help establish what state can access state income, death taxes, validity of a will, determining rights and beneficiaries.

In the declaration, you swear to the following, which is notarized: "… which place of residence I recognize and intend to maintain as my permanent home and, if I maintain another place or places of above in some other state or states, I hereby declare that my above-described residence and abode in the state of Florida constitutes my predominant and principal home, and I intend to continue it permanently as such. I am, at the time of making this declaration a bona fide resident of the state of Florida."

In summary, the Declaration of Domicile, which states you reside at a given address, is notarized and filed with the county clerk of the circuit court of residence. There's no time constraint before one can be legally declared a resident, but some residency benefits, such as lower in-state tuition at state universities may require residency for a year.

Consider hiring a Florida attorney to review out-of-state trust documents, wills and living wills to make sure they reflect Florida law. Florida statutes provide for a Living Will, which is a written declaration by an individual specifying direction as to the use of life-prolonging procedures.

Residency Proof.

Declaration of Domicile has the benefits mentioned, but it may not suffice in avoiding paying taxes to another state. More than one state can legally impose inheritance tax and collect tax on source of income. Many states pro-rate taxes up to the time you make the switch, so you could owe tax in the other state. Florida has no income tax, but most other states do and can be aggressive in collecting it. They reach out and collect the maximum on assets held elsewhere.

Intent is important. Courts have ruled your heart is where your treasure lies.

In addition to obtaining driver's license and automobile registration, registering to vote, filing your federal income tax return in Florida, filing your Florida intangible tax and redrafting your will showing the Florida address, and filing for a declaration of domicile, here are other actions you can take to help "prove" residency in overwhelming fashion:

- Convert all your memberships (social and religious) in your northern state to "nonresident" and establish membership in Florida.
- Minimize the time you spend in your northern state. Spend as much time in Florida as practical; preferably more than six months.
- Maintain most of your assets in Florida (bank, trust, brokerage, deposit box) and close similar ones up North. Have your safety deposit box in Florida.
- File an Intangible Tax return with Florida each year. Request the Registrar in the state of your former residence, to strike your name from the voting records of that state.
- Notify your tax officials of your change of residence. I sent a letter, for example, to the state tax office.
- Change your address on stocks, bonds and other securities to your new Florida address.
- Use your Florida address when registering at hotels, getting airline tickets, and on documents in which your residence is mentioned, such as leases, contracts, tax returns, subscriptions, telephone listings, and charge accounts.
- The intangible tax form requires you to fill in a space that requests you to enter when your Florida residency was established; and notes that it is the first year you qualified for homestead exemption or the first day you were qualified to vote in Florida. Know that date!

Keep in mind, even performing all the actions mentioned would not permit you to take advantage of some residency rights. If you want to attend a state university at the much lower tuition of a Florida resident, you must have established and maintained permanent legal residence in Florida for at least twelve months before the first day of the term. As proof, you will need to provide two of these three documents: your Florida Driver's License, Florida Vehicle Registration, Florida Voter's Registration. The difference in cost can save $10,000 a year if you are a resident. Florida Gulf Coast University, in 2004, had a rate of $96.86 a credit hour for residents versus $442.02 a credit hour for non-residents.

For purposes of hunting in Florida, you need to be a resident for six continuous months before applying for licenses, or have filed a domicile certificate with the county clerk. The same rule applies to fishing licenses. In both cases, active military personnel stationed in Florida are considered residents when purchasing licenses. Short-term non-resident licenses are available. If you over 65, you'll qualify for a real bargain; no license is required. Fish free!

There is no waiting period to become a resident. New residents do need to obtain their Florida driver's license within 30 days. Register motor vehicles within 10 days of accepting gainful employment, entering children in public schools or filing for homestead exemption, which provides a property tax exemption of $25,000 on your home.

Voter Registration

If you are at least 18 years old, a citizen of the United States and a Florida resident, you are eligible to become a registered voter. Voter registration can be done year round. To vote in an election, you must register at least 10 days before an election to vote in that election. We moved to Florida in mid-October, registered to vote soon after, but still could not vote in the November 4 election that year. By planning ahead, and knowing where to get forms, we could have met the deadline.

The simplest way to register is to obtain the Florida Voter Registration Application Form, fill it out and mail it in. You need to have a Florida driver's license (with your correct address), a declaration of domicile or a voter's registration card from another county. In addition to your address (legal residence), you also need to fill in your last address where you last registered to vote and address of homestead exemption property, your Florida Driver License number and last four digits of social security number.

Florida Licenses

County Tax Collector Office.

Check for the nearest County Tax Collector office, because it's where you anglers and hunters pick up your licenses, in addition to car registration. The office also takes care of manufactured home tags and titles and disabled parking permits. They have available a variety of forms you may want. Many counties have several tax collector offices. What they do *not* do is issue vehicle license plates, which is done at the Department of Highway Safety and Motor Vehicles.

Vehicle License Plates.

You'll need to buy Florida tags within ten days of residency, employment or enrollment of a child in school. Going to the county tax collector's office to do this can be an adventure, especially if you forget to bring everything you will need, including vehicle title, registration, proof of insurance, and the vehicle itself. You will also need Florida State Form 42.3 completed to verify odometer reading. A sheriff's deputy inspected our auto after we checked in, including the VIN number. The state requires VIN verification on all previously registered vehicles.

Oh, and about that adventure and learning the hard way. When we arrived at the office, several people sat waiting. Take a number. Our number was 25. With No. 20 on the board, we figured this wouldn't take long. Wrong. We watched CNN news and waited. And waited. You're looking at your watch. Time slows. Your blood pressure might even bounce. Finally No. 25 blinked on the board.

Tip number one. Don't go during the season if you can avoid it (January-April).

Tip number two. Don't go on a rainy day. VIN verifications aren't done on rainy days.

Tip number three. Trying to deal with the tax office can be frustrating, so be prepared for an exercise in patience. Smile.

After we finally reached a desk and a person, we learned we could register only one of our two automobiles, because we brought only one.

Florida requires minimum insurance coverage, including personal injury protection/no fault, so you will need proof of insurance. Typically, registration and title cost $180. As a newcomer, you will pay $100 initial registration fee for each vehicle. Add to that a title transfer fee of $33. The annual registration fee is based on the vehicle's weight but cost around $35. Add to that a $10 plate fee.

Tip number four, check the purchase date on your vehicle!

We learned the hard way if you bought a new car elsewhere, within the past six months, you will owe sales tax, or the difference of the sales tax you paid in the state in which you bought it, and the six percent Florida sales tax. In our case, that added one percent of the car's price to our fees. Make sure you buy a new car six months before moving. The use tax of six percent does apply to any motor vehicle imported from a foreign country into Florida.

Specialty plates add personality and $15 to $25 on top of the usual fees. Florida, at last count, had nearly 100 specialty plates from which to choose. You can view the various plates at the office. Samples are also available to view on the Internet at www.hsmv.state.fl.us.

Driver's Licenses.

Florida requires new residents to obtain a driver's license within 30 days of establishing residency. You are required to obtain a Florida license if you enroll your children in school, register to vote, file for a homestead exemption, accept employment, or reside in Florida for more than six consecutive months. You also need to have registered your automobile.

Driver's licenses are *not* issued at the tax collector's office; Register at the Department of Highway Safety and Motor Vehicles. We drove ten miles to the office on a Monday; not realizing the office is open only Tuesday through Friday.

Tip number one: call ahead for the recorded message of the days and hours the office is open.

We went on Tuesday. The waiting room overflowed with people. After waiting a while, an officer notified everyone the computer crashed. Also we learned that "Tuesday always gets the new drivers who turned 16 during the three-day weekend."

Tip number two: don't go on Tuesday.

Tip number three: pick a midweek afternoon, "when your cohorts are taking a nap," an officer quipped. That works. We tried our third time on a Wednesday afternoon.

Tip number four: make sure you have proof of your Florida registration, have your social security number and proof of insurance. You will need your valid out-of-state license. If you need glasses to pass a vision test, make sure you have them with you.

If you have a valid out-of-state license, you will be required to pass a vision test. Appointments are not taken. If your license has expired, you will need to take traffic law and road tests. Call for an appointment. Adults who have not had a driver's license must attend a driver education school and take all tests. Foreigners, except Canadians, also must take all driver tests. If you are 80 years old, or older, you must take a vision test to renew your license. The license, which costs $20, is valid for six years.

If you have children, drivers must be 16 years old to qualify for a license and 15 years old to get a restricted permit. First time drivers must complete a drug and alcohol education class. Most high schools offer the class. Those under 18 must also furnish a form (ESE570), which proves they are either in school or a high school graduate. Also a legal guardian must accompany anyone under 18 years old.

Florida seat belt law covers the driver, front-seat passenger, and children. Children age three and younger must be in approved infant carrier or children's car seat. Age four and five may be restrained with safety belts.

Pets.

Dogs and cats must be vaccinated and licensed every year. Tags can be obtained at veterinarian's offices

Fishing Licenses.

As mentioned earlier, if you are a Florida resident who is 65 years old or older, the good news is that Florida offers you the ultimate low-cost license. You do *not* need a fishing license. For those not yet 65 years old, most residents need a license.

For a fishing license, you are considered a Florida resident if you have resided in the state for six continuous months before the issuance of a license, and have an intent to reside in Florida and claim Florida as your primary residence; and any member of the U.S. Armed Forces who is stationed in the state (includes spouse and dependent children residing in the household). Proof of residency is a Florida driver's license, voter registration card or a certificate of domicile.

You can buy your license at all county tax collector's offices and at many bait and tackle shops. You can also buy one over the phone ($3.95 surcharge) from the state by calling 1-888-347-4356.

The Florida Fish and Wildlife Conservation Commission (620 South Meridian Street, Tallahassee, Florida 32399-1600) website, www. marinefisheries.org, summarizes regulations, provides information on licensing, permitting, fishing clinics and news of interest to anglers.

If you plan to fish, most freshwater fishing areas require a license, unless you are fishing with a cane pole. For salt-water fishing, you will need a license although there are some exceptions. Even with a license, you need to be aware of fishing limits and restrictions. For example, you must obtain a kill license to keep a tarpon. Restrictions exist on methods used to capture a number of species. If you plan to take either snook or crawfish, you must buy a special stamp and affix it to your license. The stamp costs $2. It is valid only during the times established by law for these species. Spiny lobster requires $2 in addition to the salt-water fishing license.

Florida residents may buy a lifetime saltwater license or a lifetime sportsman license. The fishing license covers saltwater fishing, while the sportsman license additionally includes fresh water fishing and hunting. Both include the fee for snook or crawfish, which otherwise require the separate fee.

Fishing Licenses Costs/Florida Resident Licenses.

Fishing license costs vary depending length of time, age and resident or non-resident. A 10-day resident license costs $10, a one-year license $12 a five-year $60. If you are age 65 or older, the license is *free*. Lifetime licenses are available for residents under the age of 65 ($300).

Vessel and Pier license fees also apply. You can check out fishing licenses on the Internet at www.floridagame.com. Also, the Florida Fish and Wildlife Conservation Commission published a handbook, "Fishing Lines," available at licensing locations. Don't forget to check for the specific seasons for various species, which differ.

Hunting License.

Hunting license rules are similar to fishing, including a free license to residents over 65 years old. There are separate permits for muzzle–loaded weapons, waterfowl hunting and for archery. Alligator permits are also a separate situation.

You must have a Florida Hunting License, Sportsman's License, Lifetime Hunting License, Lifetime Sportsman's License, or five-year Hunting License and a free Migratory Bird Permit. If you hunt ducks or geese, you need a Florida Waterfowl permit ($3 plus insurance fee) and a Federal Duck Stamp ($15). All licenses and permits are available at the county tax collector office. Duck Stamps are also available at the Post Office and some retail sports stores.

All Florida hunting and fishing licenses may be purchased with a credit card by calling 1-888-HUNT-FLORIDA (1-888-486-8356) or at www.floridaconservation.org.

Boating License.

Recreational boat operation in Florida does not require a license. Anyone born after September 1980 however must complete a National Association of State Boating Law Administrators boater education course or pass a boater's competency test before operating a boat of more than 10 horsepower.

The Youth's Boater Safety ID card, issued by the Florida Department of Environmental Protection, and another form of photographic ID, must be in his or her possession while operating a boat.

Boats must be registered and titled in the county where the vessel owner resides (at the county tax collector office). You have 30 days after purchase of a new or used boat to apply. The fee for a title is $6.25 with registration fees scaled for boat size. A Class 1 (16-26 feet) is $21.75; a Class 5 (110 feet or more) is $125.75 and various fees in between. The registration certificate must be on board the vessel when in operation.

Beach Parking Sticker.

You can save money on parking in counties that issue beach stickers. These entitle residents to park free at metered parking spots near the beach. Check to see if your county has these. You'll need your driver's license and car registration. Even snowbirds can apply by having a property tax receipt.

Florida Taxes Taxes Taxes

Income Tax.

Florida has no personal income tax! That attracts people to Florida, but as one wag said, "they get you in other ways. " Florida does have a

Corporate Income Tax, an Intangible Tax and perhaps higher sales tax than some states. Forms and information are available at www.myflorida.com/dor or call 850-488-8422.

Intangible Tax.

Florida, one of six states to do so, imposes an Intangible Tax on personal intangible property. Because it is a tax on money that has already been taxed, the governor and legislators have said they intended to repeal it. What bonanza came in 2004? The exemption for single persons was increased from $20,000 to $250,000 and for those filing joint returns the exemption increased from $40,000 to $500,000. So, if you have less than $500,000 in intangible assets, you won't owe or even have to file a return!

Individuals must file an annual Intangible Personal Property Tax Return (form DR601I). Returns must be filed by June 30, based on Intangible property value on January 1 (based on closing value of the investments on December 31). Corporations must file also, using form DR601C.

What is intangible personal property?

Intangible personal property is property whose value depends on what it represents, rather than on what it is. A stock certificate value is not the value of the paper on which it is printed, for example, but the value of the interest in the corporation it represents. Intangible property includes:

- Loans, notes and accounts receivable.
- Beneficial interest in any trust.
- Stocks, mutual funds, money market funds.
- Limited partnership interests, which are registered with the Securities and Exchange Commission and some collateralized mortgage obligations.

What is not subject to tax?

The most common items exempted from tax include money (cash on hand, cash in bank, certificates of deposits, annuities and similar instruments), trusts, U.S. treasury bills, notes and bonds, IRAs, Florida municipal bonds and funds, cash value of life insurance, and limited partnerships not registered with the Securities and Exchange Commission.

Also exempted are: accounts receivable arising from, or acquired in the ordinary course of a trade or business; franchises, real estate mortgage investment conduits (REMICs), financial asset securitization trusts (FASITs), and intangible property owned by tax exempt religious, tax exempt educational or tax exempt charitable institutions.

How much is the tax?

The tax is $1 per $1,000 of value (a 1 mill tax) on covered intangibles, after a tax cut in 2001 from $1.50 per $1,000. From the taxable amount, starting in 2004 as mentioned, there is a personal exemption of $250,000 ($500,000 for joint). The state provides a discount for payment before June 30 (four percent by last day of January or February; three percent March; two percent April; and one percent May). You do not need to pay or file if your total tax due is less than $60 before the discount.

How Can I Reduce My Tax?

You can avoid or minimize your Florida Intangible Tax by investing primarily in tax deferred investments and Florida Municipal tax-free bonds (or mutual funds). Some residents move taxable investments to non-taxable just before yearend. An example would be money from a mutual fund to cash in a Florida bank, which is excluded. The tax is based on a "snapshot" of your investments on January 1.

You can invest in Florida municipal bonds, rather than bonds from other states. Investing in the Florida bonds should be done based first on the quality of the bond. The Florida intangible tax is just 10 basis points, so its impact for example, would trim a 4.8 percent return to 4.7 percent. Ben Franklin frugality says that all other things being equal (percent return, triple A insured bond), why not save $100 each year on $100,000, because "a penny saved, is a penny earned?" I'll bet old Ben would like the deal.

If you are a large investor, check into a Florida Intangible Tax Trust with a lawyer. This is a way to avoid large intangible tax bills. The breakeven to do this is approximately $1,000 of intangible tax because the legal costs to set up the trust are about $1,000. This would mean well over $1 million in taxable investments.

Where can I get forms and assistance?

For assistance call the taxpayer division of the Florida Department of Revenue at 1-800-352-3671, or 850-488-6800. Download forms at www.myFlorida.com/dor/forms. Check the forms for the latest updates. The Department of Revenue also conducts seminars, January through May, in more than 80 cities around the state. You can check with your tax and legal advisers for specific help.

Sales Tax.

Sales tax of six percent applies to all items except food (non-prepared), medicine and professional services. Many Florida counties impose an additional 0.5 to 1.5 percent local option tax on transactions subject to sales tax, although at last count 16 of the 67 counties did not.

Florida had a tax-free week July 24-August 1, 2004. This provided an opportunity for back-to-school shoppers to save six percent on clothing and footwear up to $50 an item and school supplies less than $10.

Real Estate Property Tax (Ad Valorem Tax).

Real estate taxes vary depending on where you live, but you can save on these taxes by having a homestead exemption.

Homestead Exemption.

If you own your home, reside in it, and are a legal resident of Florida, you can apply for a $25,000 exemption from the appraised value of your property. This is another benefit for Florida residency and can typically save $400 a year on property taxes. The exemption also qualifies you for the cap on assessed value. It cannot exceed three percent or the CPI, whichever is less; each year following the year you received homestead exemption. To qualify you need to hold property as of January 1, reside in it and be a legal resident. You must file before March 1 of the year for which you are applying.

You'll need to fill out Form DR-501, which requires ownership information and proof of residence for all owners. Easy to say, but we had to dig up some of the information. You'll save time if you have everything you need to apply when you go to the tax collectors office.

If you drive, you will need to provide your Florida driver license number. You will need your vehicle tag number for all Florida vehicles. You will need your voter registration number or Declaration of Domicile (if not a U.S. Citizen or you do not wish to register to vote).

So, before working on getting your exemption, you will need to have gotten your driver's license, license plates and registered to vote. If the property is held in trust, a copy of the trust is required. You will also need your social security number and date of birth. If married, you must also provide your spouse's social security number. You need to submit, with the form, a copy of your most recently paid tax bill with parcel identification number, or recorded deed, or recorded contract for deed.

Some senior residents may qualify for an added $25,000 exemption. Florida voters approved amendment 3 to the state constitution to give cities and counties the power to grant exemptions to those aged 65 and older with household incomes $20,000 or below. Several communities have adopted the second $25,000 exemption for seniors with low incomes, including Miami-Dade county and the cities of Miami, Ormond Beach, Fort Myers Beach and Ponce Inlet.

Tip: If you've had any change in home ownership in the past year, make sure you have applied for the exemption. The Homestead Exemption is not transferable. So, if you buy a new home, you will need to file a new application in person on or before March 1.

Do I have to be a citizen to qualify? No. You must present, however, a resident alien card.

You are required to notify the Property Appraiser promptly whenever the use for the property changes (other than a sale of property). For further information on the Homestead Exemption, call the Florida Department of Revenue at 800-352-3671, or inquire by mail to Taxpayers Services, 1379 Blountstown Highway, Tallahassee, Florida 32304. Their Internet address is www.sun6.dms.state.fl.us/dor.

The Department has a free fax on demand service with 24-hour, seven-day-a-week access to more than 150 tax forms, files, statutes and other documents. Call 850-992-1676 from a telephone connected to a fax machine. A recorded message instructs you on how to retrieve documents.

Estate Taxes.

It pays to die in Florida. Although Florida has no inheritance tax, the Federal Estate Tax does apply in Florida, however, just as in every other state. If you died in Wisconsin in 2004, for example, and had an estate of $1.5 million, your estate could owe more than $60,000 in state taxes. In Florida, the tax would be zero. You might not care, but your heirs would.

Bed Tax (Tourist Development Tax).

The bed tax sometimes is called the tourist tax. If you rent your property, then you need a tax ID number and to collect three percent on the rent, up to six months. So, if you rent for six months or less, you need to collect and remit taxes to the County Tax Collector. The state also levies a six percent sales tax on this income. If you remit on time, there is a "collection allowance" of 2.5 percent to compensate for collecting the taxes. On the other hand, penalties for not remitting, or not remitting on time, can be costly: ten percent for each 30 days, plus interest.

Landlords have been shorting the county by not collecting. One estimate was a $10 million shortfall in Lee County, $3 million in Collier County, for example.

Perhaps the "dirty little secret" of taxation is Florida politicians have found creative ways to offset the lack of income from income tax by taxing tourists and seasonal residents with tourist development taxes.

Tangible Personal Property Tax.

If you operate a business, there's a tax on Tangible Personal Property, which refers to all assets used in a business or rental activity that are subject to an Ad Valorem assessment, such as furniture, fixtures, tools, machinery and household appliances used to generate income. Property is listed at 100 percent of total original cost. File by April 1.

Doing Business in Florida.

Florida offers several tax advantages for businesses:

- ❏ No personal state income tax.
- ❏ No inventory or goods-in-transit tax.
- ❏ No corporate income tax on estates, partnerships, individuals or private trusts.
- ❏ No state sales tax on electricity used in the manufacturing process.
- ❏ Plus: Low crime rate, attractive places to live and work.

In a study in Southwest Florida, 77 percent of employees were in companies with one to nine employees, 21 percent in companies employing 10-99 and only two percent in companies with 100 or more employees. In Collier County, more than 85 percent of the businesses had fewer than 10 employees in a 2003 survey. The Bonita Chamber of Commerce reported that 90 percent of member companies had fewer than 50 employees; half had fewer than ten employees. In the U.S. the 23.5 million small business owners generate more than half of all sales. Small businesses account for three-fourths of new jobs, according to the U.S. Bureau of Labor.

Inc magazine listed Fort Myers as one of the 50 hottest cities to start a small business. *Forbes* list of 200 Best Places for Business included a number of Florida cities; Naples was Number 32 on the list. If you are an entrepreneur, building a business in Florida makes good sense. Florida dominated *Inc* magazine's March 2004 Top 25 Cities for Doing Business in America, with six cities, including West Palm Beach (fifth), Fort Lauderdale (seventh), Jacksonville (eighth), Orlando (eleventh), Tampa-St. Petersburg (fourteenth) and Miami (twenty-second). Add three more on the medium size cities (150,000 to 450,000 job base) list: Sarasota (third), Fort Myers-Cape Coral (twelfth) and Daytona Beach (twentieth). *Inc* based the lists on job growth from U. S. Bureau of Labor statistics.

In *Entrepreneur Magazine's* annual list of best cities for entrepreneurs, Florida had four of the top ten in the United States, which included Fort Lauderdale (fourth), West Palm Beach (sixth), Miami (eighth) and Orlando (tenth) in the 2003 survey. Minneapolis-St. Paul finished first, followed by Washington, D.C. and Atlanta. A recent poll showed half of all Americans dream of owning a business. You can start one, buy an existing one or by a franchise. All three options have pluses and minuses.

Well, enough of the statistics, but they do illustrate opportunity for you.

Starting a Business.

You may want to start your own one-person business as so many have done after moving to Florida. In one new community of more than 400 homes, one person does painting, another does pressure washing, and another started a lawn service. Startup costs were small and they had a ready-made beginning customer base---their neighbors. The solution in Florida to being an older person, and working, may be to start a business. The older you get, the harder it is to get hired in a meaningful job.

Niche Businesses.

If you are a professional person, such as a physician, accountant, architect, dentist, engineer, or veterinarian, opportunities exist in fast-growing Florida for you to practice your profession.

Here are some of the many one-person niche businesses, some of which are almost unique to Florida, where you can "work for yourself" and "be your own boss." Many are part of an explosion of service businesses in Florida:

❖ Swimming pool cleaning service.

❖ Landscape/Lawn service.

❖ Home Watching. With thousands of homes that sit empty several months of the year, Florida has a business that hardly exists elsewhere. Alarm systems are a problem. For example, in Lee County, the sheriff said that in 2002 of 35,000 alarms just 26 were bona fide burglaries. Lightning strikes and power outages often trigger alarms.

❖ Pressure Cleaning. Most of the new homes are stucco. Pressure cleaning annually not only cleans the exterior, but also extends paint life.

❖ House cleaning service.

❖ Home helpers (non-medical in-home companion care).

❖ Pet grooming. In our area, a couple started a pet grooming business by buying a van and providing the service at pet owner's homes.

❖ Painting. Requires minimal upfront costs.

❖ Upholstery. An experienced upholsterer can contract with fabric stores; thus not requiring investment in a "storefront" or sales effort.

❖ Consultant. We provided strategic planning for businesses and associations. Homeowner and condominium associations particularly need help in strategic planning.

❖ Appraiser. Opportunities exist for property appraisers, but also business appraisers, which are certified by Institute of Business Appraisers, Inc.

❖ Handyman.

Operating a Business.

When we first moved to Florida, we were among those starting a small business. We learned the hard way you need to jump through some hoops to get into business. Some would-be entrepreneur businesses take more effort and time than others, but failing to take the steps can be costly. Here's what you need to do:

1. Decide on the right legal structure: corporation, partnership, limited liability or sole proprietorship. We chose the latter, which is the simplest. Of course, your choice determines what kind of taxes, who is liable and what forms you need to submit. A subchapter S corporation and a sole proprietorship pay taxes at individual rates.

2. Fictitious Name. If you use a name other than your own, which we did, then you must register the name with the state. The purpose of Chapter 865.09, Fictitious Name Act, Florida Statutes, is to insure a public record of the identity of a fictitious name owner.

3. State licensing.

4. Federal ID Number. If you are a business other than a sole proprietorship, you need to apply to the IRS and receive a Federal ID Number. We skipped this because as a sole proprietor, you can simply use your social security number.

Seasonal Challenges.

If you start a restaurant, huge swings in business volume are a fact of life in Florida. Business can drop 40 percent or more in summer. Even in the swimming pool servicing business, the season affects it to some degree because fewer chemicals are needed in winter to keep pools clean.

We have one powerful hint for you: don't hire for the peak. You need to develop a staffing plan, and an inventory plan for these seasonal swings. Some restaurants, for example, close for a month or more in summer. Others have working mothers take the summer off, which can be a win-win. Stores and restaurants run special events in summer to boost sales (offer two for one promotions and coupons).

Office in Executive Suite.

We recommend you crawl before you walk in a new area. Having an office in an executive office building fits that scenario. That's what we did when we first moved to Florida. We rented an office in an executive suite of offices, which offers convenience and services. This also simplifies getting into business in a new location. Operators of executive offices will tell you of the many former renters who built their business and moved on into their own office complex.

Home Office.

After a couple of years in an executive suite office, we moved our operation into a home office, along with nearly 9 million other business people. This works best for professionals who do not have a need for clients visiting the "office."

In some gated communities, however, homeowner association rules prohibit businesses operated from the home. When we built our new home, one important design element was a home office and the wiring for it to support broadband computer connections, and office equipment.

In the span of a few years, we made the leap, and paradigm shift, from the corporate office with all the people interaction, big office, big desk and administrative help and resources, to a single-person office in an executive suite, to a home office in retirement. The transition works, but each step has its challenges. Your attitude is the important factor along with an exit strategy. Who I am is not what I do.

Networking.

Networking, regardless of the business you plan to be in, remains the number one action. The quickest way to building a supportive network is to join local organizations, just as you probably did in the community up North. These include the local Chamber of Commerce and clubs like the Rotary, Lions and Kiwanis. A retailer friend, who sells hobby supplies, joined the radio control model airplane club and flies his plane at the club's field. Of course, if you're in an executive office building, the chances are the other offices are occupied by a variety of businesses, a number of which can help one another. For example, the financial planner, lawyer, and accountant often have the same clients.

Business Resources.

National business magazines such as *Fortune, Forbes, Inc, Business 2.0* along with Florida magazines such as *Florida Trend, South Florida CEO* and *Gulfshore Business* and local business publications offer an excellent resource.

Take advantage of resources, such as SCORE (Service Corps of Retired Executives), formed in 1964 as a non-profit association dedicated to entrepreneur education and the formation, growth and success of small business. TEC (The Executive Committee) is a good resource for CEOs. There are several chapters in Florida. Chapters consist of a dozen CEOs, which meet monthly, to "increase the effectiveness and enhance the lifestyle of CEOs." Check it out at www.teconline.com.

Small Business Development Centers (SBDC), which are non-profit organizations, help business owners with confidential business counseling and with low-cost seminars. The 31 college and university-based SBDC offices in Florida, are part of 1,400 national offices. Find the nearest one to you at www.floridasbdc.com.

Keyword Savvy.

A boost in your business may be just a click away, at pennies a click from a search engine. A tip worth trying: ask your customers words they'd use to describe your business or service. "Ask questions and listen" are four magic words to business success.

Chapter Four
Nifty Fifty and Life Begins at Seventy; Mental, Physical and Financial Health

"Age is a question of mind over matter.
If you don't mind, it doesn't matter. Satchel Paige, baseball
great who pitched until he was nearly 60 years old. *"How
old would you be if you didn't know how old you were?"*

Welcome to 50! Or 60! Or 70!

If you've reached 50 years of age, 70 may seem a long way off. It isn't! Time accelerates the older you get. Whether you're 50, 60 or 70, you need to plan ahead, rather than getting stuck in today's myopias. Planning in choosing a Florida lifestyle, as this book shows you, saves you time and money. What makes sense at 70, even if you are now 40, 50 or 60 years old?

Nearly a fourth of the residents of many Florida communities are 65 years old or older; and 37 percent are 55 or older. Every month, one million people turn 60 years old in the world. By 2010, nearly half the population will be 50 or older!

Will Your Nest Egg Last?

The U.S. population is getting older every year. In 1900, life expectancy was 47 years. When Social Security began (1937), life expectancy was 61 years. Now it's 77 years from birth (and more for women), but if you are 65 then expect to live to 83 or beyond. The average person will spend 20 years in retirement. The fast growing 85 years old and up population

59

group has tripled to four million persons since 1960, and will double in the next 30 years to eight million persons. The number of Americans over age 100 will double by 2010 (from 65,000 in 2003). That tells you to invest wisely so you don't outlive your income. The nest egg may need to survive longer if you do. The only options are withdraw less, retire later (or work in retirement) or save more. This chapter focuses on living in retirement and protecting the nest egg.

Generational Differences: Silent Generation and Baby Boomers.

Nearly two million "Silent Generation" (1928-1945) Americans turned 70 years old in 2000. Americans will turn 70 years old at the rate of two million each year until the surge from the Baby Boomer generation (born 1946-1964) increases the rate. This 77 million-person generation has been termed a "pig in a python" for its effect on society, because of a lower birthrate before and after it. As many as one in five Baby Boomers, will consider moving to Florida.

If you were born in the 1930s, you come from a small group. Only 20 million Americans show up in the U.S. census born during the Great Depression. Contrast that with 41 million people born in the decade of the 1950s and the 77 million Baby Boomers.

Silent Generation members continue the trek to Florida. The "silent generation" is a misnomer if you look at their impact on society, even though they had the lowest birth rate of any generation in the twentieth century. More than a fourth of the billionaires listed by *Forbes* in their July 5, 1999 issue, for example, were born in the 1930s. And a third were older than 70. They dominated corporate boards.

During the 1930s, 12 million workers were out of a job. Five thousand banks failed. President Franklin D. Roosevelt said one-third of us were "ill-fed, ill-housed and ill-clothed." Our life may have been simple and hardy, but we were not conscious of privations. You don't know what you don't know, or don't have.

In 1930, the public debt was $131.51 per person. By 1994, it had soared to $17,805.64 per person. The population then was 124 million; now it's more than doubled to 280 million. People who are 70 have lived through twelve U.S. presidents and four wars. The Silent Generation's war was the Korean War, in which 54,248 died in three years; just 3,907 fewer than the much longer and more visible (TV) Vietnam War. No parades greeted veterans from either of these unpopular wars, but most of us just wanted to get on with our lives.

All these factors create a generational attitude that differs from other generations. The Silent Generation grew up with parents of The Greatest Generation, who had attitudes of, "do your best, keep going." The Silent

Generation has been more about conformity than the more open people of the Baby Boomer generation, who perhaps air their problems. Whatever the differences, some things remain the same in approaching retirement; such as adequate funds, health, and graceful aging. So, whether Baby Boomer or Silent Generation, this chapter will paint a future picture for you and the actions you can take to enhance your future lifestyle.

The first massive wave of retirees will hit in 2008. That could be a time of higher interest rates and higher inflation, so find out how the street-smart actions at the end of this chapter will help your readiness.

Being Seventy.

Someone wrote about life begins at forty, but Oliver Wendell Holmes observed: "To be seventy years young is something far more cheerful than to be forty years old."

Of all the people who have ever reached 65 years of age, in the history of the world, half are alive today. Nine million are veterans with Florida second only to California in the number of veterans at 1.75 million. Americans think of themselves ten years younger than their real age and don't consider themselves "elderly" at age 70. "How old would you be if you didn't know how old you are?"

"If you ask me how it feels to be 70, I will answer that I feel exactly like seventy. And it is splendid." said William Lyon Phelps.

Society Shapers After Age 70!

Society shapers, after they were 70 years old, include: Socrates, Copernicus, Galileo, Ronald Reagan, Gandhi, Ben Franklin and Nelson Mandella. Golda Meir (1898-1978) was 71 when she became prime minister of Israel. S. I. Hayakawa retired as president of San Francisco State University at 70, and then was elected to the U.S. Senate. Thomas Jefferson was elected to his second term when he was past 70.

Benjamin Franklin had turned 70, and was the oldest, in working on the Declaration of Independence in 1776. He was an investor in hot air balloons at age 77. He was president of the Pennsylvania Society for Promoting the Abolition of Slavery when he was 81 years old. We can't overlook the wizard Edison who had his lab in Ft. Myers, Florida when he was 70 and beyond. Florence Nightingale lived to be 90 and accomplished much in her last 20 years. Tennyson penned, *"Crossing the Bar"* at 83.

Michelangelo was 71 when he painted the Sistine Chapel. Oliver Wendell Holmes composed "Over the Tea Cups" at age 79. Goethe finished the second part of "Faust" at 83. Verdi gave us the masterpiece, Othello, when he was 80. Titian drew his historic picture, "The Battle of Lepanto" at 98 (1575).

Success Again After 70.

Bob Hope, then 96, turned on the Christmas lights at Disneyland in November 1999. John Glenn, at 77 years old, returned to space. Paul Newman won a car race at age 70. President George H. W. Bush parachuted on his birthday at age 75 and 80. George Burns was 80 when he won his first Oscar.

Casey Stengel didn't retire as manager of the NY Mets, until he was 75. *Sports Illustrated* magazine in 2003, named 72-year old Jack McKeon, Florida Marlins manager, National League manager of the year for turning the team into an unlikely playoff entrant. The Marlins won the World Series led by a man who calls himself an "old goat," the oldest manager ever to win a world series. Arnold Palmer, golfer, turned 70 in 1999 and competed in his fiftieth Masters in 2004 at age 75. Florida State University coach Bobby Bowden at age 73 had won more major college football games than any other coach!

Life Can Begin at Seventy!

These examples do show life can begin at seventy. So, take heart! Point your ship toward adventure and accomplishment. Find a project that fits your skills and expertise, or that is something you've always wanted to do. Toss out the alarm clock, make each day one you can count on doing things you want to do geared to a laid-back Florida lifestyle. It's never too late to change, to revitalize energy, and to seek out new challenges.

"Begin doing what you want to do now. We are not living in eternity, we have only this moment sparkling like a star in our hand--- and melting like a snowflake." Marie Beyon Ray.

Planning the Future; Fifty to Seventy and Beyond.

When you look in the rear-view mirror, as you get older, entire decades seem to be identified by a few events in your lifetime. That provides you a perspective that has value, but the future is ahead, not behind. The good old days may not have been all that good! In fact, the past is gone; let it go. What does the future bring? Forecasting the future is a lot like driving in fog. It's tough to see what is ahead, but you can bet it's coming your way. As Ben Franklin observed: "It is easy to see, hard to foresee." No one can say what the future will bring, but we can adjust, plan and prepare, which will make it easier to handle the unanticipated events sure to come around the corner.

Aging Successfully.

The most vibrant older people are ones who feel useful, gerontologists say. There is an advantage to having a new starting point in life, a time "to close the door on the past, take a fresh grip on life, and start the journey afresh."

John Rowe and Robert Kahn, co-authors of *Successful Aging,* say it's never too late to change your lifestyle. They see three major issues for longevity: "A low risk of disease and disease-related disabilities, high mental and physical abilities and a desire to remain actively engaged with people." Gene Cohen, in his upbeat book, *The Creative Age-Awakening the Human Potential in the Second Half of Life,* notes one's later years can be a creative time.

We have asked the over-70 crowd in our community about how they're coping with advancing age. Time and again, we heard: "You have to have a positive attitude." A long-term study showed that people with a positive attitude lived 19 percent longer than pessimists. "Rejoice in the little things: your keys are right where you look, you hit all green stoplights, you end up in the fastest line at the store, lunch or dinner out exceeds your expectations, you receive an unexpected call from a friend, and make every moment count." Hey, even embrace Florida kitsch! Let's face it; some attractions are corny because Florida's number one industry *is* tourism. Go with the flow because swimming with the tide often makes more sense than struggling against it. Someone said, "A smile is contagious so be a carrier."

My father often quoted, when change would be discussed: "Grant me the serenity to accept things I cannot change; courage to change the things I can; and wisdom to know the difference." That age-old advice keeps on ticking. Enrich your life with a focus on the spirit of adventure; self-improvement and making dreams come true, as described in this book. Let these stimulate you to think about life after work!

Mental Fitness: Find a Project

Projects that give back to the community provide fulfillment; some projects even turn from hobbies into moneymakers. Do something you love that expresses your inner desires. Here are some examples of activities to consider to remain engaged and to connect to other people:

Volunteer on Committees. Many of the Florida county governments have Volunteer Advisory committees. This provides you an opportunity to share your expertise in helping the local government on specific issues. For example, we served on the County Productivity Advisory Committee.

Neighborhood Watch. We joined Neighborhood Watch by attending educational sessions put on by a Sheriff's Deputy at our community clubhouse. In the process we learned some valuable tips in protecting our own home. The neighborhood watch volunteers also have an annual "block party," which gets people involved.

Genealogy. A cousin, Russell Farnham, a certified genealogist wrote, "It [genealogy] can be an addiction. Realistically, we all see it as part of the aging process. It's just a shame we don't recognize it earlier in life." Everyone who has jumped into tracing family roots laments they should have started earlier when ancestors were alive. If you wait until age 65 or 70, even your parents, and other relatives, with all their family knowledge could be gone. Start now to reduce the number of brick walls you'll hit in your research. Start now in writing family sketches to use later. Go beyond just names and try to understand your ancestral families. We did and shared a book about the family with our descendants and other relatives and friends. Great project. Check out www.ancestry.com.

Crafts and Hobbies. Many retirees get into crafts of one kind or another, but even anti-crafters seem to jump into the hobby of scrap booking, now a $2.5 billion "industry," with 2,500 scrap booking stores, which offer supplies, including stickers to enhance photographs. The computer has added ease and simplicity in preserving memories.

Great Books. Several colleges offer discussion sessions. The Creative Retirement Center at International College, for example, hosts a "Great Books Discussion Group" every other Friday. The purpose is for members to share their thoughts and insights about Western world literature.

Aquacize (water aerobics). My wife, Mary, started a three-times-a-week Aquacize (water aerobics) class at the clubhouse swimming pool. This offers not only the healthy aspect, but also socializing, which perhaps is equally healthy.

Coach, Counselor, Mentor, Docent. Opportunities abound to share your knowledge, especially helping with school age children. In Florida, with the influx and growth of the Hispanic population, tutoring adults in English is a need.

Red Hat Society. Mary started a chapter in our community, one of more than 100 in Naples, among thousands in the United States. The *Red Hat* women find fun after fifty. All play, no business, no rules. They greet middle age "with verve, humor and élan." Check out www.redhatsociety.com for more information in joining a chapter and to go for the gusto.

Homeowner Association Board. I served as president of two associations and viewed the service as "giving something back." It can also be nearly a full-time unpaid stressful job!

Foster Grandparents Program. This program places senior citizens who qualify in area schools to help out in classrooms. Participants must be 60 years old, and agree to work 20 hours a week.

Master Gardener. Gardening in Florida differs greatly from up North. See Chapter Seven. Typically, achieving Master Gardener status requires a 12-week course of one day a week, and then doing volunteer work.

Community Emergency Response Team. Most communities have organized volunteer community emergency response teams to respond in a disaster. Typical training involves six 3-hour sessions for certification.

Habitat Steward. If you're interested in wildlife, ecology and habitat conservation, this may be for you. The National Wildlife Federation offers training for volunteers on topics ranging from butterfly habitat to creating a pond, which takes one day a week for four weeks to be certified. If you have an interest in Florida's three national parks, and want to volunteer, see details at www.nps.gov/volunteer.

School Volunteer. Some of our friends help out on Saturday morning with clean up at the schools. Not only does this "give something back" and help with costs, but also helps give a well-kept look that can leave a positive impression, which can indirectly help home values.

Part-time Employment. A pharmacist friend, 73, told us: "I was retired, but really got bored, so I went back to work part time." An 87-year old continues to play the piano at a restaurant. He says, "life is like a piano; it depends on how you play it."

In summary, "aude aliquid dignum," sixteenth century Latin for d*are something worthy.* Live life large! The networking involved in these projects builds friendships. We look to cultivate and nourish new friends, which usually isn't easy. We try to stay away from negative people (they'll pull you down) and look for positive, happy people who share our values.

Physical Fitness

When my grandfather turned three score and ten, he wrote: "Why should not I and everyone at 70 aspire to go on actively to the final goal? Why sit and gaze at the faded fire?" He lived to be 98. He believed the "Three Rs (reading, 'riting, 'rithmetic) that agitated the first twenty years, can give way to the three Vs to sweeten the last twenty: *vim, vigor, vitality."*

Exercise remains the single most potent anti-aging medication known to humankind. Eubie Banks, the famous composer and pianist, said when he was 100 years old: "If I had known I was gonna live this long, I'd have taken better care of myself."

Fortunately one of the best exercises, walking, requires little investment and can be done outdoors nearly year round, even during the rainy season. Brisk walking on a regular basis shows benefits. Swimming, another terrific exercise can be done year round in Florida.

Just Do It....Exercise That Is. A 2000 National Health Interview Survey showed that 64 percent of men and 72 percent of women do not exercise regularly, even though moderate activity later in life helps protect against disease and boosts memory.

Financial Fitness

Mark Twain said, "Before seventy we are merely respected, at best, and we have to behave all the time, or we lose that asset; but after seventy, we are respected, esteemed, admired, revered, and don't have to behave unless we want to."

Perhaps Mark Twain had it right, but one behavior he didn't have to worry about, you do: check your IRAs and 401Ks, because if you haven't taken money out, you must do so at age 70-1/2, or face a 50 percent IRS penalty! Not only do you want to avoid a penalty, but minimize taxes during withdrawal. The IRS says you have a life expectancy of 16 years, so it's easier to get older, than wiser.

You probably are thinking at this point, you don't need another sermon on financial planning, so we'll keep this section short, clear and helpful. We will focus on helpful hints that will not only make, or save, you money, but will also provide you with a financial checkup.

Net Worth. What is your net worth? In the book, *The Millionaire Next Door,* the authors say you should have a net worth equal to your age multiplied by your pretax income, divided by 10. If you earn, for example, $40,000 a year, you should have $200,000 at age 50. Let's say you, as a couple, have combined salaries of $100,000 plus $10,000 in investment income for a total of $110,000. At age 50, you should have $550,000 net worth using their formula. Another way to look at it is you should have a nest egg of 20 times your annual expenses not covered by pension or social security, to withdraw 5 percent a year. The traditional three-legged stool of retirement income consists of savings, social security and pensions. That nest egg must stretch farther than ever because of longer life spans we mentioned earlier, and because the value of your nest egg will diminish over time. Making up for mistakes is much tougher when you're older, so the street-smart ideas in this chapter can help you avoid costly mistakes. The lousy alternatives are to run out of money or severely adjust your lifestyle.

Grow Your Investments and Live off the Returns. People spend time preparing for retirement, and when it finally arrives, they think: "Now what?" You must manage your assets to insure you don't outlive your income. What do your assets generate in income a month? Your net worth, and any pensions, annuities, dividends, interest and social security, will determine where you can live and how well. Using the 5 percent a year withdrawal rule of thumb, you need $20,000 of investments for every $1,000 of annual income. If you have $400,000 of investments, for example, you could withdraw $20,000 annually, and your principal would never run down, although a prolonged bear market might require you to withdraw less for a while.

If you are one of the 3.8 million households with a net worth of one million dollars, or more (of 111 million households in 2003 in the United States), you could withdraw $50,000 a year for each million and probably not affect the principal. If your total worth will generate less than your needs, then you perhaps need to spend some time on retirement goals, work longer and save more! Is this something you can relate to?

Pension Woes. The lack of a defined-benefits pension underscores the need for wealth building. Many companies ended these plans in favor of employee contribution plans, such as a 401k. So, when people advise you to contribute the maximum to your IRA and 401k plans, taking the advice would be wise! Even for those of you with pensions, the pension could be in jeopardy. According to Credit Suisse First Boston, the companies in Standard & Poor's 500-stock index will be $247 billion short of what they need to finance pensions for future retirees.

Ten Street-Smart Sure-Fire Tips

The following straight-talk ideas will help you in many ways if they galvanize you to act now. The gold is in the execution.

Diversify and Allocate. The market drop and gyrations in 2000-2002, a three-year bear market, a once-in-a-lifetime event for most people, should have taught all of us a "set-it-and-forget-it" approach to our investments is unwise as is too much money concentrated in one or a few areas. Mark your calendar now so you check your portfolio balance in terms of asset allocations. Re-balance. Sell overweight asset classes and add to under-weighted areas; sell high and buy low! "Rebalancing forces investment discipline and avoids the up and down emotions of greed and fear that affect all investors," a financial planner said. If you're too busy, then find someone (financial planner) to help you.

What allocation is right for you depends on your age, tolerance for risk and other factors, but clearly your investments need to be allocated into stocks, bonds, and cash. One simple rule of thumb: your investment in stocks should equal your age subtracted from 100. At age 50, stocks would be 50 percent of your investment; at age 70 stocks would be 30 percent, although some would argue for a higher percentage. One expert argues for 90 percent in stocks in your early years and 10 percent in stocks in retirement. His theory is that at 30 years old, you have a long span of time to smooth out the downs of the market, which does not exist when you are 70 years old. At 70 years old you need to protect the principal and focus on income. Our retirement allocation is stocks 50 percent, bonds 30-35 percent, and cash vehicles 15-20 percent. Within the "stocks" category we include large, mid and small cap stocks, some foreign stocks and REITs to diversify within the category. In "bonds" we have a mix of long and shorter term, high and lower quality and laddered low-risk treasury bonds. Within "cash" we have "cash vehicles" laddered (different maturities). Does it work? Yes, although we have been withdrawing for several years, including during the stock market downturn of 2000-2002, our principal remains at the same level it was when we started withdrawals. One of the biggest mistakes investors make, experts say, is to retreat from the market, which we did not, because the enemy is still inflation. Having half your funds in stocks offers inflation protection in the long term. Having 15-20 percent cash protects us from bear market downdrafts.

What's right for you? The Internet has hundreds of calculators that can help you determine your saving level, given your age and tolerance for risk. Just remember to review periodically; and rebalance. The three-year bear market (2000-2002) caused apathy and fear. But failure to rebalance and pay attention can be costly. Further, being too conservative can be a big mistake; with life spans increasing, you could outlive your income. You may not want to contemplate your own death, but you don't want to run out of money, either, so check out your life expectancy at www. livingto100.com.

Company Stock. I loved the company I worked for and was a loyal employee who had a major part of our net worth in company stock. That's a big mistake! You may have no control over the company being crippled or destroyed, as has happened with Enron and others. Employees not only lost money on the stock, many also lost their pensions. Fortunately for us, many years ago, a financial planner advised us to diversify, which we did. If you have more than 10 percent of your total assets in company stock, diversify the excess into other stocks. Do it now!

Mutual Funds. An estimated 93 million Americans have money invested in mutual funds, perhaps half or more of all households. A financial planner told us the biggest mistake people make with mutual funds is buying last year's best funds. If you have enough money, and time, to invest in 25-30 stocks, you can avoid the mutual fund fees. If not, mutual funds make sense. Further, mutual funds are probably the best way to have some money in foreign stocks. Most brokerage firms, like Morgan

Stanley and others, have "model portfolios" that can help you, as can their financial planners.

Bonds and Bond Funds Risk. If you have money in bond mutual funds, remember bond prices are inversely related to interest rates. If interest rates rise, bond prices fall. A two percent interest rate rise could whack your bond value by 12 percent, for example, in the short term. On the other hand, if you have individual bonds, and plan to hold them to maturity, then rate changes are irrelevant except the purchasing power of your future interest payments may decline with rising inflation. We sold our bond funds and bought individual insured triple-A bonds with different maturities. Ladder your bonds, so they have a "ladder" of maturities. If you still would rather have your money in bond funds, then consider index funds where fees are lower. Bonds yield less than stocks, so fees have a bigger impact on your returns.

Buy What You Really Understand. One of our biggest winners, Chico's, came about from living in the town where Chico's is headquartered, buying Chico's clothes, attending Chico's annual meetings and getting to know the management. Florida Rock was another one. Others: Florida Power & Light, FindWhat.com, Darden Restaurants, WCI Communities, Source Interlink Company, St. Joe Company and, whoops, Winn-Dixie. Of course, past performance is no guarantee of future price appreciation; and some can go down like Winn-Dixie did. We did concentrate on buying Florida-based stocks and Florida bonds (because of tax-free advantages). Approach stock buying as though you were buying the business. Warren Buffett has been an outstanding success following that precept and patience. He said, in an interview with *Business Week*, "Success in investing doesn't correlate with I.Q. once you're above the level of 25. Once you have ordinary intelligence, what you need is the temperament to control the urges that get other people into trouble investing."

Buy TIPS (Treasury Inflation Protected Securities). TIPS were introduced by the Federal Government in 1997. TIPS adjusts the principal value of your bond twice a year in step with any CPI move. If deflation ever hits, you are guaranteed to get 100 percent of your original principal at maturity. TIPS are designed to protect you from inflation.

Continue 401(k) Contributions. Continue contributing as long as you can. Pay yourself first! Contributions are pretax, which means that a contribution of $500 amounts to perhaps only $360 less out of your paycheck for a person in the 28 percent bracket. If the company matches your contribution, then contributing to the maximum of the match is a no-brainer because of a return of 50-100 percent! You win the trifecta: pre-tax investment, matching funds, and tax deferral until retirement. Take from taxable investments before tax-deferred ones, such as 401(k) and IRA. Take advantage of the tax deferral for as long as you can. If you can afford it, contribute the maximum. If you believe you can't now, then review your contribution when you get a pay raise. Pay yourself first.

Dividend Paying Stocks. Buying dividend-paying stocks makes sense, not only because of the income, but also because of the changes in the tax code that favor the approach.

Leaving a Legacy. One of the biggest mistakes you could make could be not having an estate plan (will, living will, assignment of power of attorney, possibly a trust). If you don't have the right estate plan for your needs, taxes and probate fees can cut the value of your estate. Being a Florida resident has advantages as we have mentioned, but you still should have a will and an estate plan, regardless of your net worth. You could leave a lasting legacy to your favorite charity and at the same time reap financial benefits with a charitable remainder trust. Money that would have otherwise been paid as taxes goes to charity. You avoid immediate capital gains, increase spendable income, get a tax deduction and reduce future estate tax liabilities. Work with your tax and legal advisors to develop a money saving plan.

You can gift up to $11,000 to any individual that you choose under the annual gift tax exclusion; and $22,000 if you are filing jointly. They're not tax deductible, but the recipient will not have to pay a tax when the gift is made, and the gifts reduce the size of your estate. The amount gradually increases as does the estate tax exemption, but who knows what the next tax change will bring!

Keep Good Records. Yes, we know this one is obvious and simple. Obvious and simple doesn't mean people do it. Keeping good records will save you pain, especially when transferring to Florida. Simply balancing your checkbook and paying bills as they arrive will save you money and help with the record keeping.

Chinese Proverb (Fortune Cookie):
"Listen to the wisdom of the old." Lottery: 3, 7, 10, 14, 16, 23.

What's the most useful thing you have learned so far in these first four chapters? Jotting down key items will remind you to do them and save time and money. The list of key items will help you develop a plan, described in Chapter Nineteen.

Chapter Five
Reflections on the Beach and
Best Beaches
"Life's a beach"

On a blustery overcast February morning, I stood on the beach watching the waves that had been kicked up by the strong wind. Looking to the west, a light fog obscured any detail of the island I knew to be there. No boats sailed or motored before me. Indeed, no one was around because of chilly temperatures.

Five hundred years ago, a Calusa Indian would have seen what I saw. Felt what I felt. That does put things in perspective, does it not? Looking out to sea, the view was the same as what the Calusa saw. If the Calusa Indian looked around, he would see Indians drying fishing nets, carving wood, cooking and making shell tools. Instead of a condo, he would see a thatched hut. His food consisted of fish and shellfish. We planned to do the same for dinner.

Perhaps humans stood on the beach and felt the same serenity with the musical sound of the surf, the wind swirling the sand ... for 100 generations and 2,000 years. Living life to the fullest makes even more compelling sense when you realize you're simply one of the grains of sand on the beach and live a brief moment. What really is important? Thoreau said: "This curious world which we inhabit is more to be admired and enjoyed than used."

Background and retrospect shape perspective. We discard some ideas like so many dead leaves. Other ideas, verified in the rugged school of experience, surface from the sea to deepen understanding and strengthen the vision. Is not the secret of contentment to care more and more about less and less? There is an undreamed joy in simply being alive and appreciating the sounds of the sea and birds. It stimulates thought and stirs imagination. I have found calmness of spirit and clarity of mind to be better on the beach than anywhere else. Is this God's cathedral?

Did the Calusa Indian, gazing out to sea, have the magic moment of just "being?" He, too, watched a Pelican glide along, then dive to grab a fish. He, too, must have watched the many species of shore birds and delighted in their antics. Egrets with long necks and spindly legs walked along at water's edge. In many ways, despite TV, computers, automobiles, basic life has changed little; at least while standing alone quietly on the beach. Certainly, the enjoyment of watching the birds, the sea and the wind is timeless. The Calusa would reflect on the past as he thought about the future. Memories are one paradise from which we cannot be driven.

Calusa Indians may have first settled in the area as early as 50 B.C. Calusa Indians lived and fished long before the first pyramids of Egypt. They started building a series of mounds between A.D. 600 and 800. Sometime after 1000, they dug a 30-foot wide, six-foot deep canal on 18-mile long Pine Island. Remnants of the ancient canal, which reached across Pine Island, can still be seen.

By the time Ponce de Leon came to Florida June 4, 1513, the Calusa had become the dominant Indians in South Florida. Calusa means "fierce people." They were not only independent and fierce, but also taller, heavier and more muscular than most Indians in Florida. A Calusa Indian arrow, some say, killed Ponce de Leon in 1521 not far, perhaps, from where I was standing on the beach. A Spanish 13-year old boy, Escalante Fontanek, shipwrecked in mid-sixteenth century, lived with the Calusa for 17 years. He wrote: "The people are archers and men of strength."

The 8,000 (some peg the population as high as 20,000) Calusa Indians had communities on many of the islands off the Southwest Florida coast. Although their capital was on Mound Key in Estero Bay, the Calusa Indians had a large settlement at Pineland on the northwest shore of Pine Island.

If the Calusa Indian, standing in my place 500 years ago contemplated the future, what might he be thinking? He would have hope. Hope is a candle in the dark. Hope believes in the future, thinks the best thoughts in the worst time.

As I gazed toward the sea, I could see my image dimly in the water as the sun broke through the overcast. The Calusa believed in the afterlife. They believed a person had three souls; one in the pupil of his eye, one in his own shadow and one in his reflection in water. When a Calusa died, two of the souls left the body …. the two I could see standing on the beach … and soul in the pupil remained.

There is an Indian legend that the Mighty One created the first strawberries to tempt an Indian maiden running away from her lover after a quarrel. The berries, says the legend, had to be so beautiful the maiden would stop to pluck them and so tasty she would forget her anger. So the Mighty One gathered sweet mist from the mountains, dew from the fresh grass, honey from the bee, color from the red bird, bright speckles from the trout, and beauty from the hummingbird. The berries thus created stopped the angry maiden's flight, sweetened her temper, and led to a legendary reconciliation.

Whatever the truth of the legend, the Calusa used indigo berries for paint. And they used palmetto fronds for cordage to make nets. They made canoes by using fire to hollow out pine logs. They used empty shells for tools, and for building up mounds in swamps. The Calusa fashioned spear-throwing sticks with hardwood points, called, Atlatl, for hunting and for war.

You can get a glimpse of how the Calusa Indians lived by visiting the Randell Research Center on Pine Island (7450 Pineland Road, phone 941-283-2062), where you can see mounds (including the 30-foot high Brown's mound), a canal they dug and artifacts. The center, on land the Randell family gifted in 1996, is operated by the Florida Museum of Natural History (www.flmnh.edu). Unlike nearby islands, Pine Island has no public beaches, but is surrounded mostly by mangroves. No luxury resorts. No high-rise condos. Boating and fishing are popular. The Calusa Land Trust (www.calusalandtrust.org) has been trying to acquire any property that displays evidence of the old Calusa canal along with property to protect as preserves.

On Marco Island, archaeologists found the small elegant sculpture of a wood cat carved perhaps in 600 A.D. Ebony replicas of the six-inch figurine, which some say resembles Egyptian or Babylonian art, can be found in most of the shops.

What the Calusa left behind, whether in shell mounds or carvings, provides a fascinating archaeological detective story of a changing culture and environment of a people who, despite having a powerful society, disappeared by the mid 1700s. Every group, individual and society faces future challenges. Survivors will adapt to changes and go with the flow. Others, like the Calusa, will not adapt. Their society simply disappeared. The Calusa were apparently victims of European diseases of smallpox and measles, slavery and wars with the Europeans and other Indians. Only artifacts and mounds remain.

Standing in the Calusa's footprints in the sand provided a stress-relieving meditation moment. On this day, in February, the sun peeked through in late morning. A giant rainbow arched over the island to the south in the afternoon. And later, a little after 6:10 p.m., the sun set in a blaze of red and gold, the reflection on the water a signal of good luck and wealth.

Thoreau spent years trying to discover whole continents within him. Someone might ask, "Why does he stand there staring out to sea?" The answer: "To better understand myself." To do so prepares one to be better able to help others.

Who can tell what is just around the corner? But, we must think about the possibilities and adjust to succeed for the long term. Besides, with reflections on the beach, the longer term feels shorter and clearer. Ralph Waldo Emerson said, "The invariable mark of wisdom is to see the miraculous in the common."

Generations have come and gone. The past is gone, the future a mystery but today is a gift, which is why they call it the present, someone said. I imagined the Calusa to say, if you want to leave footprints in the sands of time, wear "work" moccasins. It's not enough to just stand and think on the beach. What does this mean to you? It means to use this book to help you develop your plan.

The Calusa would not, of course, know Banks, the poet who wrote of spirit and bright hopes and the good that can be done, but if he did, he might recite the lyrics. Of course, standing on the beach, I didn't remember all the words either, so I looked them up later. George Linnaeus Banks (1821-1881) wrote:

I live for those who love me,
Whose hearts are kind and true:
For the Heaven that smiles above me,
And awaits my spirit too:
For all human ties that bind me,
For the task by God assigned me,
For the bright hopes yet to find me
And the good that I can do.

Where are the Best Beaches in Florida?

Florida has more than 770 miles of beaches, although some claim as many as 1,100 miles of beaches. With 90 percent of the population within 10 miles of the ocean, beaches perhaps are Florida's biggest natural attraction. Whatever your interests are, with a wide variety of beaches to choose from, there's a beach for you in Florida.

Many polls are published about best beaches, but the best beach for you depends entirely upon your desires. If you want remoteness, seclusion, few people around, and a quiet serenity for reflection, then Lovers Key and Cayo Costa come to mind. If, on the other hand you want the dynamics of the social beach scene with lots of people, parasailing off shore, restaurants and beach shops, then South Beach in Miami may meet your needs. Daytona, Panama City and Fort Lauderdale beaches attract spring breakers, but so do other beaches. Sanibel beaches are among the worlds best for shelling. Windsurfers have a wide variety of choices.

We have spent sun time on scores of beaches in every sector of Florida, including Daytona, New Smyrna, St. Augustine, Deerfield, Miami, the Keys, Smather's in Key West; and Panama City, Clearwater, St. Pete, Siesta Key, Cayo Costa, Sanibel, Captiva, North Captiva, Fort Myers, Lovers Key, Vanderbilt and others in between. Let's first look, however, at how "experts" rated the beaches:

Bountiful Beautiful Beaches in Florida. In a *USA Today* 2001 survey, seven of the best 10 beaches were in Florida, based on 3,000 responses to the poll.

The Travel Channel featured their top 10 Florida beaches. One of these, Lovers Key, which was number four on their list, is a personal favorite simply because it's one of the last natural secluded places. We have visited all 10 of the Florida Beaches profiled. The program featured Parke Puterbaugh and Alan Bisbort, well-traveled beach writers who wrote the 1999 book (second edition, 2001) *Foghorn Outdoors: Florida Beaches*

1. South Beach, Miami
2. Siesta Key, Sarasota
3. Palm Beach
4. Lovers Key Beach
5. Clearwater Beach
6. Smather's Beach, Key West.
7. Sandspur Beach, Bahia Honda (south of Marathon); called "the most beautiful beach in the keys."
8. Panama City
9. Sanibel
10. Daytona Beach

Dr. Leatherman, called "Dr. Beach" (www.Drbeach.org), selected several Florida beaches in his top 10 beaches list in 2003, including Fort DeSoto Park (second), Caladesi Island State Park (fifth), and Cape Florida State Recreational Area (ninth). Kaanapali Hawaii topped the list. St. Joseph Peninsula State Park in Florida headed the list in 2002. Fort

DeSoto and Caladesi are both in the St. Petersburg area. Cape Florida is south of Miami.

St. Petersburg/Clearwater claims the "ideal Florida beach destination" in an area that is the world record holder for the most consecutive days of sunshine----768 days in a row---and with Fort DeSoto and Caladesi among 35 miles of beaches. St. Petersburg has an average of 361 days a year of sunshine and an average high temperature of 81. Fort DeSoto has 900 acres and seven miles of beaches on five islands. Caladesi, like Cayo Costa, accessible only by boat, is one of the few remaining undeveloped Gulf Coast barrier islands. It has a three-mile nature trail, in addition to beautiful beaches. A ferry travels hourly from the mainland to the island.

Dr. Leatherman, who is director of Florida International University Laboratory for Coastal Research, also has campaigned for healthy beaches. His intense interest even extends to naming his daughter Sandy and his son Beach. The National Healthy Beaches Campaign (NHBC@flu.edu) certifies beaches "based on water quality, public services, safety and water control and managed with a proactive environmental stance." The top 40 list shows 29 in Florida in 2003. Dr. Leatherman is the author of *America's Beaches*.

Our Top Three Beaches

1. Lovers Key Beach. Lovers Key State Park, 8700 Estero Boulevard, Ft. Myers, Florida 33931, phone 941-463-4588. What could be nicer than cruising down the river on a warm late-August day in Florida? We did that with a dozen friends on a rented pontoon boat from Fort Myers Beach. The boat plied its way south at mid morning in Estero Bay on calm, placid, indigo-colored water. A light breeze blew in from the Gulf to cool the warm summer temperature under a cobalt sky.

First to come in view were the live-in boats anchored in the bay, along with several abandoned derelict boats, marooned on sand bars or sunk and resting on the bottom of the shallow bay. Two boats looked like they could have been expensive at one time. We have boated down the bay many times but we always see something new. "Look at all the large new homes being built where a small older home used to stand," said one passenger. We've seen this phenomenon all along both coasts.

We stopped along the way at the Fish House Restaurant for a leisurely lunch. After lunch, we continued to our destination, Lovers Key, where we pulled in and beached the pontoon boat so we could walk the beach and look for shells and swim.

"There are many more shells and a larger variety here than on Fort Myers beach," one person on the tour said. "Yes, but not as many as at Sanibel," another replied.

Lovers Key is a fun beach to visit, but you can simply drive to the beach and enjoy the amenities as we have done on other occasions. There's plenty of parking, after you enter the state park ($4 a car). The 1,600-acre state park, which comprises four barrier islands, has 2.5 miles along the beach, acres of trails to explore and miles of mangrove-lined estuaries. The park, which was the fourth most visited state park in Florida in 2003, includes restrooms, showers, picnic tables, and a large pavilion on the beach. Guided two-hour paddle tours are offered. The locals like fishing from the beach, or in the bay; catching mullet and snook.

From highway 41, in Bonita Springs, take Bonita Beach Road west for approximately seven miles (it's three miles after Hickory Pass). Bonita Beach Road becomes Hickory Boulevard as you head north, then Estero Boulevard. Turn left into the park at the sign.

On the boat ride back through "no wake" and manatee zones, we spied some bottlenose dolphins breaking the surface. We carefully steered around them staying 50 yards or more from them; and watched while they frolicked.

2. Beaches at Unspoiled Cayo Costa. Cayo Costa State Park, Boca Grande, Florida 33921, phone 941-964-0375. A quiet peacefulness reigns on 2,234-acre Cayo Costa, one of the few islands still primitive, nearly an untouched ecosystem. No cars. No condos. This barrier island, half the size of the well-developed Sanibel Island, south of Boca Grande in a chain of barrier islands, is entirely a state park. You can reach it only by boat. If you want to stay overnight, you'll need to "bring everything." There are, however, some picnic tables and grills. Boats can dock at Pelican Bay Pass. We boated to Cayo Costa, walked the beach, and explored the clear waters offshore. Don snorkeling gear and enjoy.

After a morning on the beach, we ate lunch on the boat, and then cruised to the leeward side of North Captiva Island and to a beautiful, remote beach on the Gulf side. The state owns two-thirds of the island.

We enjoyed swimming in the warm Gulf waters. We walked north on the beach to an area staked out as a bird sanctuary. Birders would enjoy the variety and number of birds. Even in late July on a sticky afternoon, birds were plentiful. After an afternoon in the hot sun on the beach, the breeze felt wonderful on the ride back to the marina. We spotted some dolphins as we boated home to cap a great beach day.

3. An Oasis by the High Rises. Delnor-Wiggins Pass State Park offers an unusual sugar-sand beach on a barrier island on the north end of Vanderbilt beach; and a surprising seclusion, and lush wildlife habitat, from the nearby, developed area of high rises. One of the most popular beaches in southwest Florida, the mangrove forest occupies 80 percent of the park, a contrast to nearby condos. During the tourist season, however, you either go very early or wait in a long line. In 2003, the park climbed into tenth place on the most visited Florida state parks list.

Remarkably you walk just a few feet, from the asphalt of the parking lot, and "civilization," into the hammock of trees (sea grapes, sea oats, pines, sabal palms) and picnic area to the wide, mile-long beach. The Calusa Indians thrived around the pass during the 1600s. The park has five parking lots (350 parking spaces), 150 picnic tables, a concession (near parking lot No. 1), bathhouses, grills and outdoor showers. A picnic pavilion, observation tower and boardwalk access to Wiggins Pass are at the north end of the park. There's a boat ramp and good fishing at the pass. You reach this beach, at 11100 Gulf Shore Drive, Naples, Florida 34102, phone 239-597-6196, by driving west on 111th Avenue (Naples), through residential areas, directly to the park entrance. Admission is $4 to this 166-acre park, although the fee for pedestrians and bicyclists is one dollar.

Find A Secret Beach.

With so many top-rate tranquil white powder beaches, Florida does have some that may be known to the locals, but not the tourists. These peaceful beaches have the advantage of relative seclusion without the crowds and hoopla. They're free from the masses; well, almost! Most have no concessions, no restrooms. One of these is Bunche Beach, which is near the popular beaches of Fort Myers Beach and Sanibel. Standing on Bunche Beach you can see the north part of Fort Myers Beach and the boat traffic through the pass. Lee County bought the more than 700 acres that make up Bunche Beach, with a public trust buying another 145 acres of adjacent mangroves to preserve the area from development.

Bunche Beach is at the end of a one-mile road, which stops at a small, unpaved parking lot. To reach the beach, drive on Summerlin towards Sanibel. Turn left on John Morris Road and follow it to the end.

If you want to go to the beach but away from the crowd, ask the locals. That's how we learned about Bunche Beach. Even most of the locals don't know the history of the beach: it was a beach for blacks during the days of segregation and named for black diplomat and Nobel-prize winner Ralph Bunche.

Chapter Six
Florida Problems and Challenges

Problems in Paradise, or Things Your Chamber of Commerce May Not Tell You.

Even paradise has some problems. Many of them are weather-related. Hurricanes, of course! Weather experts also call Florida the lightning capital of the world. Typical summer afternoon and evening thunderstorms can bring thousands of lightning strikes. Summers are hot and humid. Sticky. Sweaty. But there are also ferocious fire ants, nasty no-se-ums, red tide, an intense sun, and other disadvantages to the Florida lifestyle that take a bit of getting used to: If it grows, it sticks; if it crawls, it bites.

Preparation and prevention minimize the problems. The more informed you are, the safer and less likely you are to have a bad encounter or accident, so here are some of the problems and prevention tips for you to avoid or minimize them.

Problems in Paradise: Hurricanes.

June 1 marks the official beginning of the hurricane season that ends November 30. Traditionally most Florida activity, however, peaks late in the season, typically August-September. In fact, more hurricanes have been active on September 10, than any other calendar day during more than 100 years of United States record keeping history. This makes September 10 the absolute peak of the hurricane season. And, the season affects Florida more than any other state. More hurricanes reach landfall in Florida than anywhere in the world, reportedly 58 in the past one hundred years.

Forecasters term the strength of hurricanes, which consist of a huge swirl of clouds rotating around a calm center (eye), in five categories, with a category five being the strongest. A tropical storm becomes a hurricane

81

when its winds reach 74 miles per hour. In the Indian Ocean they are known as cyclones. West of the International Date Line, they are called typhoons. By any name, they represent danger. Some say the word hurricane comes from the Taino Indian word "huracan" (evil spirit), which came from the Maya word "huraken" (God of Storms).

Much of the danger comes from the storm surge and resulting flooding. The categories are based on the Saffir-Simpson Hurricane intensity scale, as follows:

Category	Winds (miles per hour)	Storm Surge (feet)	Damage
1	74-95	4-5	Minimal
2	96-110	6-8	Moderate
3	111-130	9-12	Extensive
4	131-155	13-18	Extreme
5	156-	18+	Catastrophic

Category 5 hurricanes cause catastrophic damage, especially near where the center makes landfall. The Greatest Storm of the twentieth century in the United States, a category five juggernaut, smashed into the Florida Keys in 1935 and caused more than 400 deaths. The barometer reading remains the lowest on record.

The only other Category 5 storm to hit the United States was Hurricane Camille in 1969, which killed 143 on the Gulf Coast in Louisiana and Mississippi and 113 in Virginia floods. Hurricane Mitch stayed south of Florida in the Caribbean Sea. Category 4 (some claim it was a Category 5) Hurricane Andrew hit August 24, 1992 just south of Miami at Homestead. It caused at least 40 deaths, left 180,000 homeless and caused damages of $26 billion. It remains as the most expensive natural disaster. Southwest Florida experienced Hurricane Donna September 10, 1960. Since then the Southwest coast has just been brushed by hurricanes and suffered through some tropical storms

Typically NOAA (National Oceanic and Atmospheric Administration) predicts 11 to 15 tropical storms with six blossoming into hurricanes. In 1998 there were 14 named storms with 10 hurricanes of which seven hit the United States. Hurricane Georges, a Category 2 storm, and a close call for the Gulf coast, passed by in late September 1998. Hurricane Floyd, in September 1999, skirted the Florida Atlantic coast, and then dumped torrential rains on North Carolina, causing devastating flooding.

Tropical Storm Harvey in September 1999 teased, then fooled the forecasters. It nose dived due South during the night instead of going north as six different computer models said, proving that forecasting isn't an exact science. Southwest Florida received some rain, but fortunately Harvey was a dud. In 2000, eleven named storms swirled about, but only Gordon affected those of us living in Southwest Florida with some rain.

In the 130 years between 1871 and 2001, more than 1,000 hurricanes formed with 200 reaching Florida and 75 with hurricane winds (74 mph or more). Florida leads all states with major hurricanes Category 3 or above, with 24, followed by Texas with 15, Louisiana with 12 and North Carolina with 11. Although Key West is "not unduly hurricane prone," Georges pounded Key West in 1998, Floyd in 1987, and Inez in 1966; Betsy sideswiped Key West in 1965 and Isbell did the same in 1964.

"It only takes one," forecasters point out to those who have been able to dodge the hurricane bullet. The fact is that one will come along. The best advice is to pay attention to reports, educate yourself and have a plan for the safety of your family.

Most damage from hurricanes comes from the flooding, and storm surges, caused by the torrential rains. Drowning causes nine of 10 deaths from hurricanes. During hurricane season, many of the TV weather forecasters conduct hurricane seminars so you'll have plenty of information. You can keep an eye on hurricanes at www.nhc.noaa.gov, the National Hurricane Center. Their mission is "to save lives, mitigate property loss, and improve economic efficiency by issuing watches, warnings, forecasts and analyses of hazardous tropical weather." At www.hurricanes.net storm structure, watches, warnings and other basics are covered. The relief agency FEMA has lots of information on storms at www.fema.gov.

The experts say that lack of awareness and preparation adds to damage. Knowing what actions to take can reduce the effects. We need to be smart about these things. Even if your home does not receive damage from wind or water, you could still be without electricity and potable water as the result of a hurricane. Here is a brief checklist of actions to take to minimize problems:

1. Check your insurance policy to be sure your policy covers your home and its contents, especially if you have re-modeled or added furniture, appliances or computers. Do you have coverage for the replacement cost to rebuild and furnish?
2. Because flooding causes most of the damage from hurricanes, know whether you are in a flood zone, or fringe flood zone. If so, check with an insurance agent as to flood insurance. Flood

insurance is separate from your home policy. There's a 30-day waiting period, so act early.

3. Let someone know of your plans if you leave your home. Incoming calls can overload and shut down phones. (Cell phones avoid the overload problem.)

4. Prepare a 72-hour survival kit. Stock up on water (at least seven gallons per person), canned food and flashlights. Here are some other key items:
    - ✓ Battery-operated radio or television; clock
    - ✓ Batteries
    - ✓ Nonperishable food (canned meats, soups, cereal, crackers, etc.)
    - ✓ Cash! Credit cards. Put valuable papers in waterproof bag.
    - ✓ Manual can opener
    - ✓ Waterproof matches
    - ✓ Sanitary supplies (toilet paper, soap)
    - ✓ Disposable plates, glasses, utensils
    - ✓ Wet weather gear
    - ✓ Essential prescription medicines, First Aid Kit
    - ✓ Ice chest (and ice), gas grill
    - ✓ Tools (crowbar, chain saw, hammer, pliers, shovel, saws)
    - ✓ Pet food if you have pets

5. A good idea, regardless of an imminent hurricane, is to inventory your household goods. Photograph your belongings. File the photos and the inventory in a safety deposit box.

6. Hurricane cut. A palm tree with a hurricane cut (only a couple of fronds left) has a 90 percent chance of survival versus less than 50 percent for an untrimmed tree. Trim dead or weak branches from trees.

7. Plan an evacuation route; just in case.

8. If power is lost, turn off major appliances to reduce power "surge" when electricity is restored.

9. Shutter or protect, all openings to maintain the integrity of the pressure envelope in the home. If even one opening is not protected, and is then breached by the wind, the wind can blow out other openings or the roof. This causes major wind and water damage. Studies after Hurricane Andrew showed garage doors being blown, which resulted in the wind lifting the roof off. Brace the garage doors.

Problems in Paradise: Lightning.

If you hear thunder, chances are you're probably close enough to be hit by lightning even if the storm is 10 miles away. The most dangerous storms come in the months of July and August, when afternoon thunderstorms often occur almost daily.

Lightning kills more people than snowstorms, hurricanes and tornadoes! On average, 73 people die from lightning each year according to the U.S. National Weather Service. Florida experiences more lightning strikes than any other state. Unfortunately Florida also leads in lightning-related deaths and injuries. Ten people a year on average die from lightning strikes. Lightning packs a wallop of 35,000-40,000 amperes of electrical current and, yes, it can strike the same place twice. Lightning and surge losses cause an estimated $500 million in damage to electrical and electronic equipment annually.

As a rule of thumb, you can estimate the distance by counting the number of seconds between lightning and thunder, then dividing by five to get the mileage. Do you have a lightning protection system for your home? Typically grounds attached to a 10-foot rod buried two to five feet from the foundation with a minimum of two ground rods. A lightning protection system does not attract lightning, nor does it prevent a strike; but it does provide a safe path to the ground should lightning strike.

Here are some tips for you when a storm approaches:

1. Get to shelter indoors; your home, a building or a car.
2. If you can't get to shelter, crouch down with your hands on your knees when in an open area. Do not lie flat.
3. Avoid wire fences, golf carts, farm equipment or other metal conductors; and stay away from open water.
4. Use the telephone for emergencies only.
5. Stop using your computer, turn it off and unplug it to avoid possible power surges. Let's add that you need a power surge protector for your computer; and for the telephone line. Don't forget to backup your computer frequently. To avoid lightning strike effects that can render a surge protector useless, if there's a direct hit on the house, unplug appliances and computers.
6. Don't take a shower or bath during a lightning storm!

Problems in Paradise: Red Tide.

In December 1999, more than two-dozen bottlenose dolphins died in the Gulf waters of the Florida Panhandle. Some washed ashore on the Gulf beaches. Dozens died in March 2004.

What happened? Red Tide. Scientists speculate the dolphins probably ate fish infected with Red Tide. Their respiratory and nervous systems, more efficient than those of other mammals, allowed the toxin to permeate their bodies. In 1996, Red Tide killed 147 manatees.

No, Red Tide is not caused by man-made pollution most experts say, but is a natural phenomenon. No one really knows what causes it. Red Tide is a massive multiplication (or "bloom") of tiny single-celled algae. The algae blooms give off toxin.

The toxic algae blooms cause fish kills and can cause respiratory problems and skin rash for humans, although the Red Tide blooms are not life threatening. Most people have no problems enjoying the water off the beaches although some people have reported skin irritation after swimming. Red Tide can cause flu-like symptoms and itchy eyes. Further, the big stink from dead fish washed up on the beach may keep you off the beach! Also people with chronic illnesses such as emphysema and asthma should avoid the beach.

The Red Tide can be invisible but in concentrations can appear as a red-brown sheen or a yellow-green color. Outbreaks occur in the summer or early fall probably because Red Tide is usually found in warm saltwater. Shrimp, crab, scallops and lobsters in Red Tides are safe to eat because they don't accumulate the toxin, but oysters, clams, mussels are not safe until the Department of Environmental Protection says the waters are clear of the red tide.

Unfortunately, no one can predict when and where Red Tide will occur, or how long it will last. Red Tide has spread to as much as several hundred square miles.

Seaweed. Birds like it. Shell hunters like it. Beachgoers hate it. Seaweeds form the basis of the ocean's food chain, provide shelter for marine mammals and animals and can be food. Washed up on the beach because strong currents ripped seaweeds off the rocks, seaweed stinks and looks a mess. Environmentalists, however, will tell you that birds feast on the tiny marine animals caught in the algae and seaweed helps prevent beach erosion. Shell seekers can peck through the seaweed and find seashells. Sunbathers and swimmers want it removed, but doing so requires a permit.

Water, Water Everywhere and None to Drink. No, water scarcity isn't that bad, but access to fresh water is a future problem with increasing scarcity. Florida will need 9.1 billion gallons of water a day by 2020, compared with 7.2 billion gallons a day in 2003, a 26.4 percent increase. Residents will need to increase water conservation and protection. With agriculture using 45 percent of the water, new water conservation measures, use of reclaimed water for irrigation and alternate sources will need to be in place before water scarcity becomes a crisis. Homeowners can conserve in the sensible irrigation methods described in Chapter Seven. North Florida, with many springs, has an abundance of water.

Problems in Paradise: Skin Cancer Epidemic. Each year more than 1.3 million new cases of skin cancer will be diagnosed. An estimated 10,000 will die from skin cancer. Of course, skin cancer can occur anywhere, but Floridians are 10 percent more likely to develop it than people who live elsewhere because of the year-round sunny climate. Realize the Florida sun can be more intense than what many newcomers are used to, so you should cut your sun exposure time.

We're all at risk, but you can avoid problems with some key sun-safe habits: avoid the sun between 10 a.m. and 4 p.m., wear protective clothing, slather on the sunscreen with an SPF (sun protection factor) of 15 or higher, wear a wide-brimmed hat and check your skin periodically for any signs of problems. Ears and noses, probably because they stick out, appear to be the areas the dermatologists see skin cancers most often. If you or your family is prone to skin problems or if your skin is fair, you should use 25 or 30 SPF. Sunglasses safeguard the eyes from the ultraviolet rays, which can harm the eyes and cause cataracts. Don't forget to drink plenty of fluids (water) to avoid becoming dehydrated from being in the sun and running, playing or walking around.

Recent research shows you may need sunscreen even when driving your car because pre-cancerous skin lesions are more common on the left side of the face and the forehead, most likely caused by rays that penetrate car windows! The sunburn you get today can trigger the skin cancer disease 15 to 25 years down the road, as we learned the hard way. Having had a squamous skin cancer on an ear that required surgery and a skin graft, our tip to you is to follow the sun-safe practices to avoid an unpleasant experience.

Problems in Paradise: Bad Bugs.

If you think there are a lot of bugs around, you would be right. According to the Smithsonian Institute, bugs comprise 80 percent of all the species on Earth! Florida has a bug-rich environment and the bugs are winning! Make sure your home is sealed and food is properly stored. Some of these critters can be downright ornery!

Bless this house, oh Lord, we cry.

Please keep it cool in mid-July.

Bless the walls where termites dine.

While ants and roaches march in time.

Bless our yard where spiders pass

fire ants in the grass.

Bless the garage, a home to please
Carpenter beetles, ticks and fleas.
Bless the love bugs, two by two,
the gnats and mosquitoes that feed on you.
Millions of creatures that fly or crawl.
In Florida, Lord, you've put them all.
But this is home, and here we'll stay.
So thank you Lord, for insect spray!
Anon

Living in Florida means living with bugs, including some that will get into your house. We have had a toad in the toilet; a snake in the bathroom; an anole (lizard) zipping across the floor; and ants in the flour. Let's take a look at some of these and what you can do to solve the problem. Generally, however, don't forget to turn on the light before entering a dark room or the swimming pool at night; have a broom and a net handy.

Mosquitoes and West Nile Virus. Hey, you're right! West Nile happens everywhere and isn't a Florida thing. But pesky mosquitoes are endemic to Florida and a threat. The West Nile virus can lead to coma, paralysis and death. People over 50 are more susceptible, than others. Further, protecting yourself in a climate where mosquitoes reign can be critical.

In Florida, mosquitoes are around all the time; there are just more of them in the rainy season. West Nile virus isn't the only disease transmitted by mosquitoes. Saint Louis encephalitis and Eastern Equine encephalitis are found in Florida, at low levels. Malaria, dengue fever and yellow fever were serious problems that health officials do not want to see return on the wings of mosquitoes.

The Florida rainy season leaves standing water ideal for mosquito breeding. Tip: eliminate any nearby breeding sites. Drain containers in your yards that contain standing water where mosquitoes lay their eggs. These include birdbaths, cans, bottles, and tires. Other recommendations: Avoid being outdoors at dusk and dawn when mosquitoes are seeking blood, wear light-colored clothing that covers the skin, and wear mosquito repellent that contains DEET (provides approximately six hours of protection).

No-se-ums. These tiny, nearly invisible bloodsuckers have a powerful bite. These locally grown no-se-um insects (aptly named because you can't see them) are also called sand flies, biting midges and flying teeth. They, like mosquitoes, are most prevalent at dawn and dusk, especially in days of high humidity, cloud cover and low wind; or most days in summer! They're tiny enough to get through screen mesh. They love brush and overgrown lots, moisture, and, of course, humans. Use insect repellent with DEET. Some, including the Avon lady, say Avon's SkinSoSoft helps.

Ferocious Fire Ants. Don't stand in the lawn too long, or the aggressive fire ants may be at your ankles. For sure, don't sit in the grass! The best thing to do is to wear shoes and watch where you walk. What may appear to be a pile of sand in the grass may really be a fire ant mound filled with these warriors. Fire ants, quarter-inch-long insects, arrived in this country on a cargo ship from Brazil three-quarters of a century ago. They were first spotted in Mobile, Alabama, but spread across the Southeast, including Florida.

The ferocious fire ants kill livestock, family pets, ground-nesting birds, disrupt electrical equipment, ruin crops and bite people. Fire ants consider your flesh a picnic! A few people have died because of allergic reaction to fire ant bites. The sting can cause burning (hence the name fire ants), itching and blistering. If you have allergies, keep antihistamine available.

A woman who left her car in long-term parking during an extended summer trip up North, arrived home and the car would not start. She called a service company. They found fire ants caused the problem. She had parked near some construction work and had some food in the glove compartment, which apparently attracted the fire ants.

One key to controlling fire ants is to locate the nest, then apply chemicals directly to the mound. For ants inside the house, the best approach is to avoid the problem by making sure no food is available. Food particles attract and provide food for ants. Store food in tight containers. Remove plants that attract ants. Reduce moisture sources, including condensation and leaks, which is also important in avoiding mildew. Fire ants aren't the only pest ants in Florida, just the most ferocious.

Termites. Where there's wood, there's a good chance in Florida there will be termites. Termites quest for food causes $500 million in damage every year, according to pest control people. Florida, with a climate ideal for these damaging pests, accounts for a quarter of the termite damage in the United States.

Termites, which nest in the ground beneath the surface, seek out food sources, usually wood. A termite colony of 60,000 workers can consume a foot of a two-inch by four-inch board in 118 to 157 days, according to a pest control company's literature. Termites have more impact on homes than fires. You can insure against fire, but not termites. Even concrete homes are susceptible because the attics are wood, often there's wood trim. The furniture is wood. Manufactured homes can be prone to termite problems.

Fortunately, there are preventive treatments that can help eliminate the problem. We use a pest control service to protect against invasive bad bugs. So do a lot of other homeowners and associations, which explains why 30,000 people are in the pest business in Florida. New homes in Florida are protected from subterranean termites by an insecticide barrier applied during construction of the home as required by the Florida Building Code.

Love bugs. Yes, those two-by-two small black flies with red thoraxes are love bugs, also known as March flies. Two love bug flights occur each year in April/May and August/September. Love bugs usually travel during the day, and while harmless, can make a mess of your windshield. These bugs may also clog your radiator! Fortunately, the flights last only a month or so. Waxing your car helps you later in scrubbing off the messy residue, which must be removed to avoid permanent damage to the car's finish. Some clever people spread a little baby oil on the hood, bumper and grill to make cleaning easier.

Spiders. Contrary to popular belief, fatalities from spider bites are rare. In fact, in the United States, only two spiders are dangerous: Widows and Recluse spiders. If bitten by either of these two species, seek medical assistance! Most spiders help control insects and are good guys.

Snakes. We later learned that the small snake we found in the bathroom, and put outside, was a brahminy blind snake (also called a flower pot snake), and harmless. A snake slithering among the shrubs in our yard turned out to be a ring-necked snake, which is skinny, black with a colored ring around its neck. These harmless snakes can be up to a foot long. Florida has perhaps 30 species of snakes, including four poisonous ones: the Eastern coral snake, the Eastern diamond back rattlesnake, the pygmy rattlesnake and the cottonmouth snake. The chances of being bitten in Florida are very small.

You see more snakes during spring and fall when they're moving to find food and water. During the spring they're coming out of hibernation. In the fall, they're moving to a sunny place. During summer, in the wet season, they have no reason to move because food and water are where they are. Snakes may not be friendly, but generally they're more afraid of us than we are of them, a herpetologist told us. Hmm. Anyway, to move a snake outside, use a broom. If you don't know what kind of snake it is, don't pick it up! If the snake is outside, let it alone because it helps by killing lots of rodents.

Problems in Paradise: Sharks

A newspaper headline in 2001 proclaimed: Florida Top Spot for Shark Attacks. In 2000, there were 79 reported unprovoked shark attacks with 34 of them in Florida. Ten of the 79 attacks were fatal. Florida has a long coastline, a large population, a huge tourist infusion and probably more people in the water than anywhere in the world, so the attacks are relatively rare in terms of total population. In fact, you are more likely to be struck by lightning than be attacked by a shark.

Problems in Paradise: Scams

Sunshine and subtropical weather bring retirees and their money. The money attracts businesses, but it also attracts crooks, especially those who steal with a briefcase, not a gun.

If it seems to be too good to be true, it probably is, as the saying goes. Florida has had more than its share of scams, con men and swamp sales. Look out! We're from Missouri (both of us) so some healthy skepticism and "Show Me" provides some protection. Knowing some of the scams helps protect against being a victim: Ponzi schemes that pay some investors returns with money raised from later investors, sale of unregistered securities, bogus promissory notes, charitable gift annuities, pay phone deals and phony viatical settlements (in which terminally ill people sell their life insurance policies for cash).

Learn About Scams so You Can Avoid Them. The overarching theme of the scams, and the fraud in corporations, is greed and more greed. Greed overtakes sense. Thousands of people have seen their pensions and retirement money disappear in the scandals of Enron, WorldCom, and others. Investors lost large sums during the dot.com stock bubble, because they didn't diversify their investments and had too many eggs in too few baskets.

One financial expert, commenting in 2003, noted: "Securities scams have increased partly because investors looked for higher returns after the stock market downturn of 2000-2002. One characteristic of nearly all investment scams is that there is not an independent, third-party involved, such as a bank or brokerage firm."

Florida ranked first in credit card skimming in 2002. In this scam, your credit card is swiped through a special device that stores the credit card information. The data later is transferred to fake cards and used to buy items in your name you never purchased. Just read through the following sampling of the fraud sharks ready to devour your assets and you'll want to spend more time on the beach checking the water before jumping in.

A Miami man was accused of bilking 105 investors of $1.7 million in an oil and gas-drilling scheme. Four persons were charged with an $18 million currency trading scam. Don't buy penny stocks from telemarketers. In 2000, the Maricopa Investments hedge fund cheated investors out of $100 million, in Southwest Florida. A wealthy investor in Naples was bilked out of $8 million, or more, by investing in a mortgage company to "bankroll mortgages," where the con man owner allegedly sold to various lending institutions, pocketing the money and using it for high living. Evergreen Securities, Ltd, an Orlando-based scam raised $200 million before filing for bankruptcy.

After the scam collapses, the company, or agent, is often broke so there's no one left to sue or to recover funds. A neighbor bought a three-year maintenance contract. The firm "disappeared" (went bust) not long after the first maintenance visit.

Health care fraud cost Americans at least $50 billion in 2003, according to the National Health Care Anti-Fraud Association. That impacts consumers with increased premiums.

Some prominent people have been caught up in some of the schemes, including some tough shrewd investors, so err on the side of caution. The Hammersmith Trust trial ended in 2001 in Florida with six defendants found guilty in a Ponzi-type scheme that defrauded investors of $100 million. Victims suffered greatly with some losing their homes and retirement nest eggs. The con artists lived the lifestyle of the rich with luxury yachts, fleets of cars, expensive clubs and palatial homes.

Another Ponzi scheme promised tax-free returns of up to 36 percent in a company offering short-term, high-interest loans to borrowers who pledged their auto titles as collateral. New investors fueled the funds for the owners to live a high lifestyle and pay the earlier investors, as with most of these scams. The CEO of a Miami-based finance and securities company was sentenced to jail for fleecing 2,000 people who invested a minimum of $10,000 because they were told it would yield returns of 30 percent and involved "no risk" and their funds would be "guaranteed" and "insured." As with most of these schemes, money was paid to old investors for a while from new investors before the pyramid collapsed.

You wouldn't think someone would get taken in by an email from Nigeria promising to transfer $6.5 million to your account, but then people have been duped by this. Fraud in the foreign currency market bilked tens of millions of dollars from investors.

The Florida Department of Financial Services reported agent fraud is on the rise with greedy agents boosting their commissions by selling unwanted or unneeded coverage, unsuitable investments for older people such as annuities, and by "twisting," the practice of persuading clients to cash in one investment for another to the client's detriment and the agent's own financial gain. "We were suckered," one investor said in dismay. Check our powerful tips for avoiding being a sucker.

Official-looking mail gets opened but the documents inside are not government documents. One scam asked for funds to help lobby to keep Social Security from "going broke." Unfortunately, bogus charities, or charities that provide little of the money for the intended purposes, prey on retirees. More than seventy-five percent of most funds should go to programs. Ask for a financial statement. Look at income and expenses.

The greedy clearly are out there ready to take advantage with pyramid schemes, vending machine offers, and life and health insurance that don't cover what is claimed. Let's face it, a population of nearly 25 percent seniors more than 65 years old, acts as a magnet for those looking for the vulnerable, which includes seniors concerned about their finances living on fixed income and needing a higher return on their investments.

Eight Powerful Tips to Avoid Being Scammed

1. Ask questions and listen.
2. Watch for red flags in sales pitches, especially a promise of large profits. Be skeptical of promises, for example, of doubling your money.
3. Don't be a "good manners" victim because con artists will exploit your courtesy.
4. Check out strangers touting a deal too good to pass up. Con artists by definition can come across as very professional and "fool the best of them." Credentials of securities sales agent can be checked (complaints on file) at www.nasdr.com (National Association of Securities Dealers) or www.nasaa.org (North American Securities Administrators Association).
5. Peter Lynch, the whiz at Fidelity Investments, preached to invest in what you really understand. Warren Buffett, the second richest man in the United States looks at stocks as buying a business, so you must understand the business.
6. Remember, if you pay money to get money, it's a scam (as in the sweepstakes scam).
7. Ask for a financial statement, especially from charities. Check how much goes to the intended recipients. Ask for IRS Form 990. Check out charities at www.Give.org and www.guidestar.org.

8. Stay in charge of your investments and monitor them to be sure you don't have unauthorized trades or changes in your accounts. Ask questions if in doubt.

Seasonal Driving

Ever increasing traffic causes some eye-opening crashes, which makes seasonal driving dangerous. Although traffic headaches may be similar in other fast-growing communities, Florida differs because of so many tourists and out-of-state, part-time residents. Further, the high traffic volume combined with road construction, and road changes, provides challenges.

Intersections pose a major hazard. One intersection, for example, with 68,000 vehicles a day going through it, had 78 crashes in a year; another had 70 crashes. Side-impact collisions account for a third of the fatal accidents; with most of these at intersections. Red light runners cause many of the accidents. They not only don't slow for a stale green light, but also not even the yellow caution; apparently with an attitude of "I'll make the light." Too many don't.

Alcohol plays a part in 39 percent of fatal accidents, according to the NHTSA (National Highway Traffic Safety Administration). Speeding, a factor in 30 percent of all fatal crashes kills a thousand people every month. "Drivers really need to focus," a sheriff told us. "Inattention is one of the leading causes of accidents. It's that simple."

The young blame the elderly drivers. Older drivers blame the young. The residents blame the non-residents. There is plenty of blame, unfortunately, to go around. Regardless of age, or residency, however, accidents could be dramatically reduced if people would simply pay attention. There are far too many distractions: cell phone, eating, drinking, and combing hair.

A little old man was driving down the freeway when his cell phone rang. It was his wife.

"Dear," she said, "I just heard on the radio that a car is going the wrong way on your Highway. Please be careful." "It's not just one car," her husband replied. "There are hundreds of them!"

One of our neighbors, tired of the lack of drivers using their turn signals, exclaimed: "I think most of the drivers left their turn signals back home when they moved to Florida."

With nearly 3,000 people killed in Florida in auto accidents in a year, and another one-fourth million injured, law enforcement people recommend driving with an adult attitude of logical, rational and low-risk decisions. Common sense courtesy goes a long way in cutting accident rates.

The penalty for not driving properly: violation points! Pile up 12 points within a 12-month period and your license will be suspended for 30 days, 18 points in 18 months will result in a three-month suspension; and 24 points within a 36-month period means a one-year suspension. Some of the violation points: leaving the scene of an accident resulting in property damage of more than $50 and unlawful speeding resulting in an accident each mean six points; reckless driving, moving violation resulting in an accident and passing a stopped school bus each garners four points as does speeding more than 16 miles per hour over the posted speed. Speeding 15 miles per hour or less over the posted speed, open container and all other moving violations mean three points. You can receive two points for improper equipment.

Lee Trevino, in Naples for a 2004 golf tournament commented on the clogged roadways: "People come here to retire for 15 years and spend seven and a half years in their cars."

AARP conducts an eight-hour refresher course, called *55-Alive*. It will not only help your driving, but also help you gain a discount on your car insurance.

Unintended Consequences.

Everything has an effect. Even actions by bright people with high IQs, "higher" education, and expertise who you would think would know better, have resulted in some horrendous unintended consequences.

Everglades. The Everglades restoration, with the more than $8-billion remedial action underway, attempts to correct the unintended consequences of actions of the past. More than a half-century has passed since Marjory Stoneman Douglas (1890-1998) wrote *Everglades River of Grass.*

Greed perhaps caused the destruction of the beauty that brought people here in the first place. In the 1960s, the Gulf American Land Corporation began developing thousands of acres in the Everglades. After selling lots, dredging miles of canals, and constructing nearly 300 miles of roads, the company went bankrupt. Meanwhile, in an era of cheap land and real estate schemes in 1950-1970, speculators drained the Everglades, emptied ancient lakes, dug canals, built roads and brought in exotic trees in this fragile environment, which is now half the size of a century ago. The receding water meant loss of habitat for wildlife. Yet potential new unintended consequences can occur from restoration efforts to improve water flow, if the increased water flow then damages the coral reef. Even the well-intended restoration needs to proceed with care.

Reefs. Nearly a half-century has passed since Rachel Carson (1907-1964) called attention to issues in books like *"The Edge of the Sea."* The third largest coral reef in the world, which stretches along the Florida Keys, has suffered unintended damage.

Causeway. A causeway built in 1965 between Bonita Beach and Fort Myers was for a good purpose, but it blocked the natural flow of water through the bay, with a loss of sea grass, trapping nutrients and polluting the water, with the unintended consequences of a devastating effect on fish. Other causeways caused similar problems.

Invasive Trees. Engineers imported melaleuca tress from Australia more than 100 years ago to serve as an ornamental tree and drain wetlands (swamps) by soaking up water. The invasive trees crowded out native vegetation and destroyed habitat for fish, birds and other wildlife in thousands of acres. Now, expensive programs try to kill the hard-to-eradicate non-native trees and plants and recover from the unintended consequences. See the next chapter for more about invasive trees and plants.

Cutting Mangroves. Removing mangroves along the Atlantic coastline, in the interest of developments, nearly eliminated fish and fishing.

Unintended Pelican deaths. Fishermen hook accidentally scores of pelicans, but then fail to remove the hook and line from the injured bird. Worse, people who feed brown pelicans chunks of fish left over from a day of fishing unwittingly contribute to a painful death of the pelican because the pelican can't digest the bones of the larger fish. The bones stick and block the passage of food. The pelican starves. In 1975, exposure to DDT pesticides nearly wiped the pelicans out, along with eagles and other birds because the DDT caused the eggs to be thin and break.

Exotic Pets on the Loose. Burmese pythons, monkeys, South American monk parakeets, Cuban tree frogs and up to seven-foot African monitor lizards released into the wild, cause problems. More than three-dozen monitor lizards were killed in the maze of man-made canals in Cape Coral in 2003.

Growth---of Course! Unrestrained growth provides job and business opportunities, but also contributes to unintended consequences of destroying the very features people moved to Florida to enjoy. Growth takes its toll on ecosystems. Rooftops and pavement replacing open spaces, means less rainwater soaking into the ground. The runoff of nutrients provides a feast for algae, which clouds water and chokes off coral from the sunlight they need and kills off sea grasses that are nurseries to fish. More people mean more urban runoff added to that from agriculture. One answer is smart growth that ties the building of new homes and stores to infrastructure change and growth. Attaining the delicate balance between sensible growth and preservation tests all of us. A common-sense wildlife management strategy that will benefit people and nature may be hard to attain. Growth should also pay for growth (using a system of impact fees on new construction).

People are talking about it. That's a start. Learn how to help in your own yard in the next chapter

Chapter Seven
Florida Friendly Flora

*"Wherever you tread, the blushing flowers shall rise
And all things flourish where you turn your eyes."* Alexander Pope

Gardening in Florida is Different from up North. When we first visited Florida, we saw a big difference with the palm trees and flowers. We noticed the strange-looking grass but until we *moved* to Florida, we really didn't have a clue as to just how much of a difference there was in growing plants and trees.

What you did up North doesn't work in Florida, but you can enjoy gardens year round. The same grass won't grow here. Florida turf resembles the crabgrass you tried to get rid of up North. But real crabgrass can raise havoc with it. Planting is in the fall, not the spring. Prune in the spring.

Florida is upside down from up North. You can grow oranges and bananas in your back yard, but not cherries. You can have blossoms all year long, if you plant the right flowers! On the other hand, you can enjoy the beautiful and fragrant blossoms of the frangipani and the lavender-blue flowers in large clusters, of the Jacaranda tree, in May and June. Farmers harvest tomatoes in December.

How about Florida's state tree, the sabal (cabbage) palm, which is very tolerant of salty soil? Then we have bougainvillea with vibrant bursts colors in winter and spring, the firecracker plant with bright red flowers hanging like firecrackers during much of the year and the Mexican bluebells outside my office window with purple flowers blossoming each morning. A bottlebrush bush, with flowers arranged around the tips of branches like bristles of a cylindrical brush, adds spectacular color in our front yard. We couldn't wait to plant our own Mango tree so we could have our favorite fruit. Brilliantly blooming ubiquitous Hibiscus add color to our yard and our neighbor's yards.

Florida is the third most biologically diverse state with 81 different native plant communities, thirteen of which occur nowhere else in the world. These communities contain 3,500 species of which perhaps 250-275 species are found only in Florida. More than 600 species of mammals, birds, fish reptiles and amphibians inhabit the plant communities.

Even if you have no interest in gardening, this overview chapter will save you money and provide some helpful information you need if you own a home in Florida. If you have a strong interest, this chapter also provides you the best resources to strengthen your knowledge. Most of us fit into one of three levels:

1. Basics: Maintaining a nice yard.
2. Novice or Advanced Gardener.
3. Master gardener.

Level 1. Basics: Maintaining a Nice Yard

When we first moved to Florida, we learned some lessons the hard way because of the mistakes of the previous owners of the home we bought. We did not know their major mistakes, because everything looked fine to us. First, we found that half of the more than a dozen palm trees we had admired were very close to the house. This meant palm fronds scraping the roof and an easy route for tree rats. Second, we learned the fica tree that shaded the lanai did so at a price. The fica tree has an octopus root system that will clutch underground pipes and uproot concrete slabs. Removing the fica tree proved difficult. So, be careful what you plant! And where. Third, we learned that cutting the St. Augustine grass too short creates all sorts of problems.

Even if you have zero interest in spending time with the lawn or gardening, or you have someone do it for you, you will still benefit by knowing some essentials for a Florida friendly landscape that will save you money and help the environment.

If you get familiar with your plants and lawn, you can look at it and be aware of how they look when they're healthy. Then you can solve problems while they are small and before they get too big to handle. Chinch bugs, for example, cause dead areas. Before these areas spread from the infestation, use liquid insecticide.

Grass. Most lawns are Floratam, the most vigorous member of the St. Augustine grass family, which was introduced in 1973. You need to set the lawn mower high so the grass is not cut below 3-1/2 inches. Keep the mower blades sharp so you don't stress the grass. Our subtropical climate, high water table and sandy soils have no tolerance for the fine-bladed grasses you've had in the North, but Floratam grasses adapt to a wide range of soil and environmental conditions in Florida. Mow high, water deep and fertilize. Fertilize two to four times during the growing season. For South Florida, a fertilizer company suggests 14-4-14 in January, March and October; a pre-emergent herbicide in February and September. For irrigation, use one inch of water per irrigation twice weekly to get deep percolation of water and to establish strong root systems.

Shrubs. Before planting shrubs, know how big the shrubs are going to get (maximum growth), then make sure shrubs are at least a foot from your home. Shrubbery growing against your home, especially thorny and woody plants can tear up screens and scratch paint.

Sensible Sprinkling. With water a main issue in Florida, many areas of Florida have lawn-watering restrictions, but even if they don't, you don't want to over water. As much as 70 percent of home water use is for *outdoors* watering or irrigation. Southwest Florida year-round restrictions specify that people at odd-numbered addresses may water their lawns on Monday, Wednesday and Saturday; those people at even numbered addresses may water Tuesday, Thursday and Saturday. No watering is allowed on Friday. The restrictions also specify watering be done between 12:01 a.m. and 8 a.m. Even if the rules do not apply in your area, the rules do offer excellent guidelines for you. Watering infrequently with the right amount of water is better than watering frequently in small amounts. Deeper roots will develop to give a greener and healthier lawn during droughts. Here are tips to not only conserve our water resource, but also help your pocketbook with savings:

- Rain sensors override the irrigation cycle of the sprinkler system when adequate rainfall occurs. Any new system will have a sensor because Florida Statute (373.62) requires it. If you have an older system that doesn't have a sensor, add it to conserve water and save money.
- Check your system regularly for leaks, clogged spray heads, and spray heads watering driveways and walks instead of the lawn. Direct heads to where the water is needed.
- Native drought-tolerant plants need less water. We asked several Master Gardeners at the Florida Cooperative Extension Service: Why use Native Plants? The best reasons: "Native plants know how to cope with insects, drought, and poor soil. The native plants attract birds, butterflies and other wildlife." A bonus a non-gardener especially can appreciate: Most Florida native plants are easy to grow and require little water and fertilizer once established. Using Florida-friendly native plants makes environmental sense. Just look at the tremendous damage done

101

by importing non-native plants into Florida, described later in this chapter.

- Use mulch (don't put against the house outside foundation, however, because this can create insect problems).
- Water for irrigation is more effective before the sun comes up. The sun evaporates the water during the day, so water early morning before 8 a.m.

The Florida Yardstick for Florida Friendly Landscape. How does your yard measure up? The Florida County University Extension has developed a yardstick goal of "36 inches" with credit of inches for actions on right plant, right place, fertilizing appropriately, watering efficiency, mulch, recycling, attracting wildlife, controlling yard pests, storm water runoff and waterfront protection. If you qualify, you'll receive a Florida Yard Certificate and a certified yardstick sign to place in your yard.

Simply select those actions you have already taken and the ones you plan to take to reach the 36-inch mark and transform your yard into a certified beautiful oasis "that will not only conserve precious water resources and reduce pollution, but will also help save time, energy and money" according to the University of Florida.

Here are some of the actions to give you a flavor for the system:

- o Calibrate your irrigation system to apply ½ to ¾ inch of water per application. Credit: 3 inches.
- o Put a rain gauge in your yard to track rainfall and avoid unnecessary irrigation. Credit: 2 inches.
- o Create self-mulching areas under trees where leaves can remain when they fall. Credit: 2 inches.
- o Recycle grass clippings by allowing them to remain on the lawn. Credit: 2 inches.
- o Plant vines, shrubs and trees that provide cover or food sources for wildlife. Credit: 3 inches.
- o Learn to identify five beneficial insects that provide natural control of harmful pests. Credit: 2 inches.
- o Save energy by using trees and shrubs to shade the eastern and western walls of your home and your air conditioner compressor. Credit: 1 inch.
- o Use iron instead of nitrogen on your lawn during the summer. Credit: 1 inch.
- o Create swales (low areas) to catch and filter storm water. Credit: 3 inches.
- o Establish a 3-feet chemical free "ring of responsibility" or buffer zone between lawn and shoreline. Credit: 4 inches.

Copies of the Florida Yardstick are available at <u>http://hort.ufl.edu/fyn</u>. Click on questionnaire link.

If you live in an association, you may need to get approval. Keep in mind the old saying: "A rose in a wheat field is a weed and wheat in a rose garden is a weed." What it looks like to you may be different in the context of the community appearance and the rules and regulations of your association documents. If you need approval because of a planned change to your exterior landscape, the best way is to provide a written request with drawings or sketches attached.

Level 2. Novice or Advanced Gardener

Opportunities in Paradise. Although you leave lilacs, crabapple trees, forsythias, blue spruce and bleeding hearts behind, "There are thousands of plants you can grow in Florida and many more are introduced each year," according to Hank Bruce in the helpful book, *Yankee's Guide to Florida Gardening*. The author wrote he tried to "keep the information light and readable." This delightful 168-page book succeeded in providing an easy-to-read guide.

Here's a "Yankee Conversion Chart" from his book:

Up North We Had	*In Florida We Substitute*
Clematis	Passion vine
Lilac	Crape myrtle
Forsythia	Thryalis
Bleeding heart	Clerodendrum vine
Lily of the valley	Liriope, turf lily
Tulips	Amaryllis
Colorado blue spruce	Norfolk Island pine
Bearded iris	African iris

As Wae Nelson, publisher of *Florida Gardening* magazine said at a seminar, "You have to start with the basic idea that you don't grow tulips here, but you can grow gingers and things of that nature." He added, "With ornamental gingers, there are whole classes that are absolutely fantastic, knock-your-eyes-out plants, many with aromas that are outstanding."

Nelson listed the top three things for success in Florida gardening:
1. Improve the sandy soil by adding organic material.
2. Mulch heavily. Mulching conserves moisture, controls weeds, builds topsoil, and keeps the ground cool.
3. Choose the right plants. (More about this later in this chapter.)

More Than 400 Commonly Grown Florida Plants. The "bible" for plants is *Florida Landscape Plants* by Professors John V. Watkins and Thomas Sheehan, which devotes a page each to 403 commonly grown plants. The page on each plant includes a black and white sketch, technical name, family, foliage, flowers, fruits, season of maximum colors, landscape uses, habitat, light and soil requirements, salt tolerance, propagation, pests and other pertinent information.

We attended a seminar at one of the county extension services with a dozen master gardeners each speaking about a favorite plant. All recommended this book, because of the detailed information on each plant. The book has become a standard manual for university students, nurserymen, and homeowners. The book also includes a model plan illustrating uses of landscaped plants for a home. So, if you're a "gardener," pick up a copy of the book.

The half-day seminar included learning about a dozen common plants and their best features, their care and any problems in growing them: Bougainvillea, Cabbage palm, Croton, Firebush, Foxtail Palm, Gardenia, Ixora, Hibiscus, Plumbago, Dwarf Schefflera, Shell Ginger and Thryallis. Volunteer Master Gardeners shared their expertise.

Hardiness Zone Map. The United States Department of Agriculture has established a hardiness zone map based on the range of average annual minimum temperatures. You need to understand what zone you are in because of differences from north to south in Florida. Florida has four zones:

Zone	Range of average minimum temperatures
8	10 to 20 degrees
9	20 to 30 degrees
10	30 to 40 degrees
11	40 to 50 degrees

These zones coincide roughly with North, Central, South and Sub Tropical Florida. Some consider Key West "tropical."

Wildlife Friendly Garden.

Animals feed on many of the enemies of the landscape and are a food source for other wildlife. Lizards and frogs feed on mosquitoes, other insects and other bad guys, so having anoles and frogs around, and sharing your garden with these tiny guys, helps control the bad guys; a good thing!

Trees, shrubs and plants provide food and shelter for butterflies, birds, anoles, and frogs. Cocoplum, firebush, dune or beach sunflowers, and wild olive produce berries that lure hummingbirds. Our firebush, for example, attracts butterflies, while birds like the berries that follow the flowers.

Who doesn't want birds and butterflies of all kinds around to brighten the yard? By converting a few square yards of lawn to native vegetation you can save water and help the environment by adding habitat for birds and other wildlife.

Florida Native Plant Society. The Florida Native Plant Society (FNPS), organized in 1980, promotes the preservation and restoration of native plants. Chapters exist throughout Florida. A member, Rufino Osorio, who has more than 500 plants in cultivation, wrote a book, *A Gardener's Guide to Florida's Native Plants,* that explains site preparation, planting and maintaining a garden along with discussion of wildlife in the garden, pests and diseases. The book includes color photographs and information on 350 plants.

Level 3. Master Gardener

Find Out How to Be a Master Gardener. The Florida Master Gardener program began in 1979 by the University of Florida in the county-located extension services. You can pick up an application for the program at your county extension office.

Each county operates its own program and training which varies somewhat, but typically involves more than 50 hours of intensive instruction on basic plant science, plant identification, propagation pathology, soils and garden related areas, such as problems; weeds in landscape and woody ornamentals. Other topics include fruit, vegetable and herb identification, and principles of landscape design. One county has classes one day a week for eight weeks. Another starts in mid-January for 12 weeks of intensive training.

Upon completion of training, and passing an exam, participants become certified Master Gardeners by the state of Florida; and are qualified to return at least 50 hours of volunteer service. The service includes: staffing the phones, work in plant clinics, conducting research to answer questions by residents, and arranging and participating in workshops. The certification does not transfer from county to county, or state.

Master Gardeners present annual 10-week Spring Workshops, sponsored by the University of Florida Cooperative Extension Service in some counties; and various seminars. If you're into gardening, here's a chance to also give back by sharing your expertise with others and be involved with people who have a common interest.

Resources

Valuable Resource.

If you have an interest in having a garden, or simply in making sure you plant the right shrubs, trees and landscaping for your home, you won't find a better way to get answers than to visit the University of Florida Cooperative Extension Service in your county.

Each of Florida's 67 counties has one, so you can get professional advice just around the corner. Each County Extension Service is part of a publicly-funded statewide educational network that links resources of federal, state and local partners to provide lifelong learning programs, information and research. We have visited several of the University of Florida Cooperative Extension Service offices and have been amazed at the knowledgeable help readily available.

The Extension Services have a wealth of information and offer a variety of services including testing your soil sample. The service also includes the Master Gardener program. The planned hands-on demonstration gardens show you what can be accomplished using Florida's native plants and materials.

The Lee County Extension Service employs more than a dozen people, for example, and has more than 200 volunteers. The Collier County Extension Service also employs more than a dozen people, and has many volunteers. For more information, go to www.ifas.ufl.edu.

The Institute of Food and Agricultural Sciences (IFAS) also has 14 research and education centers in the five IFAS districts in Florida.

Summary, Resources. The three books mentioned (*Yankee's Guide to Florida Gardening, Florida Landscape Plants* and *A Gardener's Guide to Florida's Native Plants)* and the Extension Services, are valuable resources, not only for those wanting to grow native plants, but those simply wishing to learn more or add diversity to their garden as we did.

For inspiration, check out the dazzling color in *Florida's Fabulous Flowers* and *Florida's Fabulous Trees*. The excellent bi-monthly *Florida Gardening* magazine, P.O. Box 500678, Malabar, FL 32950, provides topical articles of interest, and ongoing help, to home gardeners in Florida.

From the Gorgeous Good Guys to the Bad Guys: Orchids

Collier County Florida, a hotbed for orchids, with an active association, has more orchid species than any other county in the United States, including Hawaii! One of every seven flowering plants on earth is an orchid according to *Taylor's Guide to Orchids*. Within Florida are 118 species of wild orchids, more than half of which are in the Fakahatchee Strand. Susan Orlean's best selling book, *The Orchid Thief* describes the beauty of the Strand, and tells of Orlean's search for the elusive ghost orchid in a story of an orchid fanatic who's caught stealing rare orchids. Nicolas Cage and Meryl Streep starred in the movie, which paints the Strand in unflattering strokes. Royal Palm Tours (www.royalpalmtours.com) developed a tour that includes visiting orchid growers and a swamp walk in through the Fakahatchee Strand in search of endangered wild orchids. You have to be really into orchids to slog through the muck of the swamp, although the swamp is not as bad as the movie makes it out to be.

According to the United States Department of Agriculture, only poinsettias surpass the orchid as the most popular potted flowering plant. Sales exceed $100 million.

Bling Bling Orchid "Garden." Our neighbor has a colorful orchid collection that would be the envy of Rex Stout's (1886-1975) fictional detective, Nero Wolfe, known for his collection of orchids in the plant rooms above his brownstone. Nero is not an orchid geek; he's an aesthete who collects orchids because they are beautiful. So, too, is our neighbor Steve Bookbinder, who has an advantage because his orchids hang in his sunscreen cage, which provides forty percent shade.

As Archie Goodwin, Wolfe's cohort in the long-running series of mystery novels by Stout says: "As many times as I had been there, I never went in the plant rooms without catching my breath." More than 350 orchids of different species and colors hanging in the neighbor's lanai/ pool area can also take your breath away.

A good book on orchids is *Taylor's Guide to Orchids,* which is a practical guide with some excellent color photographs. Neighbor Steve recommends *Wild Orchids of Florida* by Paul Martin Brown.

Meet the Bad Guys

Some non-native imports have wreaked havoc with Florida's ecology, as invasive plants take over native plant communities like saw grass marshes, wet prairies and aquatic sloughs. Eliminating them is tough, and costly. Meanwhile, we can help by not planting these, or volunteering to help in plant removal. By getting involved in preventing the spread of exotic plants, you will be saving yourself money. Control of unwanted plant species costs taxpayers millions of dollars each year. The exotics degrade our natural areas and wildlife habitat, which affects our lifestyle.

How can I help? Identify the "intrusive" plants in your yard and replace them with native plants. Some of the invasive plants were unknowingly planted and maintained by homeowners. You may also want to volunteer for one of the existing programs or projects. One chapter of the Florida Native Plant Society, for example, spends two workdays in spring and fall, removing invasive exotic plant species. Other chapters get involved in similar ways. This is a powerful way to fight biodiversity losses.

Top Ten Invasive Plants. Here are the top ten invasive, and dangerous plants according to the Florida Department of Environmental Protection. They refer to these as "biological pollution," because they grew out of control. Invasive plants threaten wildlife habitats and displace native plants. Some exotic plants can cause allergic reactions to people. The State of Florida, and many counties have spent millions of dollars attempting to rid the state of invasive exotics. Many counties have also restricted, by law, the use of invasive plants. Although Collier County, for example, has prohibited 12 exotic species, the Florida Exotic Pest Plant Council lists 126 non-native plants that pose problems. See the list at www.fleppc.org.

The more these species grow and spread, the tougher and more expensive ridding them becomes. By knowing what these are, and the problems they present to Florida lifestyle, you can find ways to help either eradicate or prevent new invasions. Reportedly, Florida spent $56 million in 10 years to treat Hydrilla, but despite this, the acreage doubled!

1. Melaleuca. This imported tree from Australia, first planted a hundred years ago, had a positive purpose of draining the swamps (wetlands) that turned into a nightmare as the invasive tree crowded out native vegetation and tens of thousands of acres of habitat for birds and wildlife. The ugly Melaleuca's blossoms stink like rotting potatoes.

2. Brazilian Pepper Tree. This large evergreen shrub tree, imported as an ornamental in the 1840s, grows so dense it prevents growth of other vegetation. It even re-sprouts after pruning and fire. It can cause respiratory problems and skin rashes.

3. Australian Pine. With its shallow roots, the Australian pine uses up surface water; thus no dew water makes it to the atmosphere to return as rain. It causes increased beach erosion.

4. Hydrilla. The slimy algae-like hydrilla, and water hyacinth were brought here as ornamental plants but ended up choking our waterways. The hydrilla, which sprouts arm-like offshoots that can grow up to 10 feet a day, destroys fish and wildlife habitats in its path. One "natural" way we helped control this pesky non-native invasive plant in our community lake, was by releasing carp into the lake system. The carp eat the plants and trim back the masses of unwanted vegetation.

5. Water Hyacinth. This floating plant chokes waterways. It is "one of the worst weeds in the world."

6. Cogon Grass. Fast-growing weed, more aggressive and harder to get rid of than kudzu; has invaded 30 of the 67 Florida counties. Dominates all other species except large trees.

7. Torpedo Grass. Exotic weed from Australia that is tough to control.

8. Kudzu Vine. This twining wood vine has become a rampant weed: "the vine that ate the south." Oddly, this weed was thought to be a savior by putting nitrogen back after farming but with no natural enemies, kudzu took over!

9. Air Potato Vine. This tall-climbing vine, forms potato-like tubers and can quickly engulf native vegetation. Gainesville has an annual Great Air Potato Roundup attended by as many as 800 people to "take back their natural areas one potato at a time."

10. Lather Leaf. This low twining shrub can form a thick mat of tangling stems, which can grow over native vegetation.

Others: Downy rose-myrtle, earleaf acacia, climbing fern, woman's tongue, java plum, carrotwood, and catclaw mimosa.

As every master gardener will tell you, "When landscaping, you can help by not using invasive plants!"

Chapter Eight
Florida Wildlife

As with many of the other chapters that follow, we'll tell you about our top three favorites and provide you information you need on the identification and understanding of the "popular" and easy-to-see Florida wildlife, especially the creeping, crawling creatures! Before talking about the wildlife, however, let's first look at the base of the food chain and the heart of what makes paradise possible: the mangroves. And, yes, birds are wildlife, but you can check them out in the next chapter!

Mangroves and Estuaries. Mangroves are what paradise is all about. The mangroves, nicknamed "walking trees" for their exposed roots that appear to tiptoe through the swamps, trap leaves or whatever floats in along with leaves and twigs from the mangroves. The leaves of the mangroves provide a major source of nutrition for the marine animals that begin their life in the backwater before entering the Gulf. Mangroves shed more than four tons to the acre, so the food chain begins with one cell amoeba, then plankton. The mangroves, which are highly salt tolerant, begin a food chain from the bacteria that assist in decomposition of the leaves, which are eaten by microorganisms, which are eaten by fish, which are eaten by larger fish. You can't mistake the unforgettable smell of mangroves, which is more pungent in the humid summertime.

Red mangroves are closest to the water, then black mangroves behind them and finally, farthest from the water, white mangroves. Nearly half the 500,000 acres of mangroves in Florida are in the Everglades.

The mangroves, which are critical to the health of estuaries, provide refuge for lobster larvae, fiddler crabs, sea trout and snook that hide from predators. The shallow waters provide a nursery that is home to soft corals, mollusks, crabs, crustaceans and small fish. The tangled mangroves provide a maze that keeps the big fish from getting at the little guys. The mangroves serve as rookeries. Mangroves also buffer the mainland against destructive storms, prevent erosion with their root system and filter the water to maintain quality and clarity. Wading birds patrol along the edges looking for a meal! Without mangroves, much of the coastal wildlife would decline.

Estuaries, unique bodies of water, contain a mix of salt water from the ocean and fresh water from the creeks and rivers. The rivers broaden as they move to the estuary and the habitat changes to the food chain in the brackish water. The mixing provides a rich soup for plankton. Perhaps 90 percent of fish in the Gulf spent part of their time in an estuary.

Developers and officials in the area from Miami to Jupiter, for example, nearly killed fishing by cutting mangroves as development progressed. The people at the time didn't see the bigger picture, or the unintended consequences of the actions. This spurred people on the Gulf side to "save the mangroves."

Top Three Wildlife Favorites

Amazing Alligators (State Reptile). When I first held an alligator, I was amazed at the soft feel of its skin, which appears hard and rough, but isn't. Holding a 5-year old alligator was a new experience. Fortunately, the cold-blooded predator took to my warmer body and didn't wiggle or spray me with Gator-"ade"! This alligator had been held many times before.

We had taken a tour to the Everglades with tour guide "Gator Steve." We had stopped in Everglades City to visit an alligator park/gift shop. Mike, the proprietor, after a group walked around and looked at his alligators, asked: "Who wants to hold an alligator?"

No one stepped forward. "Try a small one first, then work your way up to a bigger one." Anyway, someone had to do it.

"Hold it like you would a small child," Mike said. Yeah right.

I learned the trick that all alligator wrestlers know and use. The alligator can crunch with its powerful jaws with great power, *but* the muscles have no power to open the jaws. Hold the jaws closed, which turns out to be easy, and you are in control!

Alligators, which have been around for a couple of hundred million years, grow to 12-13 feet long, but typically the female grows to 8-9 feet. These top-of-the-food-chain predators can weigh 500 pounds and live more than 50 years, but reaching six feet may take 10 years. When hatched (the female lays 20-60 eggs in a nest of soil, leaves and vegetation in June/

July), after two months incubation, the young come out fully developed and eight inches long.

The swamp food-chain cycle: Insects eat plants, frogs eat insects, alligators eat frogs, and alligators feed-fertilize-the plants. Alligators can survive and grow on a small amount of food.

Author and Alligator

Alligators, part of the crocodilian family, come closest to a living dinosaur but they are just a third or less of the dinosaur length. Nonetheless, next to man they're the top predator in the Everglades. Named state reptile in 1987 by the state legislature, the 23 species no longer are endangered. Crocodiles, which have pointier snouts and two large exposed teeth on both sides, live in salt water and brackish water, because they have desalinating glands, which alligators lack.

Alligators, with 80 sharp, white, spike-like teeth, eat fish, turtles, mammals, snakes, and birds, but rarely people. Only ten humans, reportedly, have been killed in Florida by alligators (since records were kept starting in 1948). Wildlife officials say alligator attacks are infrequent and deaths even rarer. State records show 265 people attacked in 52 years, with just nine deaths.

Alligators look for water. In summer they can stay under water 15 minutes. In winter, the time stretches to an hour or two! Warm weather awakens cold-blooded alligators from their winter sluggishness. With warm days, their blood warms up and they start to move around more. Peak activity continues into June. As they search for food and mates, they turn up in unusual places; swimming pools, carports, lawns and in small community lakes. Before taking a dip in the pool at night, first turn on the pool lights and check the pool, especially in the spring drought.

If one strays into your yard, don't feed it, leave it alone, call for help and stay out of the water because another one may be around!

During a June "drought month" visit to the Everglades, alligators had clawed out "wallows," or "gator holes." The gator holes fill with groundwater. Other animals congregate at the holes to get water; and to be eaten if they get too close to the gator!

Gator Steve said: "The first rule to know about alligators in the wild is don't feed them. An alligator can bite the hand that feeds it. Worse, once fed, the reptiles lose their fear of humans."

"How can you figure out how big an alligator is if you just can see its head?" we asked. "Estimate the distance from the nose to the middle of the eye in inches. For every inch, the alligator will be about a foot long."

Alligators lie in sun to warm up and digest food. With a cold-blooded metabolism, their activity and food level depends on outside temperature: the warmer the temperature, the higher their metabolism. Although alligators were placed on the Endangered Species list in 1973, they were removed from the list in 1987. More than one million of them reside in Florida, with their only real threat being humans. In addition to hunting alligators, fast-growing building development by humans, and pollution, continues to encroach on the alligator's habitat.

Only licensed hunters can legally hunt alligators. The hunters captured and killed 5,000 alligators in 1999. For one week in September, the state issues 500 permits for hunting by bow and arrow (or means other than guns). More than 7,000 apply, so they select the "winners" by a drawing.

The state issues permits to alligator trappers when it receives complaints about a large gator or one that has lost its fear of humans. A large one was removed from a small lake in our gated community. Small ones are in the lake, so swimming in this lake and others where alligators are present, is not a prudent thing to do.

At a nearby community, a 10-foot alligator chomped on a volleyball that had strayed from a volleyball game. The alligator kept the ball clinched between its teeth for more than three hours as it swam around the lake. As a player said: "The ball bounced over the net and went into the lake. The alligator saw the ball and swam to it." Another player said: "I think he thought he had something to eat and was trying to drown his prey." One player had his video camera with him so filmed the alligator. His video made the evening TV news.

On a sadder note, an 11-foot bull alligator snatched an 85-pound golden retriever from a lakeside in St. Petersburg in 1999. In June 2000, an alligator grabbed a 46-pound Dalmatian that had bounded into a lake near Seminole for a swim. The devastated owners could do nothing but watch. The Conservation Commission reports dozens of alligator attacks involving pets every year.

Safety Hints:

- Don't feed the alligators, because not only does this make them lose fear of humans, but also it is against the law.
- Don't disturb nests. Females can be aggressive if threatened.
- Keep your distance. Alligators can move fast for a short distance (run 40-50 feet faster than a galloping horse).
- Keep pets and children away from alligators.
- Don't swim in lakes with alligators. I photographed a 10-foot alligator in the lake behind our home just 25 yards off shore. Swimming in the lake would not be a good idea!

Alligator trivia: An alligator was involved in the first toilet ever seen on TV, which was on the *Leave it to Beaver* show. Wally and Beaver had a baby alligator, which they kept in the toilet.

Delightful Dolphins.   (State Saltwater Mammal). Named state saltwater mammal, dolphins delight us by playfully twisting and turning before sliding back into the water with a giant splash. The bottlenose dolphin (the term is used interchangeably with "porpoise") lives to be 30 years old and grows to 12 feet long, although most are six to eight feet long. Dolphins, which are grayish in color, but darker above and a lighter color below, weigh typically 400 pounds. The dolphin not only is intelligent, but also has keen eyesight, remarkable hearing and makes a wide variety of clicking sounds. Warm-blooded dolphins breathe air, give birth, and nurse and care for their young for two to four years. The friendly dolphins travel in family groups and normally slice along at 5 to 10 miles per hour but they can boost the speed to 25 miles per hour. They eat 15 pounds, or more, of fish a day!

We see them cavorting nearly every time we go boating or take a pontoon boat tour. On every tour, our pontoon boat stayed carefully at a distance to avoid stressing the dolphins, but typically they swam alongside! We slowed to a crawl as we watched them and they watched us!

More than 400 inquisitive, friendly dolphins inhabit Tampa Bay. We have not boated in Estero Bay (Fort Myers) without seeing dolphins near Big Carlos Pass. One captain said he could almost guarantee seeing dolphins because the flow of water through the pass brings a lot of fish, which the dolphins love to eat.

By the way, how does a dolphin make a decision? Flipper coin.

Marvelous Manatees (State Marine Mammal). The fascinating West Indian manatee, named Florida's official marine mammal in 1975, remains on the endangered species list. Some see the manatee as among the crown jewels of Florida's wildlife treasure chest. Others see the manatee as a loafing oaf, grazing on sea grass for eight hours, and 200 pounds, a day. The gentle manatee, averaging 13-feet long and weighing more than a ton, moves slow, which exacerbates the problem with boats, because they can't move quickly out of the way like a dolphin. Touching a manatee feels like a wet football.

The battle of boaters and environmentalists over manatee speed zones continues to percolate. As with development growth versus no growth, the smart stance is one of balance and some compromise from the extreme positions on these issues. An environmentalist claimed, "The most common cause of death for manatees is being struck by boats and barges." Boaters quickly disputed this with statistics that supported red tide and natural causes leading death reasons, but boats appear to cause up to a fourth of manatee deaths.

You can see manatees in dozens of places in Florida. We watched them on a boat ride around Marco Island, on a kayak outing on the Orange River (near Fort Myers), in the Indian River (near Cape Canaveral), at Homosassa State Park (90 minutes north of Tampa) and several other places. At Homosassa, which calls itself "The Manatee Capital of the World," you can see them from an underwater observatory without getting wet.

So the alligators lurk like some readers of emails, dolphins play uninhibited like children and manatees graze peacefully all offering a Florida contrast of amazing wildlife.

A Less Visible Three

Here are three that are less visible than the top three. Florida has some unusual wildlife concentrated in some small areas, including the Florida panther, key deer and Florida black bear. Your best chance of seeing one of these is the key deer on Big Pine Key.

Florida Panther (State Animal). The Florida panther, with fewer than 100 alive (one report says 87), has to be the most endangered predator in North America. Survival of the large (six feet long), long-tailed pale brown panthers (the state animal), which are relatives of mountain lions and cougars, depends heavily on preserving space for them to breed, eat and roam. An adult male requires a range of 200 square miles; a female 100 square miles. Loss of habitat has been a major cause of the decline. Most of the adult panthers known to exist live in South Florida. Their food source includes deer, wild hogs, small alligators, raccoons and rodents.

Typically, a Florida panther starts life as one of up to four one-pound blind kittens that stay with their mother for two years, and live 12 to 15 years.

The Florida Panther National Wildlife Refuge, which was established in 1989, comprises 26,400 acres 20 miles east of Naples, a few miles from where we live. The refuge, bounded on the south by I-75 and on the east by Highway 29, in Collier County, is within the Big Cypress Watershed, and on the northern end of the Everglades. Highway 29 has three elevated panther crossings. The chances of you seeing the very secretive panther in the wild are not much above slim and none. The refuge is closed to the public although there are plans for a trail. Two Florida panthers converged on the Corkscrew Swamp Sanctuary, where officials reported that a kitten was raised to maturity in 2003. The Caribbean Gardens Zoo in Naples has three Florida panthers.

Judging from the occasional road kill on Highway 29, despite under road panther crossings, and "Panther Crossing" signs, clearly someone saw the panther. We have driven Highway 29 scores of times and never glimpsed a panther. Some people have seen a panther by driving on Jane's Memorial Scenic Drive in the Fakahatchee Strand Preserve State Park, which is south of the refuge. It provides a boardwalk. The Strand and the Florida Panther Refuge are also home to many rare orchid species.

Key Deer. The tiny key deer is a subspecies of the Virginia white-tailed deer and is the smallest (25 to 90 pounds) of all white-tailed deer; and found only in Big Pine Key and surrounding keys. This three-foot tall, protected deer numbers 500-700 today. They're tame, forage in the garbage cans and have recovered from being an endangered species. Scientists at the Key Deer National Wildlife Refuge have been establishing populations of key deer on nearby Sugarloaf and Cudjoe keys, south of Big Pine. You can stop at the refuge and take a half-mile self-guided tour on a trail that winds through the refuge. Early morning and evening are the best times for viewing. Check www.thefloridakeys.com/parks/deer.

As we were driving to the Keys on one of our trips there a few years ago, traffic stopped on route 1 in Big Pine Key. Why? A key deer leisurely crossed the road and everyone wanted to see it! Unfortunately, automobiles on U.S. 1 also account for half the key deer deaths. Two underpasses a mile apart, and completed in 2003, should reduce highway deaths and prevent them from crossing the highway. The speed limit in the area is 45 mph, so watch for the deer. If you want to see the deer, stop in at the refuge, but look don't feed as it is illegal to feed key deer.

You can find white-tailed deer in all Florida counties, with a large population in the northern part of the state. Some areas have 25 to 30 deer per square mile. Although the average deer weighs 100 pounds, deer size increases the farther north you are; Wisconsin deer typically weigh 130 to 150 pounds.

Florida Black Bear.

Despite the Florida Black Bear population declining from 12,000 to an estimated 3,000, the bear isn't on the government's endangered or threatened list. Many of the bears roam the same habitat as the Florida Panther, not far from where we live in the Big Cypress National Preserve. The Florida Fish and Wildlife Conservation Commission estimates that more than 500 live in the preserve, but diminishing habitat and road kills take a toll. In 2002, a reported 132 black bears died on the roads, despite crossings under Interstate 75.

Three From the Sea

Sailfish (State Saltwater Fish). The striking-appearing sailfish leaps like a high-jumper on steroids. Sail fishing, is popular in Fort Pierce, Miami, and the Keys during the colder months. Ernest Hemingway landed a nine-foot one-inch sailfish off Key West in 1924.

Tarpon. Tarpon, the magnificent game fish, which lives for decades, hangs out at Boca Grande Pass. Anglers say that few experiences match catching a tarpon in shallow water on fly or light tackle. Imagine a free flyer five feet long in six feet of water leaping seven feet in the air!

Florida Sea Turtles Nesting. The turtle-nesting season starts in April, usually toward the end of the month. Florida turtle time volunteers, patrol the beaches looking for nests. When they find one, they mark it with yellow tape to keep people away from these endangered reptiles.

Loggerhead turtles, named for their large heads, scooped out 61 nests on Fort Myers Beach and 575 nests on Sanibel and Captiva Islands in 1998. Lee County, in total, had 865 nests in 1998 but fewer in 1999. Volusia County beaches had 570 sea turtle nests in the 1999 season.

After dinner at a beach restaurant on a beautiful evening in late April, we walked the beach to the spots where we had seen turtle nests the year before. We were probably a few days early, because we didn't see any. We thought we spotted a turtle in the sea. We did see dolphins frolicking offshore, their fins slicing through the water then silently disappearing. Although the turtle-nesting season starts in April, it lasts into September. A few days later, a volunteer spotted the first nest April 28.

The female turtle, with her paddle-like limbs (with no distinct toes), drags herself slowly up the beach from the ocean to beyond the high water line (high tide), and then digs a nest in the sand with her flippers. She deposits 100 or so eggs. The eggs incubate in the warm sand for two months before hatching. So the first hatchlings come in the peak of summer in July.

The temperature of the nest determines the sex of the hatchlings; with cooler nests yielding more males, warmer nests more females. The hatchlings are about the size of a quarter. Only a handful of eggs and hatchlings survive the threats of fire ants, ghost crabs, raccoons, birds and careless people.

The reddish-brown loggerhead turtles have thick armor-like shells, toothless jaws but powerful jaw muscles. The turtles, which can grow to three feet in length, and 200 to 350 pounds, eat clams, crustaceans and encrusting animals attached to rocks and reefs.

The giant sea turtles are protected in several ways. Beachfront residents, for example, are prohibited from shining lights on the beach during the nesting season. Hatchlings are drawn to the water by natural light, but become disoriented by artificial light. Environmentalists say porch lights, street lights and headlights kill hundreds of hatchlings each year.

The diminishing nesting grounds, mostly because of shore development, threatens the species' survival. The green turtle is nearly extinct. Only one green turtle nest was found in 2001. These large sea turtles, which can live to be 70 years old, were here before we were, so we need to respect their needs. Turtle fossils have been found that date from 200 million years ago, so they were here not only before us, but also even before the dinosaurs. We have seen turtles in the small lake near home, but not these large, captivating loggerhead turtles that emerge from the ocean during the nesting season.

A number of years ago, we traveled to the Cayman Islands. On Grand Cayman, we saw hundreds of turtles of all sizes, including the leatherback turtle, in pens at a large "turtle farm" facility. Even though the loggerhead turtle is large, the leatherback is even much larger. This largest of all the turtles can grow to 1,200 pounds! The pens on Grand Cayman held some of the largest we've ever seen, but you can't help but feel sad for these creatures in captivity. The Florida turtles live in their natural habitat. We need to protect the turtles, which is why volunteers patrol the beaches looking for nests to guard and keep safe.

Chapter Nine
Florida Birds

More and more people have been flocking to the hobby of birding. The U.S. Forest Service said birding is the fastest growing outdoor activity with 71 million bird watchers in 2001, up from 21 million 20 years before. The biggest growth has been in the 50 and older age bracket, as you can see by simply looking at a group of birders. Florida attracts birders like a magnet strengthened by the power of 300 bird species migrating south to Florida during the winter to add to the more than 175 bird species already here. Florida has many different bird habitats and different bird species north to subtropical south, because of the length of the state. More than four million bird watchers flocked to Florida in 2001 according to the U.S. Fish and Wildlife Service.

Birding has three main interest levels: Level 1. Basic Information and Casual Interest; Level 2. Birder; and Level 3. Florida Master Naturalist. Let's look at each of these.

Level 1. Basic Information and Casual Interest.

You may not want to take up birding, but you do need to have some basic information so you aren't embarrassed when friends and family from the North visit.

"What is that ugly bird there by the canal, grandpa?" asks a visiting grandchild.

"A wood stork. You're right that they are a bit ungainly on the ground, and sort of a dirty white and black, but when they fly they are a sight to behold in gracefulness with neck extended and legs straight behind."

"Cool."

So, even if you don't get hooked as a birder, knowing the most common birds will make you appear, if not an expert, at least not a newcomer or tourist. So before you go all atwitter, here's the short course on how to identify the commonly seen birds. If you *do* know anhingas, egrets, ibises and herons then you may want to skip to "our favorite bird" paragraph.

Wood Stork

Let's quickly note that more than 9,000 bird species exist in the world, so don't be alarmed if you don't know them all! Even knowing the 475 species in Florida presents a challenge for a master birder. We'll describe only the commonly seen birds so that you have the "basics" and give you some tidbits about them. A handy thing to have, if you have the interest, is a plastic laminated "cheat sheet" that depicts the commonly seen birds on both sides. A laminated, beach proof, waterproof reference guide that depicts many local bird species, folds to a handy size.

Wading Birds; Long Necks, Bills and Stilt-like Legs. Nineteen species of wading birds, more than any other state, call Florida home. Most are year-round residents.

Long-neck white birds. The smaller ones are snowy egrets, unless they have a long curved pink bill, which means they're probably ibis!

Snowy egrets have black legs and "gold slippers" (yellow feet) and a shaggy plume on head and neck. There are, however, many species of egrets. The cattle egret, for example, which you can often see in pastures and habitats away from water, has a dull orange or yellow bill and dull orange legs and smaller than a snowy egret. When it flies it tucks its neck in close to the body, unlike the larger snowy egret, which holds its neck in an "S" curve in flight.

If the white bird is large (three-feet tall) then it's likely a great egret, a wading bird with elegant plumes or a great white heron. How can you tell which, because people often confuse the two similar species? The great white heron is larger with yellow legs and a single head plume from behind the eye. They generally live only in south Florida and the Keys. John Audubon claimed a first in identifying the great white heron as a separate species, when he was in Key West.

122

Grey-blue long-neck birds. The smallest of these (egret-sized) is the little blue heron, although youngsters are white and turn slate blue when adults! The large one, reaching as much as four-feet tall, is the great blue heron, which has a blue-gray back, wings and belly. You can distinguish in flight by the way its thin legs stretch out behind. It has a black plume from behind the eye. The tri-colored heron is similar but you can tell it from a great blue, because it has a white belly.

Little Blue Heron

Wood Stork. This endangered bird sports a coarse charcoal neck and head, with pink legs and long bills. The population of wood storks has dropped drastically in the past 50 years. They need shallow wetland areas and plenty of fish. Corkscrew Swamp is one of the few remaining habitats suitable for wood stork nesting. The wood storks nest in December-March. They leave in June, depending on water level. Adult wood stork legs, usually a dark gray color, turn pink during the nesting season. The black scaly featherless head earns the bird the *iron head* nickname.

Anhinga or Double-Crested Cormorant? What about those dark birds that perch on a limb and dry their wings? They're either an anhinga or a cormorant. If they have a straight bill, the bird is an anhinga. Another tip: when drying their wings, the back of the anhinga wings look like black and white piano keys. Cormorants have solid colors. These birds swim underwater to catch fish with their razor-sharp beaks. Some call it the snakebird because when hunting, only its long thin neck and head protrude from the water, which makes it look like a snake. If it looks like an Anhinga, but the bill has a hook in it, the bird is a cormorant.

Birds on the beach: Sea gulls, terns and others. If you're on the beach, you'll see flocks of small birds and a squabble of gulls. Let's look at some key identification characteristics. Simply sitting on the beach will provide opportunity to watch gulls light on the

Anhinga

123

water to feed and terns dive for food. The heavier-bodied gulls with short beaks, contrast with slender Terns and their sharp beaks. Identifying the species of gulls and terns, however, with nearly three-dozen each, can be challenging. Some, like the ring-billed gull are easy to spot because of the ring around its bill. You can distinguish the laughing gull with its black head.

Among the flocks of gulls and terns, you can easily distinguish black

Laughing Gull

skimmers by their large beaks, with a red-orange coloring along the base of the beak. They are the *only* bird with a lower mandible longer, than the upper: so they can skim along the water and scoop up fish.

Sandpipers have long legs, short necks and long beaks and peck away at the sand. In flight, they wheel and swoop in unison. The six-inch size little guys, nervously darting about, with legs pounding away at high rpms, are sanderlings, the most common of beach birds.

Brown Pelican. No one has a problem identifying a brown pelican, especially as they dive-bomb and plunge into the water. On the other hand no one can figure out which is male and which is female! Only the pelicans know for sure. Gulls hassle them for food. The brown pelican, a big bird with a wingspan of 6-1/2 to 7-1/2 feet, excites viewers with its spectacular dives for fish, bill first, into the water. Adults have white heads with pale yellow crowns, brown-streaked back and tail, black legs and feet. They nest in large colonies on mangrove islands. Have you noticed how many businesses and developments start with the word "Pelican?"

White Pelican. The white pelican is not only distinctively white, but also much larger than the brown pelican with a wingspan of up to nine feet. These birds are very sociable and fish in a group, unlike brown pelicans. It has a bright yellow-orange pouch for feeding beneath its long, flattened bill.

Common Moorhen. The moorhen looks like a duck with a short, red bill tipped with yellow. You can distinguish it from the similar looking coot, by a line of white feathers on the flanks and the red bill. Simply stated, coots have white snoots! The moorhen moves its head back and forth when swimming.

Other Birds.

Muscovy Duck. You'll see a few of these waddling around, sometimes near shopping centers. With the black and white color and with warty red facial areas around the eyes, you can bet you're looking at a muscovy duck, which is genetically different from other ducks. They don't swim much because their oil glands are underdeveloped compared to other ducks. The males are twice as big as the females after just three months and can weigh up to 12 pounds.

Osprey. Often mistaken for a bald eagle, because of its brown body and white head, you can distinguish the osprey from an eagle from the dark eye stripe and it's white from the head under the belly. This fish catcher, much more common than the eagle in Florida, lives high in the trees and on platforms atop poles erected for them. Florida has the second highest eagle population (Alaska first).

Roseate Spoonbill. You can't miss the roseate spoonbill, when you see one, because of its pink coloration (from eating shrimp) and the spoonbill. They walk slowly in shallow water and move their bill sideways to catch fish.

Now that you can pop up the answer to relatives and friends visiting for the above birds, you'll at least appear to have some knowledge. That wasn't so hard. Identifying the 360 or so species flying around, perching on a tree limb or wire or roosting, however, can be difficult. For that, you need to step up to another level and arm yourself with some gear! Before talking to you about Level 2, let's ask you what is your favorite bird? Our answer, before living in Florida was the Bald Eagle. Florida has 1,000 nesting pairs, up from fewer than 100 just 30 years ago. It still ranks high, if not first, but….

Other than the Eagle, what is our favorite bird?

Watching a blue heron flutter in for a landing, seeing a pelican sweep his wings back for a dive into the water to nab a fish, spying an elegant snowy egret walking in shallow water, observing an ibis with it's long pink beak pecking into the grass, looking at a wood stork in graceful flight; all are favorites. But since moving to Florida, we have become infatuated with the official bird of the state of Florida: the mockingbird….and how he can sing! This bird has become a favorite, especially after an April evening, when I heard what I thought was a cardinal, then a meadowlark. I stepped outside and looked up to see a grayish bird sitting on the corner of the fireplace chimney. His beak was open, his throat vibrated from his exertions as he sang away.

An anole occupied one of the two chairs nearby, so I sat in the other chair. Under a cloudless blue sky, warmed by the fiery ball sinking toward the horizon, and listening to the bird sing, you can forget about life's problems for a few minutes. The Frank Sinatra of birds continued his thrilling trilling. Sometimes confused with a loggerhead shrike, you can't mistake this bird with the vocalizations: a mockingbird. He's slightly bigger and less stocky, than the loggerhead shrike, although both birds have grayish undersides. The tail is bordered by white feathers. There are splashes of white in the wings that can be seen in flight.

The mockingbirds, which are virtuoso mimics, are relatives of the thrushes. Male mockingbirds may sing as many as 150 different songs. They not only mimic a wide variety of birds accurately but also pick up on noises such as dog barks, frog calls, cricket chirps and human whistles.

Northern Mockingbird

They mimic so accurately you can't tell them from the real thing! Usually the mockingbird gives the call in groups of three or more. I tried a whistle, but the bird continued his own one-bird vocal stream. He ignored me, and the anole, because he was focused on a mate. Clearly, his lack of success in finding one was our gain as he sang and sang.

The male mockingbird will continue to sing to attract a female even into the night. During courtship, the male and female do a mating dance on the ground with their heads and tails erect and their wings spread. They run toward each other, and then retreat. They repeat the run and fly into the air. Nesting begins in March in Florida. It continues into late summer. Nests usually are only five to eight feet above ground in shrubs. The mockingbird builds the nest with a base of twigs, and then lines it with fine leaves and grass. The three to five eggs, which are blue, speckled with brown, incubate in 12-13 days. Two weeks later the young will fledge. During the season, the mockingbirds will have three broods.

Mockingbirds eat insects and fruit. They have an unusual way of capturing insects called "hawking." They quickly flash their wings when walking on the ground. Then they slowly lower the wing to watch for any insect startled by the movement. They're great pest controllers! The next day, as we took a morning walk, the mockingbird seemed to go along with us with a serenade. Of course, it wasn't the same one, but many scattered throughout the bushes and trees. The experience will make you want to become a birder.

Scrub Jay. Some believe this bundle of blue, gray and white feathers should be the state bird, rather than the mockingbird. The scrub jay is the only bird of the more than 475 bird species in Florida that lives exclusively in Florida. The little guy fits in well because he's been called the bluebird of friendliness.

What is your favorite bird?

Summary, Level 1. Knowing how to identify just these birds will give you enough information to answer questions and at least appear knowledgeable. You can take some simple straightforward steps to move to the next level to get to know more of the bird species in Florida.

Be Kind to Our Feathered Friends; Learn to Co-Exist.

- Keep your distance.
- Avoid colonies during nesting season. (It's illegal to harass nesting birds.)
- Don't startle birds; use slow, steady calm approaches.
- Walk around groups of birds rather than forcing them to fly.
- If you're in a bird sanctuary, be quiet so you and others can hear the bird songs.

Level 2. Birder

Get ready to spread your wings! Step up to Level 2.

If you feel a real thrill to see a rare or reclusive bird species you've never seen before you may want to step up a notch. Seeing a crested caracara, a purple gallinule, limpkin, blue-gray gnatcatcher, marbled godwit, magnificent frigatebird and male painted buntings, with bright blue, red and green colors that look like Christmas tree ornaments (female painted buntings are lemon/lime), may inspire more study. Or, if you start to identify places of your favorite bird sightings, as in: "That's where I saw my crested caracara," you should follow through on Level Two!

If you want to go to the next step in identifying birds, get a copy of a field guide and a pair of binoculars, then attend a bird program at a refuge. Being a birder requires very little other than a pair of binoculars and a bird guidebook, so you participate without breaking the bank. There are no dues, no golf clubs, no green fees and no fishing gear.

Binoculars. For binoculars, get a pair with seven to 10 magnification and an objective lens of 35 to 42 millimeters. The larger the lens, the greater the amount of light the binoculars gather. Set the focus on an object 30 feet away. If you wear eyeglasses, get binoculars that have rubber eye cups that fold back. You can get a good pair for $50, but you'll see birders and master birders with top-notch binoculars that cost up to 10 times that. A pair of Audubon Equinox 8 x 42 premium binoculars from Eagle Optics (www.eagleoptics.com) cost $230. At www.optics4birding.com, a non-commercial site, you'll find helpful information for making an informed buying decision.

Field Guide. Many consider *The Sibley Guide to Birds* by David Allen Sibley the "birder bible" ($35). Phil Nye, a master naturalist, recommends Sibley's Eastern North America version, which is pocket size and easy to take along with you. Sibley describes and illustrates 650 species in 432 pages, a bargain at $19.95. Stan Tekiela organized his *Birds of Florida Field Guide* by color. *Favorite Birds of Florida* by Dick Schinkel and David Mohrhardt has 125 full-color illustrations with text for each.

Other Equipment. Serious birders take along a camera. Also don't forget the sunscreen and mosquito repellent.

So, where should we go birding?

Birder's World Magazine rated J.N. "Ding" Darling National Refuge third, Everglades National Park fourth and Corkscrew Swamp Sanctuary fifth among the top 15 places to go to see birds. No other state had three spots (Southeastern Arizona was first and Cape May, New Jersey second). Chapter Ten describes visits to the three Florida top-rated sites, along with some other hot spots.

Florida has been developing the *Great Florida Birding Trail.* Special highway signs on major highways direct you to parks designated as official birding sites. The trail will run 2,000 miles and include 400 birding sites. The guides for the east and west areas have been issued with guides for the Panhandle and South Florida to follow. Guides can be bought in bookstores, downloaded or picked up at key nature center "gateways," including in the east Ft. Clinch State Park (Fernandia Beach), Merritt Island National Wildlife Refuge (Titusville), and Tenoroc Fish Management Area (Lakeland); and in the west at Paynes Prairie Preserve State Park (Gainesville) and Fort Desoto State Park (St. Petersburg). The gateways also provide loaner binoculars, if you didn't bring along a pair. The east section consists of 135 sites in 18 counties. The west trail has 117 sites. *The Guide to the Great Florida Birding Trail*, edited by Julie A. Brashears and Susan Cerulean, is available in bookstores. The book describes each site from a birder's point of view. It includes directions, hours of operation, seasonal birding opportunities and essays by state experts to help you understand different species and conserving habitats. For details on the trail, see www.floridabirdingtrail.com/guide.htm.

Birding also leads you to the natural beauty inherent in the birding sites and to other activities readily available at most sites, including beaches and nature trails for hiking. On your *to-do list* of things you want to do in Florida (Chapter Nineteen), you can combine goals with multiple benefits (visiting a lighthouse, kayaking, or fishing).

Major bird festivals occur in October in Marathon, Port St. Joseph and St. Petersburg. The five-day Space Coast Birding and Wildlife festival is in Titusville in November. The Everglades Birdfest is in January with festivals at Pelican Island and Suwannee River Valley in March, Tallahassee in April and St. Augustine in May. The three-day "Big O' festival, at Lake Okeechobee runs in April (www.bigobirdingfestival.com). In short, no matter where you live in Florida, you have a birding festival closer than a short bird flight.

Several state parks have beginning birding programs, such as at Lovers Key State Park. Audubon master naturalists conduct programs at Corkscrew Swamp.

Let's look at one of these. We attended, along with eight other people, a half-day seminar at Corkscrew Swamp led by Phil Nye, master naturalist. This program consists of "classroom" time in the Blair Audubon Center to review the basics, to view a slide presentation of 89 species of birds found in the Corkscrew Swamp, and to learn clues to identify birds. Impressively, Phil easily identified each of the birds, without notes. Armed with the information, the ten of us spent the remainder of the morning on the boardwalk, in the swamp, looking for bird species. We fell far short of a group who two days before chalked up 46 species!

Learning how to identify birds isn't easy, but the challenge can be very rewarding because you see something new each time. The clues to look for are silhouette (shape and size), plumage (and colors), behavior (how it flies, forages), habitat, and it's unique voice and song. You may need, however, just one or two of the clues to identify the bird.

Songs. Some birds can be easy to identify from their sounds, which they use to defend their territory or attract a mate:

- Chickadees. They say "chick-a dee."
- Whippoorwills say, "whip-pour-will."
- Laughing gulls sound like human laughter
- The yellow warbler goes "sweet, sweet, sweet, I'm so sweet."
- Mourning doves sound depressed.

Bird sounds have inspired composers because birds produce sound like flutes, oboes and tubas. Listen to a tape of bird sounds like *Bird Songs of Florida* by Geoffrey A. Keller ($14.95), or better yet go with an expert into the field and listen.

When should we go birding? Anytime! Check seasonality, because more species of birds populate Florida in the winter months. Call ahead to visit sites that can be visited only by appointment, or during special hours. At Merritt National Wildlife Refuge, for example, a space launch trumps the park and closes it. If you're interested in birding festivals and events, check the Florida Birding Trail for a current list.

Certification. *Wings Over Florida* awards free birding certificates at five achievement levels, starting with level 1 Beginner (50) and going up to level 5 Elite Florida Birder (350 species). Request an application online, or mail to Florida Fish and Wildlife, 3400 Drane Field Road, Lakeland, Florida 33811-1299, or email to wof@fwc.state.fl.us. They will send you a handy little booklet; *Checklist of Florida Birds* that will help you keep track of "the spectacular range of bird life" in Florida. The book lists 485 species.

Level 3. Florida Master Naturalist

Corkscrew Swamp Sanctuary offers an adult education course twice during the year, in partnership with the University of Florida Institute of Food and Agricultural Sciences (UF-IFAS), to qualify as a Florida Master Naturalist. The course consists of classroom instruction, field trips and practical experience in interpretation about Florida's freshwater wetland habitats and wildlife. Five other county locations also offer the Freshwater System Module. The class lasts six weeks and costs $200. Florida Museum of Natural History at University of Florida conducts the Coastal System Module in Gainesville. The course is offered also at five county locations. Completion of the course results in a colorful award patch, pin and certificate.

Turkey Vulture

Graduates volunteer and share their knowledge with others and help "foster principles of sustainability, connectivity and biodiversity to assist others to understand and respect Florida's natural world as a community to which we all belong."

Register at www.masternaturalist.org.

Email for more information at info@masternaturalist.org.

Trash Collectors and Large Birds. If you want to see all the following large birds, you'll need to do your watching in Florida!

If you have watched a turkey vulture spiral high in the sky, riding the thermals and updrafts, you can see why the Wright brothers gained inspiration more than a century ago for their invention. You can recognize this graceful soaring bird by its large size and the V-shaped wings. On the ground, as nature's scavengers of road kill, with their bald red head, they don't look graceful, but they serve a purpose by getting rid of dead flesh of road kill and other decomposing animals that could spread disease. The Turkey Vulture Society (www.accutek.com/vultures), organized in 1994, is looking into the health aspects of the bird's ability to absorb bacteria.

The crested caracara, a unique raptor, looks like an eagle in flight. Called the "Mexican Eagle" sometimes, the bird is a symbol in Mexico. The bird has a black crown that ends in a crest, with the rest of the head white except for a red featherless face and yellow legs. The bird feeds on small prey (lizards, large insects, birds, small mammals) and steals carrion from their distant relatives, the vultures. Sometimes they stand on the backs of turtles and wait for them to stick their necks out! They've nailed bats in the air. Your only real opportunity to see one is in South Florida in open bushy areas with palms and cabbage palm; scrub habitat that scrub jays also like. We saw two of these unusual birds in rural Hendry County.

Ah, the magnificent frigatebird with its eight-foot wingspan and the bright scarlet gular pouches of the males that they puff up to football size to attract the notice of female birds. We have watched these remarkable birds in the A-B-C Islands off Marco Island, in the roosting mangrove islands outside of Charlotte Harbor and in Pine Island Sound. You'll find them mainly along the South Florida seacoast. The birds have a hard time getting airborne so they don't land on the ground, or even in the water, but in the mangrove trees. With their pointed wings and forked tail, the birds ride the offshore wind and hover over potential meals. The frigatebird is also a bully and a pirate, often stealing prey from terns.

Finally, whooping cranes, after an absence of 71 years, returned to Florida in 1993. The endangered crane, tallest bird in the world, resides in Kissimmee Prairie with 80 surviving today.

What about flamingos? You can see them at the Lowry Park Zoo and Busch Gardens in Tampa, Sunken Gardens in St. Petersburg, Sarasota Jungle Gardens and Parrot Jungle Zoo in Miami!

Chapter Ten
Wildlife Refuges, Nature Centers and Parks

"Take nothing but pictures, leave nothing but footprints."

Wildlife Refuges, Nature Centers. More than 540 national wildlife refuges grace the United States plus state and organization-owned refuges. These refuges, which contain nearly 100 million acres, provide outstanding opportunities to enjoy wildlife. We'll share with you some of our adventures in visiting refuges in Florida, simply to give you a flavor. Some of the best wildlife refuges, and the very first one, are in Florida. President Theodore Roosevelt established the first one, March 14, 1903, on three-acre Pelican Island. In 1903, the American flag had 45 stars, the nation had just 8,000 cars, and the average wage was 22 cents an hour. One in 10 adults could not read or write. Roosevelt went on to create 55 wildlife refuges to "preserve breeding ground for native birds." At the time, plume hunters nearly wiped out some bird species for their plumes. Today, more than 700 bird species, 220 mammal species and 250 reptiles find refuge in these cornerstones of conservation. More than 37 million people visited the refuges in 2003, helped by 37,000 volunteers.

The Pelican Island National Wildlife Refuge now has more than 500 acres and a boardwalk with an 18-foot observation tower. The refuge hosts a birding festival in March.

State Parks. In 1999 the National Sporting Goods Association awarded Florida State Parks its first-place gold medal. The 151 properties at the time, under the umbrella slogan, "The Real Florida," comprised 500,000 acres and got 14.6 million annual visitors.

In 2003, Florida had 157 state parks. Truly, the parks represent something for everyone. More than 18 million people visited Florida State Parks in 2003 to enjoy the beaches, hike, bike, canoe, fish, swim or visit a lighthouse. Consider the parks have 1,600 miles of trails with more than 350 miles for hikers only and more than 240 for cycling. If you want to canoe, the parks have more than 1,000 miles of canoe trails. How about horseback riding? Eight parks provide overnight stables: Florida Caverns, Jonathan Dickinson, Little Manatee River, Lower Wekiva River, Myakka River, O'Leno, Rock Springs Run and Wekiwa Springs. Several others have equestrian trails. Half the parks have trails with interpretive signs, which describe the cultural heritage and ecology. Florida has 36 state forests with more than 800,000 acres.

The entry price for the most-visited parks at $5 for a car with as many as eight visitors is truly a bargain. You can buy annual passes for $40 for a single person, or $80 for a family (up to eight in a car).

You can order a pamphlet with a map and facilities, or download a version in PDF format. More than 30 individual brochures are available for specific parks. For a complete list of the 157 state parks and a map, log on to www.FloridaStateParks.org, or call 850-488-9872 to obtain a park guide. If you're interested in camping at parks, check out www.ReserveAmerica. com, or call 1-800-326-3521. The site lists 60 campgrounds in Florida.

National Parks. Florida has only three national parks, but what they lack in quantity is more than made up for by unique qualities: Biscayne, Everglades and Dry Tortugas. You will relish the contrast of the timeless wonders with the commercial developments nearby.

Biscayne National Park's 173,000 acres are 95 percent underwater, with shallow reef and colorful coral!

The 1.5 million acres of the Everglades stretch across three southern counties of Florida (Dade, Monroe, and Collier) with three main entrance areas at the east (near Homestead, Florida), Shark Valley and in the west at Everglades City. Approximately a third of the Everglades is in Florida Bay and the Gulf of Mexico.

Everglades and Biscayne parks made the top ten list of "most endangered" by the National Parks Conservancy Association. Dry Tortugas National Park (and Fort Jefferson) can be reached only by boat or seaplane and is the least visited national park.

In your list of things to do, make sure these three are on your list! Chapter Thirteen describes one of our visits to Dry Tortugas National Park. Although not a "Park," Big Cypress Preserve, north of the Everglades, comprises 729,000 acres, twice the size of Rhode Island! Seminole and Miccosukee Indians live in the preserve.

*"The clearest way into the universe is through
a forest wilderness..."* John Muir

Top Three Places to Visit

J. N. "Ding" Darling National Wildlife Refuge. Sanibel-Captiva Road, Sanibel Island, phone 941-472-1100.

We have visited the J. N. "Ding" Darling National Wildlife Refuge many times. We have been delighted. We have been disappointed. We learned the hard way when you should visit. *February. At low tide. In the morning.*

February is the best month for birding. February also is the best chance to see the huge American crocodile, believed to be the only one this far north. The downside of going in February: it's also a peak month in the tourist season. More than 334,000 vehicles cross the Sanibel Causeway toll in February alone, so that does mean crowds. Dense traffic can mean slow going for tourists, brisk business for tollbooths. Ding Darling hosts almost a million visitors a year. "February is the busiest month of the year," a refuge ranger said.

If you are not a birder or knowledgeable about the ecology and birds, stop at the center first. Better yet, go with a guide. We went with a group with Martin Packard, a noted birder. He has identified 396 different birds during his years of bird watching. He has been birding on Sanibel since 1973.

"I've come to Ding Darling many times, but this was so informative and enjoyable," one in the group said.

"There's so much to see when you have a guide who sees and points out things you don't see!" Another said. "An amazing array of exotic birds."

On this visit we saw the huge female crocodile just yards from the road. We saw rarely seen reddish egrets and roseate spoonbills. We watched white pelicans fish together as a team, using a different system than the individually diving and fishing brown pelican. We saw double-crested cormorants, anhingas, tri-color herons, ospreys and many others. We saw, on a walk near the end of the five-mile drive, a zebra long-wing butterfly, flitting above alligators. We watched a pelican tuck in its wings and nosedive into the surf, then bob quickly to the surface before taking a big gulp to swallow the fish it caught.

A good way to see the wildlife is by canoe or kayak, which you can rent at the refuge.

The refuge, named for Pulitzer Prize-winning cartoonist J.N. "Ding" Darling, occupies nearly half of Sanibel Island. If you go, remember the refuge closes on Friday to let the wildlife rest!

Captivating Corkscrew Swamp Sanctuary, 375 Sanctuary Road, Naples, Florida, phone 239-348-9151. Have you ever seen the rare purple gallinule? No? Neither had we. In fact, we didn't know the bird existed until a February visit to the Corkscrew Swamp Sanctuary, several years ago, after we moved to Florida. We visited the sanctuary on a late afternoon under an azure sky on a balmy day, perfect for a walk in the woods. We later moved close by and visit the 11,000-acre, Audubon Society-owned-and-operated Corkscrew Swamp often. It's off the beaten path, but an easy excursion fifteen miles east of I-75 from Exit 111, between Naples and Immokalee.

Florida Monthly Magazine named Corkscrew Sanctuary and its Blair Audubon Center as the best nature center in Florida! *Birder's World* Magazine ranked the sanctuary fifth in the top 15 birding spots in the United States. *Florida Monthly* Magazine cited Corkscrew as the Number One Nature Center in Florida. We have visited the Sanctuary more than a score of times, yet always see something new. The Sanctuary celebrated its golden anniversary in March 2004.

The sanctuary, famous for the largest nesting colony of endangered wood storks in North America, also has the largest remaining stand of majestic bald cypress trees in the world. These towering trees, some of which are more than 500 years old, soar 130 feet to form a cathedral-like canopy. Cypress "knees" poke out of the water. These "knees" (roots) add stability for the trees.

After looking at the exhibits in the Nature Center, which nestles in the pine flatwoods, we headed out on the 2.25-mile boardwalk that winds through a variety of distinct habitats of the pine flatwoods, wet prairie, peat marsh, pond cypress stand and tropical hardwood hammocks, with half the sanctuary the ancient cypress forest. Each habitat supports a range of flora and fauna to see. The swamp actually is a slow-moving river that flows southwest toward the Gulf of Mexico.

We didn't see much for the first mile. Florida has two extremes that dominate the weather with a wet summer and a dry winter. During this visit a drier than normal winter affected wildlife. We saw just one stately wood stork. We did see a great blue heron, some ibis, and a raccoon.

A dark-brown Barred Owl sat quietly resting in a tree. Then, instead of a *"whoo,"* the booming baritone barred owl calls with something that sounds like *"who cooks for you, who cooks for you all."* Florida has five species of owls that control rodent population: eastern screech, great-horned, barred, barn and burrowing owls.

We saw snowy egrets, little blue herons and ducks. A little further along the walk, a movement caught our eye and we watched Florida's most common hawk, the red-shouldered one, swoop from a tree. We could hear the shrill call: ke-arr, ke-arr. We saw a turkey vulture perched on a limb.

More than 200 species of birds have been spotted in the sanctuary. So, we saw perhaps twenty percent of them during our visit, but the purple gallinule highlighted the tour.

The Audubon Society, which first purchased the property in 1954, completed a six-year campaign to raise $6.7 million to improve the sanctuary. The money funded the new boardwalk that replaced a shorter one, the Blair Audubon Nature Center, which includes a theater, classrooms, nature store and café, and a unique innovative "living machine" water treatment system. The Society conducts environmental education programs and has rangers spaced along the route to answer questions.

You walk more than the 2.25 miles because of spurs you can take to observation decks. Fifteen interpretive displays along the boardwalk help explain what you see. Benches along the boardwalk give you a chance to sit and absorb the peace and tranquility of the woods. We have visited many times in all seasons, but your best chance to see the most is January to April. Each time we have visited we have seen something new. During one visit, we were surprised to spot a black-crowned night heron.

Every year in March, the sanctuary conducts a one-day fund-raising Bird-A-Thon. The staff starts before dawn to identify as many species as they can, which in 2003 totaled 104 species!

Black-crowned night heron

Only rainwater feeds Corkscrew (no springs or lakes). The clean and pure water has a tea-like color from tannins from the leaves. We pointed to an area on the water surface that looked like an oil slick. We asked an Audubon boardwalk naturalist: "Is that an oil slick?"

"No, it isn't pollution, but resin leached from cypress seeds, branches and needles."

Lots of air plants (epiphytes) clung to the trees. Air plants grow on other plants without soil. The air plants use their roots to attach to trees and get moisture and nutrients from the air and rain. All have spineless leaves. Half the 18 Florida species are endangered. An evil weevil from Mexico (the metamasius callizona) threatens air plants. The weevil particularly likes the giant, cardinal and twisted air plants. Large air plants were very visible because the cypress trees had lost their needles. Many air plants catch water, which is then used by other animals, including frogs and mosquitoes.

"Where are all the wood storks?" we asked. A khaki-clad Audubon naturalist replied: "There's not enough water for them this harsh dry season, so they decided not to risk nesting. Last year we had wood storks here on nest during a gentle dry season with more than 2,500 new storks to fledge before the rainy season." (In 2004, few wood storks nested because water levels were *too high.* Wood storks have not nested, or abandoned nests, in 12 of the past 40 years.)

We began to wonder if the visit would be worthwhile. Little did we know that nature's riches were up ahead on the trail at Lettuce Lakes; wide shallow "bowls" of water, which are a favorite for wildlife, especially in the dry spring months. Water lettuce, a floating aquatic plant, covers the water. The sights at Lettuce Lakes brought excitement, education and a desire to return to this remarkable sanctuary.

We rounded a bend and saw a dozen photographers lined along the boardwalk rail in the Lettuce Lakes area. Here there was a shallow pool of water. "What is going on?" we whispered to a ranger. He pointed: "There are two purple gallinules. They are very rare here."

The bright iridescent purple birds stood in shallow water fifty feet away. The purple on the head and neck looks so rich as if painted by an artist. The purple contrasts with an olive back and a yellow-tipped red bill. One hopped up on a small branch sticking out of the water. Click. Zip. Click. Cameras with lens a foot long and the diameter of a coffee cup saucer, almost in unison, clicked and whirred as film automatically advanced. The bird went *cluck, cluck, cluck.* Sounded just like a chicken. The purple gallinule's feet spread the bird's weight so it can walk on lily pads and on other floating vegetation.

Nearby were a couple of alligators. Two red-bellied turtles sat sunning on a partially submerged log. We saw anhingas, resting on branches,

Purple Gallinule

spreading their black and silver wings to dry their feathers. We watched one swimming with just its head out of the water, which shows why it's nicknamed "snakebird."

Territorial ibis fought over limb space with more than a score of the white birds in a tree above a large motionless alligator resting in the shallow water. She might have been thirteen feet long. The birds and animals congregate around the water.

Snowy egrets decorated a tree like fat candles.

Raptors circled lazily above in thermals.

On another visit we ran into a river otter sunning on the boardwalk. On yet another visit, with friends, we watched a great white egret standing patiently looking down in the water as an alligator soaked up sunrays nearby. Then, the great egret in a splashy flash jabbed his yellow bill into the water, coming up with a fish.

"Why do birds nest above alligators?" our friend asked. "Because alligators provide protection from raiders like raccoons."

We visited in early March 2004, not expecting to see much because unusual rainfall in the "dry" season caused high water levels. The wood storks had left, as had some of the migratory birds. We were halfway on the boardwalk, however, when a war broke out in the trees; at least it sounded that way with the red-shouldered hawks screeching and limpkins adding to the racket with their distinctive, piercing Banshee wail: kre-ow, kra-ow, repeated over and over. The long-necked, long-legged limpkin, which has no close relatives, flies into Corkscrew because of its fondness for the freshwater apple snail found in the swamp. Limpkins, once hunted to near extinction, have recovered, but these wading birds are still relatively rare. You'll find the two-foot tall limpkin only in Florida in the United States.

On our first visit, a naturalist said, "This is one of the most beautiful places in Florida." We agreed and soon moved to a new home close to the sanctuary! We live where the temperate zone and tropic meet.

The entrance cost is $10 per person. Also be sure to spend another dollar for the guidebook. Bring along camera and binoculars. Stop in at

139

the "Swamp Theater," which depicts the daily and seasonal changes in the swamp.

To get to the sanctuary, take I-75. Get off at Exit 111. Go fifteen miles east on State Road 846 (Immokalee Road) to the sanctuary entrance. If you can't make the trip, take a virtual tour on the Internet. Go to www. audubon.com, and then click on Local Audubon Resources, then Audubon Sanctuaries, then Corkscrew Swamp.

Everglades National Park. Visiting the Everglades really means at least three different visits to the entrances at Gulf Coast, Shark Valley and Coe (Homestead) and the four visitor centers: Gulf Coast, Shark Valley, Coe, and Flamingo. You can get to Flamingo only by entering the park at Coe, or by boat.

"There are no other Everglades in the world. They are, they have always been, one of the unique regions of the Earth, remote, never wholly known." Marjory Stoneman Douglas (1890-1998) in *Everglades River of Grass.*

I have succinct advice about visiting the Everglades. Don't.

Now that I have your attention, let me modify that advice. Don't visit until you have read this chapter, checked out the National Park Service's excellent pamphlet, *Everglades National Park,* or logged on to the website www.nps.gov/ever. You'll get much more out of your visit. We found *Motorist's Guide to Everglades National Park* by Florida National Parks and Monuments Associations, Inc, (10 Parachute Key #51, Homestead, Florida 33034, phone 305-247-1316 www.nps.gov/ever/fnpman.htm) an informative, valuable aid.

The first wise counsel from any park ranger; "Stop and get out of your car." Everglades, unlike perhaps Yosemite or Yellowstone, is not a "drive-through" park. If you don't stop at Royal Palm four miles from the Coe Visitor Center, for example, you will risk missing a remarkable variety of wildlife within just a half mile of the center. We'll tell you more about that later, "after the break" as they say.

Although, as a resident you can visit in the off-season and avoid the crowds, you also won't see much wildlife, mosquitoes will attack you, afternoon thunderstorms pop up frequently, and the heat can be oppressive. Migratory birds leave. Wildlife disperses. Alligators disappear into the water. Go during December-March, with peak enjoyment usually late February. The least "buggy" time to go is in January.

We believe the best way for a first visit to the Gulf side is an escorted bus tour, which can be in the off-season. For the other two entrances we recommend you drive on your own, and go in late February-early March, to see the most different species of birds and wildlife.

President Truman established the park in 1947 to "protect the unique and fragile ecosystem." The park, third largest of all the national parks, has the world's largest mangrove system and 137 miles of coastline. This national jewel provides a habitat for 1,500 varieties of plants and wildlife, including 68 threatened or endangered species. The habitat maintains a delicate wildlife balance of the hunter and the hunted. More than 400 species of birds inhabit the park, which is the most significant breeding ground for tropical wading birds in North America.

The Everglades, now half its original size at 1.5 million acres once stretched from the lakes south of Orlando all the way to Florida Bay, as a slow-moving 60-mile wide river of grass on a slightly-sloping (a few inches per mile), three-mile thick base of limestone between two limestone ridges on the east (Miami) and Gulf (Naples) coasts. The porous limestone bedrock acts like a large sponge and is the source of Southern Florida's drinking water. No spot in the everglades exceeds eight feet above sea level. The "river" has an average depth of six inches!

Everglades East. Gulf Coast Visitor Center, 102 Collier Avenue, Everglades City, Florida 34139. Holding a five-year old alligator highlighted an event-filled, daylong escorted tour of the Everglades on a warm day in early June. We have often found the best way, for starters, is to join a tour that provides an overview. You can go back later and spend time at the places you liked best, or that offer specific experiences. So, our first visit to the Everglades on the west side, came in the Pelican Tours van, driven by our guide Gator Steve. He picked up a small group of us at 7:40 a.m. and returned us to our community at 5 p.m. In between, Gator Steve treated us to a busy day visiting many places. You simply can't do that on your own.

On the way to the Everglades, we stopped for a short visit to the 779,000-acre Big Cypress Preserve. Big Cypress, just north of the Everglades, is at a higher elevation and waters move slowly toward the Everglades and Florida Bay. We have returned to Big Cypress a number of times. Big Cypress, unlike the Everglades, allows hunting and off-road vehicles. The visitor center offers an interesting 15-minute film.

We walked on the 2,400-foot Boardwalk into the Fakahatchee Strand (Copeland, Florida; phone 239-696-4593), adjacent to the Big Cypress Preserve, to view a large alligator sunning itself near the end of the walk. We walked past tall cypress trees, many festooned with blooming "air plants," or bromeliads. Nets are provided to cover your head if bugs become a problem. Bugs were not bad because the heavy summer rains had not begun. Fakahatchee Strand, about 15 miles long and five miles wide, has the deepest slough in the Everglades region and more wild orchids than anywhere in the world. You can take a road trip on Janes Scenic Drive, an old logging road, starting off Highway 29, three miles north of U.S. 41.

A trip in early June has the advantage of avoiding crowds and hassle, with the off-season for tourists. "Summer is for Floridians," someone observed. Going in June does have the disadvantage, as mentioned, of having many of the birds gone on their migration, although we saw egrets, herons, ibis and osprey, we did not see any wood storks, snail kites, or roseate spoonbills.

After the walk, we were back in the van headed for a one-hour leisurely, "Jungle Boat" ride through the 10,000 islands. The pontoon-boat rounded a bend and a half dozen raccoons scurried through the mangroves to stand on their hind legs begging for a handout as the boat approached with its two-dozen passengers. We watched a chocolate brown and white osprey dive toward the water on a food foray for fresh fish.

"The Seminoles say when the sawgrass blooms, there will be a bad hurricane," the guide said. "That did happen in 1960 with Hurricane Donna after the sawgrass bloomed."

Back in the van, we rode to Everglades City, once the Collier County seat, and an alligator park/gift shop, where we watched a large pen full of big alligators.

We stopped at the old Spanish-stucco train depot, built in 1928, now the Seafood Depot Restaurant, for lunch with appetizers of....what else?......gator bites. After lunch, Gator Steve took us to the pier where airboats lined up like taxicabs. We hopped in a small 6-passenger one. The 454 cubic inch Chevy engine, looked like it might power the boat to fast speeds. Chris, the airboat captain, asked: "Do you want to go fast or really fast?" The two English kids in our small group shouted: "really fast!" We held on for a wild one-hour ride. Chris, an experienced airboat captain, whirled the airboat around in some 180-degree turns, zipped past mangroves by just barely missing them and, finally, spun the airboat into a water throwing 360-degree spin. Why go to Disney World?

Next we visited the smallest (seven by eight feet) post office in the U.S. at Ochopee. The postmaster hand cancelled a post card for us. The building isn't much bigger than an outhouse. Ochopee is Indian for "big field." On the way to the post office, we saw a large Florida panther replica along the roadside. Few people will see the real thing in the wild.

Gator Steve then drove us south on State Road 29 to the 150-acre Chokoloskee Island and the historic Smallwood old Indian trading post, which is now a museum. Ted Smallwood came to tiny Chokoloskee (pronounced by natives *chuck-aluskee*) in 1891. Before he arrived, the final stages of the Seminole wars played out in Chokoloskee in 1858. Smallwood established the trading post in 1906. No road connected the island to the mainland until 1956. Memorabilia fills Ted Smallwood's Store and Museum (360 Mamie Street, phone 239-695-2989).

Chokoloskee's colorful history includes residents in 1910 gunning down infamous Ed Watson, who reportedly murdered several people in the area. Some say he earlier also murdered Belle Starr when he went up North. Totch Brown wrote a book, and several songs, that talk of this fascinating Florida frontier. He also made his living hunting alligators for their hides, even after it became illegal to do so. Smallwood's descendants recently sold some nearby property to the Indians for a million dollars, which is ironic because once upon a time the Indians controlled it all.

On the way home, we stopped just off U.S. Highway 41 and watched five manatees frolic near a bridge. This was a rare treat because there are perhaps fewer than 3,000 left in all of Florida. This event-packed trip targeted areas for us for many future visits to the Everglades, Everglades City and its restaurants; and to: Fakahatchee Strand, Big Cypress Preserve, Smallwood Museum and Museum of the Everglades (105 West Broadway, Everglades City 34139, phone 941-695-0036). Housed in a restored laundry, the museum displays artifacts and photographs that tell the historical story; along with the old laundry equipment.

Everglades National Park 40001 State Road 9336, Homestead, Florida 35034. Phone 305-242-7700. Before you reach the park, signs encourage you to visit the privately owned Everglades Alligator Farm, on the edge of the Everglades at 40351 Southwest 192nd Avenue, Florida City, Florida 33034, phone 305-297-2628, www.everglades.com. The farm started with airboat tours, which it still offers, but highlights their 3,000 alligators.

The main visitor center for the 1.5 million-acre Everglades National Park is near Homestead off State Road 27. From the main center, you drive four miles to the Royal Palm Center. Stop!

Did we say we were lucky? Wow, when we walked out on the boardwalk of the Anhinga Trail, so many bird species greeted us we felt like VIPs; cormorants and anhingas drying their wings, with some of the birds perched on the boardwalk fence, stately great blue herons, wood storks, great white egrets strutting in all their mating plumage and little blue herons. We saw a four-foot tall great white heron, which is found only in south Florida in the U.S. Add to that several alligators including one halfway across the blacktop walkway! Roseate spoonbills. Snowy egrets.

Great White Egret,
Mating Plumage

The half-mile Gumbo Limbo Trail, also at Royal Palm, offers glimpses of wildlife and plants in "a jungle-like environment."

After spending time on the trails, and enjoying all the wildlife, we pushed on toward Flamingo, but turned off at the sign to the Pa-Kay-Okee Overlook. A short walk on a boardwalk brings you to an observation platform to get a panoramic view of the sawgrass prairie the Indians called "pa-ha-okee" (grassy waters).

When we arrived at Flamingo, 38 miles from the Coe Center, we thought the place strange. Buildings spread along the shore. The visitor center perches up a ramp on a second floor. Vehicles with empty boat trailers crammed the parking lot of the marina, which is separated from the visitor center. Two boat ramps separate boats going into the back bays from those going into Florida Bay. Your first step should be a visit to the center and a chat with a park ranger about how to best spend your time in Flamingo. Pick up a map that shows the many hiking and canoe trails.

Xanterra Park Resorts operates the lodge, 24 cottages, rentals, restaurant and marina and guided tours. The 102-room Flamingo Lodge, open year round, operates full service from November through April. The Guy Bradley Hiking Trail connects the campground to the center. Plume hunters killed Guy M. Bradley (1870-1905) near Flamingo. He was the game warden of Monroe County, according to a plaque at the visitor center.

Flamingo, which is open all year, offers world-class fishing.

After lunch at the park restaurant, we walked over the lock bridge to check out a 70-year old crocodile, lounging on the bank. The southern Everglades is the only place in the world where you'll find both crocodiles and alligators. "We have an estimated 50,000 alligators in the park," a ranger said. "Crocodiles number just 400 or so."

The best way to enjoy the Everglades at Flamingo is by boat, so we joined three dozen other people on the *Pelican* tour boat for a two-hour backcountry cruise through the canal to Coot Bay and Whitewater Bay. *The Bald Eagle* tours Florida Bay. The sail boat *Windfall* takes you on a sunset cruise for $20.

Great Blue Heron

Although we didn't see the bountiful wildlife of Anhinga Trail, we did see great blue herons peering intently at the water ready to spear a fish, anhingas preening and drying their feathers, several alligators and a young crocodile along the canal banks. They ignored us. When we pulled into Coot Bay, a flock of coots greeted us. As we approached Whitewater Bay a passing boater yelled, "Dolphins ahead." The captain circled a couple of times, apparently hoping dolphins would cavort in the bow wake, but no dolphins split the surface.

The marina rents kayaks $27 for a half-day, canoes, fishing gear (including poles), binoculars and even ice chests.

Flamingo Marina has several 40-foot houseboats for rent for a real getaway. Newer ones rent for $525 for two nights ($1375 for a week), older ones for $475 for two nights ($1115 for a week), November through April. If you want to rent one during the season you need to make reservations three months in advance!

If you plan to tackle the canoe trail from Flamingo to Everglades City, you're better off starting at Everglades City because of the prevailing north winds. Even so, the seven to 10 day trip "requires energy and stamina."

Broward County Audubon sponsors a birding festival at Flamingo in January (www.browardaudubon.org). With 347 species, according to Audubon, Everglades at Flamingo offers some opportunities to spot many species of birds. Check out www.flamingolodge.com.

Everglades, Shark Valley. The Shark Valley entrance is 35 miles west of Miami and east of Naples on U.S. 41 (35 miles east from State Road 29), phone 305-321-8776. On our way from Miami, on a late February day, we spotted a dozen airboat tour businesses strung along U.S. 41.

Chapter Six described the many unintended consequences of actions taken in Florida. Shark Valley, however, offers an example of an unintended benefit. Oil companies came in and drilled for oil. In the process they built what is now the 15-mile loop trail that provides the public a window into the flora and fauna of the Everglades. The ponds, which were borrow pits for the limestone used to build the road base, attract wildlife. The park does not allow vehicles on the trail, but you can walk it (takes seven to eight hours), bike it (takes two hours or so), or do as we did and take the narrated two-hour tram tour, coupled with a short walk. The tram cuts traffic and protects park resources by avoiding the congestion of automobiles.

During our tram tour, on an ideal non-buggy day with temperatures in the 70s, we looked at a remarkable amount and number of species of wildlife. Anhingas stared at us with mating-season bright blue eyes. Egrets displayed their plumes. We saw three soft shell turtles.

Several alligators lounged in the sun with young alligators swimming nearby. In one instance we counted 18 small, a-few-months-old alligators near their mother. Mom hissed so we moved on. Don't mess with a protective mother alligator. They're why the tour guides jokingly call bicyclists "meals on wheels."

Ibis

Large numbers of wood storks arrived for feeding time. Most of the wood storks nest in Corkscrew Swamp to the north. Roseate spoonbills displayed pink colors. We lost count of all the alligators, but saw scores along the road. Just past halfway on the tour, the driver stopped the tram to allow us to spend 20 minutes or so at the 65-foot observation tower. We climbed the ramp to the top to be dazzled by a sun-soaked panoramic view. You can see 10 miles in every direction. Directly below us, two large alligators soaked up sun on the canal bank.

As we approached the end of the tram ride, we passed along a canal teeming with birds. So after we stopped, we walked along the canal to take photographs as the egrets, anhingas, purple gallinules, ibises and herons posed, like people lined up at a single's bar. So, bring your camera and make sure you walk to this area of wildlife concentration. We could also clearly see Florida gar in the water. Other people spotted bluegill and largemouth bass.

The tram departs hourly between 9 a.m. and 4 p.m. and costs $12.75.

Everglades Restoration

Once viewed as a "worthless swamp," people's viewpoints started changing with the 1947 landmark book by the "mother of the Everglades,"

Marjory Stoneman Douglas, *The Everglades- River of Grass.* This visionary of the Everglades lived 108 years and wrote extensively about the region. She served on committees to create Everglades and Biscayne National Parks. She helped spearhead legislation to protect the parks.

The $8.4 billion Everglades restoration plan, which will take more than 30 years to complete, has projects to collect, store and redistribute fresh water to put back into the *River of Grass* where it can replenish aquifers and wildlife habitats. More than 1,000 miles of canals and 720 miles of levees cut the natural sheet flow of the original 18,000 square miles of wetland ecosystem by 70 percent. The canals, levees and 200 water control structures interrupted the vast free-flowing river of grass. The population in the 16 counties of South Florida of 500,000 in the 1950s now approaches 7 million to further impact the Everglades. The massive restoration program requires filling in canals, removing roads, and eradicating exotic plants to "re-plumb" seven decades of drainage and damage. The ribbon of U.S. 41, the Tamiami Trail, acts as a "tourniquet" as it stretches across the heart of the Everglades from Naples to Miami, a park ranger said. "Elevating parts of it will open water flow." It's all about water!

An early project, started in 2003, will re-establish natural sheet flow to the Ten Thousand Islands, and connect ecologically the Florida Panther National Wildlife Preserve, Belle Meade State Conservation Lands and the Fakahatchee Strand State Preserve. As of 2004, the phrase "when all is said and done, more is said than done" applies. Talks and delays continue. Show me. Results count.

Critics express concern about private property rights (land being taken by eminent domain) and the huge amount of money that might otherwise be spent on nearby poverty stricken areas, such as Immokalee. If the panther preserve area cost works out to more than a $1 million for each Florida panther, could that money be better spent on the children who are "food insecure" with either inadequate food or unhealthy diets?

In addition to the 1.5 million acres of Everglades National Park, large tracts of land (and water) perch just north of the park in state and national refuges with a total of more than 1.2 million acres, including Big Cypress National Preserve (729,000 acres), Arthur R. Marshall Loxahatchee National Wildlife Refuge (147,000 acres), Rookery Bay National Estuarine Research Preserve (110,000 acres), Fakahatchee Strand State Preserve (75,000 acres), Picayune Strand State Park (69,975 acres), and CREW (Corkscrew Regional Ecosystem Watershed) Land and Water Trust (60,000 acres), Panther National Wildlife Refuge (26,400 acres), and Collier Seminole State Park (6,400 acres). Several of these continue to buy land. Most have recreational opportunities and native wildlife and plants to see.

As Theodore Roosevelt said: "The nation behaves well if it treats the natural resources as assets which it must turn over to the next generation increased, and not impaired, in value."

The Next Three to Visit

Pssst....Want to hear a secret?

Can you believe it? Many people, even in nearby Miami, don't know about Biscayne National Park, a stunning marine ecosystem. If the locals aren't aware of it, surely it is a secret! To reach it, you go by the well-known Homestead-Miami Speedway. You can't beat the price; entrance is free to this underwater park! No restaurants, no motels.

The Dante Fascell Visitor Center, completed in 1997, is nine miles east of Homestead, from U.S. 1 Highway, on Southwest 328th Street (North Canal Drive), phone 305-230-7275. www.nps.gov/bisc. The park also is approximately 21 miles from Everglades National Park. We stayed at the Hampton Inn in Florida City, halfway between the two parks, for several days of visits to the parks.

At the visitor center, we boarded the *Boca Chita* tour boat, along with 40 others, on a picture-perfect February Saturday for a trip to Boca Chita Key and to the Fowey Rocks lighthouse. Captain Tom suggested we change our schedule and visit Fowey Rock lighthouse first, at the farthest edge of Biscayne National Park, and five miles northeast of Boca Chita, because of the remarkably calm morning seas.

The rusting Fowey Rocks lighthouse, one of a string of six reef lighthouses, rises out of the sea today to provide a marker for divers to the reef to see the colorful fish and coral. Lighthouse lovers cringed to see the deterioration of the lighthouse, which badly needs a paint job. The scores of birds perched on it have coated the lower part white.

Boca Chita Lighthouse

After circling the lighthouse for a photo opportunity, we headed back to see the 32-acre island of Boca Chita Key (silent mouth in Spanish).

Here's the skinny on the "secret treasure" of Boca Chita; it's the tapered 65-foot ornamental lighthouse, built of coral rock.

Mark C. Honeywell (1874-1960), industrialist and founder of the Honeywell Company, owned the island 1937-1945. He built the lighthouse to help his yacht captain with navigation to the island. The Coast Guard, however, nixed letting Honeywell light the unofficial lighthouse!

Honeywell, who invented the thermostat to regulate heat, wintered at Boca Chita, until his wife died, when he apparently lost interest in the island. Fire destroyed the main house in the 1960s.

We ate a leisurely lunch in the picnic Pavilion (which rents for $100 for half day). We walked around to explore the small island, climbed the lighthouse and watched the boats cruise by the island. For a time, this island must certainly have been paradise for Honeywell. If you have ever dreamed of owning your own island, feasting your eyes on this one will evoke envy.

Boca Chita Pavilion (middle right)

Overnight docking for boats, if you can find a spot in the small lagoon: $15.

You can camp (tent camping only) for $10 a day for two tents at Boca Chita and at nearby Elliott Key.

The park, with more than 44 keys (islands), contains the longest stretch of mangroves on the East Coast, in ecosystems of mangrove forests, bays, keys and coral reef. Biscayne National Park has a portion of the world's third-longest coral reef, which stretches south along the Florida Keys, and called the "enchanted braid" by author Osha Gray Davidson (1960-), in his book by that name. The complex marine ecosystem of the coral reefs has been destroyed "at an alarming rate," he said.

"Although coral reefs represent less than two-tenths of one percent of the area of the global ocean, approximately one-third of all marine fish species are found in this tiny zone." Home to fishes, shrimp, snails, crabs, sea stars, urchins and sea plants, this colorful, underwater world offers a snorkeling paradise with a rainbow of tropical fish that inhabit the fragile coral reefs.

149

Captain Tom noted the need "for saving the reefs and that requires understanding them better." He pointed out scarring of the sea grasses and coral by careless boaters. Boat propellers cut sea grass blades and roots, which reduce food for sea life and on which manatees graze. Recovery from damage can take 10 years. The bay, with snapper and grouper, provides great fishing, but over-fishing has been a concern. The 20 miles of coral reef, with patch reefs that occur only in this area, beckon for wonderful diving and snorkeling among coral, fish and shipwrecks in clear water.

To get the most out of the three-hour glass-bottom boat tour, you need calm sunny days to see the brilliantly colored tropical fish. The park offers tours at 10 a. m. The captain said the views in Biscayne were "much better" than at John Pennekamp State Park to the south, at Key Largo, where dozens of charter boats take more than a million people out to the reef, nearly 100 times the number going from Biscayne National Park. Pennekamp State Park tops the list of most-visited Florida state parks. At Biscayne, just two boats operate, one of which is a glass-bottom boat. If the conditions aren't best for viewing, the boats don't go out. Biscayne National Underwater Park, Inc., which has the concession, faces a Catch 22 of needing more visitors, but wanting to avoid too many visitors! Although the aquatic park attracts 500,000 visitors a year, more than 85 percent come into the park by local private boats. The park ranks high on the National Parks Conservation Association list of the top ten most endangered parks.

"The world of the keys has no counterpart elsewhere in the U.S., and indeed few coasts of the earth are like it." Rachel Carson

Six Mile Cypress Slough.

Gee, Six Mile Cypress Slough (pronounced slew) sounds like a title to a song. And, if you go you will hear songs in the 2,200-acre Slough Preserve! Birds. Animals.

We took a self-guided tour of this preserve, in Lee County (Ft. Myers) at Penzance Crossing on Ben C. Pratt Six Mile Cypress Parkway (between Colonial Boulevard and Daniels Parkway) in Fort Myers, on a hot afternoon in August. The preserve does offer guided tours at 9:30 a.m. and 1:30 p.m., Wednesday and Saturday. The only cost is to feed the parking meters at the rate of 25 cents for 20 minutes. This jewel dotted with hammocks of trees, wildlife and birds puts you into a world apart from the nearby bustling surroundings, even if only a small fraction in size of the big refuges.

Pick up an "Explorer's Companion" in the entrance area. It indeed is a helpful companion in understanding this crowded ecosystem "where every available niche, or job is filled by plants and animals adapted to life in a complex wetland." The 1.2-mile boardwalk winds through the five "communities" of the preserve, but you'll walk farther because of the short walks to overlooks of Gator Lake and ponds, like the Otter Pond and the Wood Duck Pond.

A naturalist, who said he visits the preserve often, said this was his first visit in which he did not see an alligator. Also, of course, the larger variety and numbers of birds are in the winter. On the other hand, we enjoyed seeing the colorful dragonflies and damselflies. They're fun to watch, unless you are a mosquito. We saw several varieties, including red ones and pink ones. We heard, and then saw, a pileated woodpecker and watched a few herons and egrets wading in the ponds.

Signs identify each of the five distinct "communities." The Pine Flatwoods Community, for example, is the fringe area of the slough, with slash pines and myrtle. With a visit in the summer, the cypress provided a dark green canopy to shade us from the hot August sun. Summer also meant few people, so we stopped and watched and listened. You start to see more; much more.

We were intrigued with the "patches of paint" on the tree trunks. We learned these are unique plant forms. Lichens are a "combined relationship of an alga, which produces food and a fungus, which provides physical support. Neither could exist without the other."

The water of the slough moves slowly toward Estero Bay, so it provides a waterway for otters, alligators, turtles and raccoons to travel. The slough acts as a kidney, filtering runoff before reaching Estero Bay. A loud rapid drumming above us caused us to search for the source. "There he is, a pileated woodpecker. Look at that flaming red crest." A knowledgeable birder standing next to us said: "He's the largest woodpecker known to exist."

The birder joked, "You can identify us (serious birders) along the way because we seem to wear these funny brimmed hats, canvas vests with pockets and carry large cameras." Clearly we didn't qualify as serious birders, dressed in baseball caps, polo shirts and shorts, but we appreciated his sense of humor and helpful insights. We did enjoy seeing all the birds, but it helps to have knowledgeable people around to deepen and richen the experience.

Near the end of our tour we saw small twisted trees, which turned out to be pond apples. During summer the large, greenish-yellow "apples," which we saw, are eaten by turtles, squirrels and raccoons. The trees also provide a habitat for air plants (epiphytes growing on the pond apple branches).

Located alongside a busy highway, and nestled among residential developments, the nine-mile, one-third mile wide wetland ecosystem, has a non-profit advocacy group, Friends of Six Mile Cypress Slough, working to protect the slough and educate people about the habitat.

Oh, and about that song, here's a start of one free gratis to Jimmy Buffett:

"Six Mile Cypress Slough

Herons, egrets and ibis, too."

Whatever the season, there's something to see, so we returned when the migratory birds arrived. Some birds, just like some of our residents, begin their trek south in September. During the season more birds call Six Mile Cypress Slough home and the preserve also attracts many more people. You can tour this Lee County park on your own, or go on a guided tour at 9:30am and 1:30 p.m. There's no entrance fee, but parking is $.75/hour. Bring quarters. For information call 941-432-2004.

Merritt Island National Wildlife Refuge (and Space Coast). Route 402, 3.5 miles east of Titusville, phone 321-861-0667. If you're a birder, then plan on visiting Titusville during the five-day Space Coast Birding and Wildlife Festival, held at the Brevard Community College in Titusville. The festival includes dozens of workshops, seminars, field trips and kayak paddling adventures, and airboat and pontoon boat tours.

If you aren't a birder, a visit to 140,000-acre Merritt Island National Wildlife Refuge, which butts up against the Kennedy Space Center, can be a part of a visit to the many nearby attractions. Half the refuge contains brackish estuaries and marshes. The refuge is a gateway for the Great Florida Birding Trail.

We stayed at the Holiday Inn Titusville, on one visit to check out the Cape Canaveral Lighthouse, immerse ourselves in the allure of strange wildlife that beckoned us to Merritt Island, and, of course, tour the Kennedy Space Center. On one of the trips I couldn't resist stopping at the airport home of the Valiant Air Command War Birds (6600 Tice Road, Titusville, Florida 32780) to watch an old C-47 fly. I made my first parachute jump out of one of them years ago, so the visit brought back memories of a different time. If you are interested, click on www.vacwarbirds.org, or call 321-268-1941. They have an air show in March. They find and preserve historic aircraft, including a Grumman Wildcat that was at the bottom of Lake Michigan for 50 years.

On our way to the Cape Canaveral Lighthouse, we passed by cruise ships in Port Canaveral, and by the Delta Command launch towers.

Pelican Island, home of the very first National Wildlife Refuge is close by. This was the last known brown pelican nesting area on the East Coast in the early twentieth century as plume hunters nearly wiped out birds. The hunters nearly brought the dense colonies of great and snowy egrets to extinction. The egrets ranked as most popular because of the flowing plumes, which are at their finest during breeding. Four egrets provided an ounce of feathers.

The year 2004 began the next century of the National Wildlife Refuge system, a collection of public lands and waters set aside to protect wildlife that expanded in its first century from three acres on Pelican Island to nearly 100 million acres! You can kayak the three miles to Pelican Island through shallow, clear waters from Wabasso Causeway. Rentals can be obtained from Adventure Kayak of Cocoa Beach, Cocoa Beach, phone 321-480-8632, www.advkayak.com. Don't forget bottled water, sun block, hats, binoculars and camera!

You can take seven-mile Black Point Wildlife Drive through this 140,000-acre refuge or go on guided tours during the season, which starts in November as birds migrate, through March. The refuge supports 21 wildlife species listed as endangered or threatened, the most of any refuge in the United States. Reportedly, more than 330 bird species have been sighted with wading birds and waterfowl in the salt marshes, bald eagles in the pine flatwoods, warblers and songbirds in the hardwood hammocks, and the threatened Florida scrub jay in scrub habitat. Winter bird population peaks in winter with 100,000 waterfowl. Eight species of herons and egrets stay year round.

A 90-minute narrated pontoon-boat eco-tour on the Indian River Lagoon provides you a good overview. An airboat ride on the St. Johns River offered more fun than education, but the Rivership Romance cruises daily on the historic river. See at www.rivershipromance.com. Space Coast Nature Tours offer twice-daily narrated tours on their boat, the Skimmer, from Titusville Municipal Marina.

If you have time, combine the visit with a tour of the adjacent Canaveral National Seashore. You can see loggerhead turtles above the high-tide line in summer along with many wading and shore birds.

The Kennedy Space Center (www.kennedyspacecenter.com) runs two-hour bus tours and shows Imax movies that vividly give you the feel of space. A $34 ticket gives you two days and includes the Astronaut Hall of Fame. Other places to visit include: the Astronaut Memorial Planetarium and Observatory, 1519 Clearlake Road, Cocoa, phone 321-634-3732; Astronaut Hall of Fame, 6225 Vectorspace Boulevard; American Police Hall of Fame and Museum, 6350 Horizon Drive, Titusville, phone 321-264-0911; and Brevard Museum of History and Science, 1463 Highland Avenue N, Melbourne, phone 321-632-1830.

Other Parks to Visit

As we said at the outset, Florida has a wealth of parks. We have shared with you our top favorites, but you have many more from which to choose. A trip to Northwest Florida at Port St. Joseph, for example, puts you in the heart of the Forgotten Coast with an opportunity to not only attend a bird festival at St. Joseph Bay State Buffer Preserves Center, 2915 Highway C-30, Port St. Joseph, but use it as a base to see nearby parks and lighthouses. Port St. Joseph is an hour east of Panama City and two hours southwest of Tallahassee. Nearby tours to Wakulla Springs State Park and St. Marks National Wildlife Refuge also offer birding, hiking, fishing and an opportunity to see lighthouses.

Chapter Eleven
Recreation: Golfing, Boating, Fishing, Shelling, Swimming, Hiking Anyone?

Participating in recreational activities as a resident differs from how you do these as a tourist. For example, tourists don't join bowling leagues or softball leagues, nor do most snowbirds. Golfing differs because of the promotional incentives that save you money on golf fees and cart rental. Florida, some say, "is all about sun, water and golf." But there's more!

Golfing.

More than 1,000 Golf courses dot Florida like the measles. "Build-it-and-they-will-come" applies to this golf-rich area. Collier County has more golf holes per capita than anywhere in the world. Southwest Florida has more than 150 golf courses. Jacksonville, home of World Golf Hall of Fame and PGA Tour headquarters, has 50 courses. The Villages, between Ocala and Leesburg has 171 holes of golf. At last count Walt Disney World Resort had five courses and 99 holes of golf. Palm Beach County, with 160 courses, claims to be "Florida's Golf Capital." In a nutshell, you have your choice of world-renown challenging golf courses. A quarter of the top 100 golf teachers in America are in Florida according to *Golf* magazine, January 2004.

You have three basic choices for golf as a resident. Which you choose depends on your level of interest in golf and your pocketbook:

Level 1. Play the public courses and live in a non-golf course community. You will have the advantage of more value in buying a home and lower fees (not maintaining a golf course). This works especially well for the occasional golfer. Naples, for example, has 15 public golf courses out of the more than 50 total plus another dozen that are semi-private and offer public access. A check of other communities shows similar ratios. Some private courses open to the public in summer.

Level 2. Buy a membership at a private course, but live in a non-golf community, which has the advantages of Level 1 plus the potential of a less-crowded course with more convenient and available tee times. Some clubs offer memberships for as little as $3,000. Works especially well for the golfer who plays more frequently than Level 1. Some non-golf communities do have putting greens. In fact, some homeowners have installed putting greens in their backyards.

Level 3. For golf fanatics, the golf course may be the deciding factor of where to live. Golf is boss, but you need to be able to play 2-4 times a week without getting bored with the course. If you live in a country-club lifestyle golf course community, a small membership assures easy access to the course. One community offers a golf membership with your home or upgrades worth $4,500. The non-golfer can live in the community but not pay the membership. But you are "paying" for the golf course nonetheless because golf course land and development costs are in the home price. The choice of living in a golf community appears to rest with the level of commitment to golf. If golf is your passion, then living in a golf community makes sense. Further, the club will have a professional available for golf instruction and pro shops. One community, with a Jack Nicklaus-designed course, and exquisite luxury homes (read "million dollar") limits members to just 275. No tee time problems there! If you're an avid golfer, and flush with dollars to spare, this would be the ultimate. The super level of level three includes the 200 rounds-a-year golfers. For your selection of a club, check into the reputation and financial status, quality of the course design, playability and conditions of the course. Does the club have professional golf staff? Can you get out as you get in? Is the course a Certified Audubon Cooperative Sanctuary? (Only two percent of courses are certified.) And, of course, can you afford it?

Golf fees vary depending on the course, but in 2004 ranged from $70-$135 for 18 holes of golf, although some offer special reduced rates for play after 12 p.m. and after 3 p.m. One example: $70 before 1 p.m., $56 for 1-2:30 p.m. and just $28 after 2:30 p.m. One course offers a $20 reduction if you have a Florida driver's license. For residents, much lower rates are available during May through December, along with incentive coupons. At a public course with 300 golfers a day in the season, "100 would be a good day in summer" according to the starter.

Boating.

Like many clichés, the old one about the best days of a boater's life being when he buys the boat and when he sells the boat has some validity. A friend, who had sold his boat, noted one in the marina named *Endless Pleasure.* He exclaimed: "More like *Endless Agony.*" Boat maintenance became a hassle for him, along with figuring out the tides and navigating the shallow waters. These are new skills for some boaters from the North. Saltwater, and its effects, may also be new to freshwater lake boaters. Few boaters can say they have avoided running aground on a sand bar; caused by the changing tides and shallow bays. Props get tangled on seaweed or nets. Lightning strikes present a major problem in the lightning capital of the country. And, of course, you contend with simpler things like running out of gas or burning up batteries. On the other hand, you can boat year-round in Florida, including being on the water in January and February when temperatures up North are at zero! Yes, yes, we do have some cool days, but if the wind whips up you can always duck behind a mangrove island. And a day on the water escapes the troubles of the world with a breeze, smell of saltwater and schools of fish surfacing on the water.

What about the big powerboats? They peaked in the 1980s as speed, noise, manatee zones and lack of slips, took their toll.

If you listen to the weather forecast, you might never take the boat out, because the forecast may sound discouraging if you don't know in Florida forecasts cover a wide area and most rain is scattered and lasts only half an hour or so. Often rain shows up at 4 p.m.

As with most activities you have three basic levels to consider in boating:

Level 1. Why buy a boat? Rent as needed or join a club so that someone else covers the insurance, does the maintenance and clean up after boating, and storage. You don't have to worry about finding a scarce boat slip or the maintenance. An alternate to membership in a club is a fractional ownership. Before going boating in the shallow bays with changing tides, try going first with a charter boat so you can get a good understanding of the area. If you go out at low tide, you can see all the "land" (sandbars, and the like) to avoid. We attended, and graduated from the "USPS (United States Power Squadron) Boating Course" put on by the local power squadron. If you boat at all, do this first! Finally, remember the wise old sea captain's advice: "First-time boaters should not be first-time boat buyers."

Level 2. Buy a boat, but live in a non-boating community. Several cities have major boat shows but the biggest is in February in Miami. If you're thinking about a new boat, or just looking to have fun, tour buses make it easy to go to the Miami boat show. A bus trip gives you the opportunity to share views and compare notes with other interested boat buyers, which will save you money and help in making the right selection. The bus ride also solves parking and traffic problems.

Level 3. Buy a home in a boating community with a direct access, or on a canal or Intracoastal Waterway, or river, or lake. Have your own boat davit, or be in a community with a marina and boat slips for the residents. To find your way, pick up a copy of the Cruising Guide by Claiborne S. Young for your area. This sprightly written book has comprehensive charts, navigation information, ratings on marinas and location. See www. cruisingguide.com. You might fall in love with a sailing boat and live on it with freedom to go where you want and take your "house" with you. You might buy a trawler and take the Great Loop, leaving Florida in the spring, reaching Canada and returning down the Mississippi on a five month to a year tour. In your cruiser, you can explore the 1,200-mile Intracoastal Waterway that stretches from Key West to Norfolk, Virginia. Called "The Big Ditch", this federally maintained navigation channel of canals, bays protected by barrier islands, and rivers, offers a rich variety of settings. The waterway is protected, easy to navigate and with lots of services. In Florida, stop at St. Augustine, Titusville, Cocoa Beach, Melbourne, Vero Beach, Fort Lauderdale, Miami and Key West. The Atlantic Intracoastal Association provides information at www.atlintracoastal.org. You may want to attend Captain's License School. If you go out make sure you have all the safety equipment on board and that you file a trip plan and leave it with someone who knows when to expect you back.

Fishing.

Lookie What I Found! How about this! You can walk out into our back yard, cast into the lake and pull out a seven-pound large-mouth bass. No boat. Not much gear. A neighbor caught one of more than eight pounds. (The Florida record is just over 17 pounds.) Another neighbor hooked a 40-pound carp. Our lake is a small one of 155 acres. Larger lakes nearby of Lake Trafford and Lake Okeechobee have good fishing as do the more than 7,700 lakes that dot Florida like blue emeralds embroidered on a green tie. Several Florida cities and counties claim to be the Bass Capital of the World. Consider this: more people fish than play golf or tennis combined, perhaps following the bumper sticker philosophy of "Life's short. Fish hard."

Level 1. You can simply fish from the lake or the piers and not invest in a boat.

Level 2. Guides and charter boat captains can save you time and money regardless of the fishing you do. With their training in navigation and first aid, their knowledge of fish movement from fishing every day, and knowing what the fish are hitting on, this can be a smart way to avoid the hassle of renting a boat and doing it yourself. Another alternative is to join others on one of the large boats that go out from many marinas. One supplies rod, reel and license and a half-day fishing for $50. Attending sports fishing shows allows you to brush up on connecting fishing lures to hooks, leaders and swivels, fishing boats and attend seminars by experts.

Level 3. Invest in a boat either for deep-sea fishing or a smaller one for freshwater fishing. Buy a home, or condo, in a maritime community, among like-minded people. Check out www.sportfishingflorida.net for current conditions in seven salt-water fishing areas in Florida, articles on fishing, species identification, marine forecast, tides and other vital information. For fishing destinations Matlacha (pronounced mat la shay), claims to have "The World's Most Fishingest Bridge." For tarpon fishing, the preferred spot off Boca Grande has a tournament every year. The famed Pine Island Sound is the only Florida location in 2003 to make *Field & Stream* magazine's list of America's hottest fishing spots.

Golfing, Boating and Fishing Communities.

We compared three communities of the same size (each with approximately 330 acres) with three distinctly different lifestyles, housing densities and location.

One non-golfing community has 420 single-family homes with 150-acre lake. A similar golf-course community has half the land taken up by the golf course and a mix of condos, villas and single-family homes with more than 500 units. A maritime Gulf-front community has a marina some high-rise towers and single-family homes, with total units above 600. Of the three, the Gulf-front community has the most expensive units.

Seashells by the Seashore.

Anyone can go shelling for nature's bounty of shells. You can do it on the beach, from a boat or even diving. The best shelling is at low tide or when the tides are moving in or out. You'll quickly learn the most common shells and develop the "Sanibel Stoop" from bending over and collecting shells, such as calico scallops, sand dollars, fighting conch, lightning whelks, augurs, king's crowns and coquina. You can make colorful ornaments with shells, candleholders, mirror and picture frames.

159

The Calusa Indians used shells as cooking utensils, weapons, tools, and for necklaces.

Level 1. With 1,100 miles of beaches, you have a plethora of places to pick up the treasures of the sea. You need to abide by one rule: Take no live shells. If in doubt, do without. The best time to go shelling is early morning at low tide after a storm.

Level 2. For more serious shelling, most people end up on Sanibel Island, home of the country's best shelling. The east-west orientation of the 13-mile long, 2.5-mile wide island, results in waves rolling in gently so they don't smash the shells. The island acts as a hook to catch shell as rougher water propels them ashore. To understand shells, and learn how to identify them, stop in at Bailey Matthews Shell Museum, 3015 Sanibel-Captiva Road, phone 941-395-2233. Raymond Burr, a co-founder, also led a fund-raising drive for this museum, which has the world's third largest collection of shells. The museum has an astounding collection of more than one million shells, more than 30 exhibits and an interesting 30-minute video, *Mollusks in Action,* which plays every hour.

The Horse Conch, the state shell, can grow to two-feet long. The fluted pink-lined mollusk shell, with an orange aperture, made a great signaling horn for the Calusa Indians. The word "conch" comes from the Greek word meaning shell.

Level 3. You can begin by casually picking up shells, getting intrigued and becoming an avid collector and docent, helping as a volunteer at the Shell Museum and constructing shell displays. That's what happened to Norm, who started collecting in a casual way, visited the Bailey Matthews Shell Museum and ended up as a volunteer docent at the museum. He also built shadow boxes on one entire garage wall to display his personal collection at home, including some pricey shells. Neighbors could get a quick education by stopping in, viewing the collection and having Norm describe them. Clearly, he took his new passion to the next level! Don't overlook the shelling cruises to the pristine barrier islands to find elusive shell species.

Kayaking.

Level 1. We had never been in a kayak and knew nothing about it, but after a few minutes instruction, we were out on the water paddling across a bay. In the universal quest for happiness, sitting in the kayak soaking in the sun and sights, we felt an inner peace, a calmness that made the paddling worth the effort.

On one trip we paddled a kayak across shallow water from Captiva Island to historic Buck Key. Our midmorning trip took us across the shallow water of the bay toward Buck Key, where we paddled into a tunnel cut through the mangroves for mosquito control. Only the swoosh of paddles broke the quietude. We had to weave through thick walls of mangroves. Dark water lapped at their claw-like roots. When we emerged after a mile of many right and left turns, we stopped to enjoy a tranquil view of the water with the sun shimmering on gentle waves. Schools of mullet darted by. We enjoyed the soothing sounds of the water, the salt-air smell, and the sun warming our skin; and forgot civilization for a quiet time. We drifted a while, relaxed and renewed like a phone on its charger.

On another trip we kayaked up the Orange River near Fort Myers to see the manatees and watched them, as a guide described: "thrust their snouts above water to suck air."

Level 2. Kayaking lets you see parts of Florida inaccessible to most visitors, especially back country trips to remote areas in almost any part of Florida. Numerous paddling locations exist. Check these out at www. kayakguide.com. The state parks have more than 1,000 miles of trails for canoeing and kayaking. For your kayak trips, don't forget to bring water and high-energy snacks, hat, sunscreen and sunglasses.

Level 3. If you are into kayaking in a big way, then consider buying your own kayak, especially if you live on a lake. You can easily carry today's light kayaks on top of your vehicle or you can buy an inflatable kayak and carry it in a bag! You could consider several kayak adventure trails, such as the 99-mile trail connecting Everglades City and Flamingo, the west and east of the Everglades National Park. Outfitters in Everglades City will provide a kayak and gear for under $700 for your weeklong trip; and pick up the kayak on the other side. If you go, leave from Everglades because the prevailing winds will be with you. You'll need to take a gallon of water per person per day and food. The trip can take seven to 10 days.

Canoe and Kayak magazine named Tarpon Bay (Sanibel Island) through Ding Darling Refuge one of the top 10 places to take a canoe or kayak. *Paddler* magazine ranked Sanibel and Everglades City in the top 10 in the United States, because of easy access to wilderness habitat and abundance of wildlife.

The first half of the Great Calusa Blueway kayak trail, from Bonita Springs and the Imperial River, up through Estero Bay to Matanzas Pass, opened in 2003. Work continues to complete the part going farther north through Pine Island Sound. The trail, dotted with mangrove islands, sparkling inlets, tidal flats, delights the senses with an abundance of wildlife. Water depths range from a half a foot to just over three feet. For details, and a map of the trail, go to www.greatcalusablueway.com.

161

Who Needs Viagra, Just Go Swimming.

Did you know swimming was an aphrodisiac? Two studies show that swimming can help revitalize your love life, whatever your age. Really. At least that's what a couple of "experts" say.

Dr. Phillip Whitten, editor-in-chief of *Swimming Magazine*, and author of *The Complete Book of Swimming*, found regular swimmers have a more active and enjoyable sex life. He studied swimmers age 40 and over. These swimmers made love more frequently than their non-swimming peers. "If you want an active and rewarding sex life, start swimming," declares Whitten.

Dr. Jane Katz, former Olympic swimmer and author of *Swimming for Top Fitness,* says swimming helps one enjoy other people and other sports, "including love making." According to Katz, the sensual swimmer knows how swimming heightens physical strength, flexibility and awareness of one's body: "Swimming helps one feel temporarily sexier, since it affects hormonal balance."

The National Spa and Pool Institute (NSPI) CEO Roger Calvin, not surprisingly, supports the view of these studies. NSPI, an industry trade association of 5,200 pool builders, retailers, distributors and service professionals, points to the many health benefits of swimming. The association, understandably, would like to sell more pools. Sex sells, so they've latched onto these studies! Certainly swimming clearly provides good exercise and if it increases your love life, well, that's a bonus. Happy swimming!

Level 1. For casual swimming you can use the community pool. Nearly every gated community has one.

Level 2. Many of the pools built in Florida serve more for a dip and cool off than swimming. Many with "swimming" pools, use the community pool for water aerobics, because it's also a social gathering, and for swimming.

Level 3. When we had our home built, we had the standard pool design extended by 10 feet to provide a lap lane. You can swim when you want to and keep in shape. When I was growing up, I tried to emulate world record holder Johnny Weissmuller (1904-1984) who synchronized six beats of the legs for every two arm strokes to win the free-style events even though he was a rugged 190-pounds.

Bowling.

We couldn't find any studies that tied sex into bowling, like swimming, and it isn't much in the way of exercise, but it does offer fun and camaraderie. We had not bowled in a quarter century, but friends persuaded us to join a six-team community league of "Nifty Fifty" people. As a tourist, you don't think of Florida as a place to bowl because you came to enjoy the outdoors, not the indoors! As a resident, however, bowling can offer a diversion, especially when followed by a dinner at a different restaurant each week in the 33-week season.

Levels 1, 2 and 3. All right! All right! The levels are obvious. Rent shoes and use the house ball and bowl once in a while. Get involved with a league. Buy your own ball and shoes.

Hiking (and Walking).

Level 1. You can hike countless places in Florida, especially in the parks and refuges described in Chapter Ten. Walking, a healthy thing to do, and a way to Ponce de Leon's fountain of youth, can be done anywhere, year round in Florida.

Level 2. For the hiking enthusiast, hiking trails in Florida provide an almost unlimited number of specific adventure trails. State parks have 350 miles of trails for hikers only.

Level 3. For serious hiking check out the 1,300-mile Florida National Scenic Trail (www.floridatrail.org), The Florida Trail Association's (5415 SW 13th, Gainesville, Florida 32608, phone 1-877-HIKE-FLA) goal is to develop the continuous hiking trail, a footpath surrounded by forests of palms, pines, cypress and oaks in areas abundant with wildlife. The trail starts at Big Cypress National Preserve, which is north of the Everglades, and 52 miles east of Naples, to Gulf Islands National seashore in Pensacola. If you hike it, you can earn an End-to-End Trail Certificate and a patch. The best time to try this multi-month trip is January-April. Call, or write for the packet of maps and Florida Trails Data Handbook.

Biking.

Most places in the parks where you can go hiking, you can also go biking. The state parks have 240 miles designated for cycling. No mountains, however, for mountain biking! Boca Grande offers a great asphalt bike trail that follows along Railroad Avenue. Many of the counties provide Bicycle Guides, with maps of bike trails within the county.

Head injuries cause 75 percent of bicycle deaths, so you'll want to wear a helmet! Florida law requires anyone under age 16 to wear a helmet. The law also requires at least one hand on the handlebars while riding and no headsets, headphone or other listening device other than a hearing aid (Florida statute section 316.2065).

Other Recreational Opportunities.

Communities also offer a wide variety of other less-strenuous activities to occupy your time, including horseshoes, lawn bowling, bocce ball, and shuffleboard. If you're not ready for those, then our community, and many others, have tennis courts, an outdoor basketball court and a sand volleyball court. Participating in those will boost your endorphins.

You can play tennis at various competitive levels, from a casual game to tournaments. Many of the communities play one another in often spirited tennis tournaments. If you are a serious tennis player, look for communities that have lighted Har-Tru courts, adult and junior clinics, pro shop, interclub team play, night events and stadium seating (or stands).

Chapter Twelve
Fun Florida Day Trips

"Peculiar travel suggestions are dancing lessons from God." Kurt Vonnegut.

We have visited interesting places on our own, and we have joined others on a bus tour to visit other places. Some destinations lend themselves to one approach or the other, as we have mentioned. The camaraderie of a group really livens up some visits and adds to the fun. Some of the happiest moments of our lives are when we do something important with others, so we want to thank those who were on trips with us and added to the enjoyment of the trip. A bus tour also pinpoints areas or attractions or parks where you want to go back and visit and spend more time.

When preparing your list of things to do and places to go during the next five years, consider adding to your list the trips in this chapter. Our fun day trips may inspire you to jot these down when you do your list in Chapter Nineteen.

Top Three Trips

Cabbage Key, Koreshan State Historic Site and Florida Cracker Motor Coach Tour.

Seize the Moment: Cabbage Key Adventure.

On our anniversary day, we headed toward Punta Gorda, not knowing what to expect. How could we know we would have a day of enriching our lives with people we had never met and going where we never had been?

We had planned to celebrate our anniversary in Naples, but the afternoon before our anniversary day a small one-column, one-inch notice of an all-day boat trip to historic Cabbage Key caught Mary's eye. On one of those spur-of-the-moment decisions, we said: "let's do it!" Cabbage

Key was one of those places we had always wanted to go, but just never got around to doing. This was our chance. Seize the moment.

We made it to Fisherman's Village Marina in Punta Gorda in time to pay the fee and board the King Fisher Fleet's *Good Times Too* boat before 9 a.m. We looked forward to visiting and having lunch at the Cabbage Key Inn, built in 1938 as the winter home of novelist and playwright Mary Roberts Rinehart 1876-1958). You can only get to the 100-acre island by boat (or seaplane).

The 2-1/2-hour trip, sponsored by the Peace River Center for Writers, turned out to be a hoot, and lived up to its billing as a "literary passage; Charlotte Harbor to Cabbage Key." The non-profit center has more than 350 members. But you don't need to go with a group, as the tour boat operates daily.

Some of us sat in the main cabin; others sat on the top deck and the bow area, until a short-duration rainsquall forced everyone inside. Our trip celebrated National Estuaries Day, so a naturalist told us about estuaries ecosystems along the way. Captain Ron, of the *Good Times Too,* told us about the harbor as we pulled out.

"We're in a delicate estuary ecosystem," Captain Ron said. "The brackish water is where the fresh water of the rivers meets the salt water of the sea. It may look dirty, but if you get a glass full of the beautiful tea-colored water and hold it up to the light you can see through it. You're in Charlotte Harbor, which is fed by the Peace and Myakka Rivers. The term *estuaries,* refers to protected near shore waters, such as bays, lagoons, harbors. They are the cradle of the ocean, because 70 per cent of fishes, crustaceans, and shellfish spend part of their lives in estuaries. The mangroves provide a protected nursery for the fish."

Yes, we have heard similar summaries on similar trips in many other bays and estuaries, but the explanations bear repeating because of the need to understand our natural treasures.

Pelicans glided past, then abruptly dove into the water to scoop up fish in their enormous bill and throat patch. Raucous laughing gulls hassled them for food. We saw dozens of pelicans, only 10 years removed since being upgraded from an endangered species. An elegant great blue heron stood silently and unmoving in the shallows, as though a sentinel. Cormorants posed for tourist photographs atop pilings. A few great white egrets and dozens of snowy egrets flew near the mangroves. The naturalist noted that the snowy egret, much smaller than the great white egret, was the only bird around to have yellow feet.

"Golden slippers," I thought. Not yellow feet: After all, this was a literary cruise.

At the end of the nineteenth century and early in the twentieth century, snowy egret plumes were so popular for hats, the birds were hunted almost to extinction.

At one point, the naturalist took the microphone to point out a magnificent frigatebird soaring just above the boat. Frigatebirds. Why not a sport team? A ditty danced in my head:

Frigatebirds, frigatebirds, what a sight!
Frigatebirds, frigatebirds, fight, fight, fight!
Yea, team.

(Just kidding. They thought it was bad, too.)

Frigatebirds aggressively chase other birds to steal their prey so "fight, fight" isn't too far from reality. The large black-plumage frigatebird sailing above us, from its roosting place in a nearby mangrove island, soared in quiet flight on a more than seven-foot wingspan. You could see his red inflatable throat sac, which identified him as a male. "Wouldst that I could accompany him!" John James Audubon once said. We, like Audubon, 170 years later, could only stare and watch.

"Port bow, port bow," the naturalist shouted into the microphone. "There's a dolphin." That sparked two things. People in the main cabin scurried to the left side of the boat to catch a glimpse and the Center's executive director, read a poem about dolphins.

During the boat trip, we cruised past mangrove-fringed islands, and passed along the north end of Pine Island. We could see the pier and docks at Bokeelia, the small town on the north end of Pine Island. We could see to the north the lighthouse at Boca Grande on Gasparilla Island.

Soon we would be at Cabbage Key, once owned by Mary Roberts Reinhart. She fulfilled a dream of many, after visiting Useppa Island, by buying her own island nearby in 1929 for $2,500. She later built the main building high on an Indian shell mound, which at 38 feet above sea level, is one of the highest points in Southwest Florida. She named her island after the palms. Reinhart not only authored more than 50 books, but she was more popular in the United States than Agatha Christie. Rinehart was named "America's Mistress of Mystery" in 1921 and honored by the Mystery Writers of America in 1954 for "outstanding achievement." A graduate nurse, she and her husband, who was a doctor, had three children. She was the first female war correspondent (WWI for *Saturday Evening Post*).

As we approached tiny Cabbage Key, tucked in between Pine Island and Cayo Costa Island, and near the eastern shore of Cayo Costa, we could see small cottages near the docks, but no beach. Although Cabbage Key does not have a beach, it's just a short boat ride to Cayo Costa with its six miles of beautiful pristine beach. Chapter Five describes Cayo Costa beaches.

The present Cabbage Key owners, Rob and Phyllis Wells, have lived on and maintained the island resort charm for more than a quarter century. You can count on quiet, because there are no telephones, no televisions, no radios, no cars, no roads, nor grilling or barbequing because there's no fire department. No cares! The seven cottages and the six-room Inn nestle in among live oaks, palm trees and tropical vegetation in this rustic sub tropical paradise. Signs along the nature trails identify the flora and fauna.

On the day of our visit, large banners at the dock and at the Inn announced "Red Neck Fishing Tournament." Fish in the area include sea trout, snook, redfish, grouper and the silver king of game fish, the tarpon. In addition to fishermen coming in to weigh their catch, three other tour boats were coming to make this a crowded day in an otherwise un-crowded time of year.

The inn has a unique décor of autographed dollar bills that paper the ceiling, walls, beams and columns. Visitors and celebrities from all over the world have taped a dollar bill to add to thousands of dollar bills people have put up over the decades. As the story goes, the bar inspired Jimmy Buffett to write *Cheeseburger in Paradise.*

For lunch, we ordered the special, announced by a busy waiter, which was a grilled mahi mahi (dolphin) sandwich. It came with French fries or potato salad. Nothing special. "We probably should have ordered a cheeseburger and French fries," Mary said. "When in Rome......."

On the return journey from Cabbage Key, members of the Center for Writers read some of the poems they wrote. Our favorite poem was the only one written *during* the trip. A woman read her short zippy poem that made the point in a clever way, that she might have been better off bringing her lunch. Not only did she receive deserved applause, but also some knowing, head-nodding chuckles.

Captain Ron announced as we passed through Jug Creek Pass on the way back, an area in Randy Wayne White's books. White, who lives on Pine Island, is the most popular author to come out of Southwest Florida. He has written a number of novels with a Florida setting, including *Everglades.*

A guitar-strumming folk singer sang some of the songs he had written. The poems, and singing, whiled away the slow journey back and also primed our mental pumps to add to the fun. A woman writing a book on Mary Reinhart pointed out to us the coincidence of our names, Stan and Mary, the same first names of Stan and Mary Reinhart. Some things, like this trip, are just meant to be. Well, speaking of poets, Shakespeare had a thing to say about *to be.*

Our advice to the poets aboard the boat:

Good, better, best
Never let it rest.
Till your good is
Better than your best.

The late Erma Bombeck wrote in *If I Had My Life to Live Over:* "Mostly, given another shot at life, I would seize every minute...look at it...and really see it! Live it! And never give it back." This was a day for us to cherish and enjoy as we seized the opportunity and enjoyed a serendipitous journey, with people we didn't know to a place we had never been. We learned a lot and learning should not stop until you do. We've shared some of what we saw and learned with you, but go see for yourselves.

If You Go.

Cabbage Key Island, P.O. Box 200, Pineland, FL 33945, phone 239-283-2278. The seven cottages rent to vacationers for $145 to $239 a night. The inn has six rooms. Boat dockage overnight costs $1.50 a foot. Cabbage Key is at Channel Marker 60 in the Pine Island Sound. www. cabbagekey.com

King Fisher Fleet, Fisherman's Village Marina, Punta Gorda, Florida 33950, phone 941-639-0969. Take exit 164 of I-75, three miles west to Fisherman's Wharf. Look for it on the right. The tour we took, minus the literary part, is available daily, 9 a.m. to 4 p.m. along with other boat tours.

www.kingfisherfleet.com

Koreshan Kicker

Koreshan State Historic Site. U.S. 41 at Corkscrew Road, Estero, Florida 33928, phone 941-992-0311

Thomas Edison, Henry Ford and John Burroughs trekked down the 30 miles or so from Fort Myers to the Koreshan plantation in 1914 in a brand new Model-T "Tin-Lizzie." The journey took them a while. Ford had the Fort Myers dealer deliver three of the cars, one for each of this trio of friends. Harvey Firestone participated later.

We made it to the Koreshan settlement the same distance in less than a half-hour, on a warm day in September, more than a century after Dr. Cyrus Reed Teed, who called himself Koresh, arrived in Fort Myers. Koresh translates to "shepherd."

We saw much the same thing these three famous men saw, minus the Koreshan people. The "kickers," in looking at these old buildings, are the surprising turn of events and stories behind what is now a State Historic Site. Fascinating oddities enhance a tour of this unusual place. A simple walk through the place is a century time warp, but there are mysteries and "kickers" that make this more than a visit to look at some old buildings.

Developers must have eyed enviously the 300-acre Historic Site, on the northwest corner, until the Koreshan Unity Foundation donated it to the state in 1961, to preserve this strange page of Lee County history. The Koreshan Unity Foundation still owns valuable property across the street from the historic site. Pelican Sound gated community borders this oasis of the tranquility of a century ago, which is alongside heavily traveled U.S. 41. In fact, standing by the old Koreshan general store, you can watch twenty-first century vehicles whizzing nearby, one century alongside another century.

If you visit, the more you know about this peculiar story, the more you will appreciate looking at some of the buildings. The two Koreshan machine shops intrigued tinkerers Ford and Edison. The small machine shop, built in 1905 and operated for many years, still has the old belt-driven machines. Nearby is the Power House, where the Koreshans later installed a Fairbanks-Morse unit to provide electricity to the commune. The Koreshans built most of the dozen buildings that remain in 1905.

After the Burroughs, Edison and Ford visit, Burroughs, the famous naturalist, wrote that the group enjoyed the plantation but thought the people "had a screw loose somewhere."

Peculiar? Take Damkohler's "cottage" and the story of this guy. Born in Germany in 1825, he immigrated to the United States, after looking for gold in Australia. He had the wanderlust. He moved often. He lived in Missouri, but finally came by boat to Estero from Punta Gorda, where the railroad ended. He paddled up the Estero River, staked out a site in 1882 and built a simple "home." You can see this small one-room cottage today. He homesteaded 160 acres, and then bought 160 acres from the state. Now get this, folks, a decade or so later, he sold 300 acres to Koresh for just $200! How did that happen?

Koresh (Dr. Teed) had traveled by rail to Florida in 1893 to search for a new location to be his "New Jerusalem." A site near St. James City on Pine Island, which appealed to him, was too expensive. He toured by boat and left some Koreshan literature at Punta Rassa. Later that year, Gustave Damkohler sailed to Punta Rassa for supplies. He read the literature, and read about the Koreshan's desire for land in Florida. Gustave wrote to Koresh and invited him to visit. Koresh accepted the invitation and returned in 1894, along with four women. The group traveled by boat (a sloop) to Gustave's place, after a train ride, to Punta Gorda. Six people, including the women, stayed in the little cabin! Now when you see the place, marvel at that piece of news, realizing a hard freeze occurred in December and then again in February 1895.

Gustave, seemingly entranced by Koresh's "lustrous brown eyes" and "resonant voice," as Koresh explained his "Universology," exclaimed: "Master! Master! The Lord is in it." And so he joined up and sold nearly all his land to Koresh. What happened to Gustave in just a few years? He buried five children and a wife there. Only one son, Elwin, remained who refused to join the Koreshans; probably because of the celibacy rule. Anyway, Elwin left and traveled from Florida to Alaska! Old Gustave followed his son and died in Alaska in 1905 at age 80, the year the train rails finally stretched to Fort Myers.

What about Koresh, also known as Dr. Cyrus Reed Teed, founder of Koreshan? His life has more twists and turns, than the road along the Snake River. He served in the medical corps during the Civil War. A practicing physician in New York in 1869 at age 30, he had an "illumination" from a beautiful woman, while he was in a trance. From this "spiritual awakening," he formed his unusual religious beliefs, which adversely affected his practice. Patients went elsewhere. He gave up medicine in 1880 and switched to religion He founded his first "church" in Moravia, New York but it failed financially within two years. He persisted and had a small following, but then his wife, Fidelia, died in 1885. He moved to Chicago, where a small group became the Koreshan Unity in 1887. From Chicago, he went to Florida in 1893.

For some, Koresh was a charismatic speaker with a "hypnotic voice." For others, he was just another in the long line of religious zealots with curious beliefs. The "curious" religious belief that invoked not only skepticism in the little community of Estero, but later even violence, was the earth was a hollow sphere. Instead of living on the outside of the globe, we live inside! Even educated people joined and believed they lived inside of the globe. Burroughs wrote while these were people of culture and refinement, they were also "Florida fanatics" who "defy common sense and the exact demonstrations of science." Other tenets included a belief "reincarnation is the central law of life," and man lives "best by communal principles, including celibacy." They lived by the Golden Rule and believed the Bible as interpreted by Koresh. He believed he was immortal.

The Koreshans had a self-sustaining pioneer settlement with a bakery, a weekly paper "The Flaming Sword," a store, machine shops, a successful printing business and a 15-piece orchestra. They farmed on

125-acre Mound Key. Where did the money come from? Wealthy and educated people joined and put all their assets in the communal pot to be immortal!

At the turn of the century there were about 50 Koreshans in Estero. Fort Myers had 947 people at the time. In 1903, the Chicago group came to Estero to provide the peak population of 250, including 42 children. In 1907, Koresh and his group got involved in Lee County politics. One opponent said: "Teed is not the first rascal who has made religion a cloak for his designs against the property and personal liberty of others." The Koreshans ran candidates for Lee County commissioner. The political confrontations led to Teed's downfall. In one, he was beaten. In a weakened condition, he moved to a cottage to recover, but died in 1908 at age 69. In a bizarre turn of events, a hurricane in 1921 washed the cottage and the mausoleum where he was interred out to sea.

After Koresh died, power struggles and dissension split the sect, so when Edison, Ford and Burroughs arrived in 1914 the Koreshans were in decline. Today only the buildings, photographs and stories remain. Take the story of "The Last Koreshan," Hedwig Michel. A Jew, she fled Nazi Germany in 1940, at age 48. She arrived eventually at the Koreshan settlement, which had dwindled to 35 elderly Koreshans. She cared for them, operated the store, and worked to have the state accept the site as an historic one (which the state did in 1961). She had the headquarters built in 1979 across the street. She died at 90 in 1982, having given 40 years of her life as "The Last Koreshan." She said, "There is no last, we shall continue."

Check out Koresh's house because it is filled with informative photos and news items. The paintings of Teed's son decorate the "Planetary Court" building. Upstairs are seven bedrooms, one for each of the known planets at the time and for each of the celibate "sisters."

You can tour the site, simply by pulling up to the Park Ranger kiosk and handing over $4 "per vehicle." The site also includes campgrounds, a volleyball court, and a boat ramp. Canoes and kayaks can be rented to paddle down the Estero River or to historical Mound Key, known for being the capital "city" of the Calusa Indians.

Florida Cracker Motor Coach Tour

If someone told you a tour bus ride would take you to Palmdale, Felda, LaBelle and Immokalee, you might figure that would be dull. You would be wrong!

We left early morning on a cool October day for an event-filled, 10-hour day of a treasure trove of eclectic events. One tour member, even before the tour was over, said," This is the best tour I've ever been on." His wife added: "If people knew about this everyone would sign up."

Ron Drake of Royal Palm Tours, created this unique tour, which is not a typical tourist outing. It combines ecology, history, economic development and fascinating behind-the-scenes views and personal stories of fourth-and fifth-generation Floridians.

The tour features towns that generally line up north to south, on Highway 29 in rural Collier, Glades and Hendry Counties. Although tourism ranks as the number one Florida industry, agriculture is first in these counties. Most of the stops on the tour are to small family-run businesses, run by open, honest people descended from Florida old-timers, who had a strong "take-care-of-one-another" attitude.

On the way to the first stop, we saw not one, but two-crested caracaras, an eagle-like vulture found in this country only in central Florida.

Florida "Cracker" comes from years ago when the cowboys cracked their whips in rounding up wild cattle. Florida was first in this country to have cattle, which were brought here by the Spaniards. Punta Rassa became a shipping point for cattle. Crackers today trace their roots to the early settlers. They greet people as "y'all" and eat grits. Well, we don't know about the grits, but "y'all" was the phrase of the day.

Our first stop, Gatorama Wildlife Park, founded in 1952, is just off Highway 29 on Highway 27 (6180 U.S. Highway 27, Palmdale, Florida 33944, www.gatorama.com). Rather than go on the tourist tour, owners Allen and Patty Register took us through their alligator farm buildings, where they process 30,000 alligators! None of us had ever seen so many alligators in one place. Alligator farming has been legal since 1986.

"The gators, fed a daily diet of chicken and grain-based gator food, are ready to market in two years." Allen said. "Farm production is used for leather goods and alligator meat." The gators, when harvested for meat and hide for leather goods, are less than six-feet long. Later, we stood outside looking over a small lake with large alligators and crocodiles in the 15-acre attraction. Several 12-foot long alligators sunbathed on a small one-palm-tree island. Then, there's Goliath, a 14-foot crocodile banished to solitary confinement because of bad behavior.

No visit would be complete without gator tail delicacies. Patty cooked the gator meat herself using a light flour coating. "These gator bites are much better than the restaurant variety," Dave, a tour member, said. Patty in addition to the gator farm ownership is also on the county economic development board. She said, "The tours have a multiple effect, with visitor-related jobs added in a rural area that provide disposable income. That boosts local spending."

Neither Glades, nor Hendry County, has had this "tourist" boost like coastal counties, yet there are a myriad of diverse interesting events among the small rural businesses and farm communities.

Our bus pulled into the back of the storefront where Renee, a fourth-generation beekeeper, greeted us to explain the beehives and the history of the business started by her grandfather in 1921. The LaBelle operation began in 1954. We filed into the back room, where the beehives are processed. "We extract and bottle all the honey sold in our store," Renee said. They also make candles from beeswax for sale in the small shop. We sampled the kinds of honey, each with distinct taste differences. A consensus favored Sea Grape. The group walked back to the bus for the next stop and a Florida Cracker Lunch.

When the bus pulled up to the unprepossessing blue metal building for lunch in Fleda, some raised eyebrows looked a skeptical question: Is this the place? We filed into the restaurant and into a back room where owner Buddy Taylor had set up a long table for us. Nearby was Kenny Stewart filling Gator Hammock Sauce bottles. This visit was definitely behind the scenes. Lots of bottles of five versions of Gator Hammock Sauce were arrayed on the table. Buddy started out passing around swamp cabbage, called heart of palm by city folks. We sampled the sauces with it. He also gave us Swamp Cabbage Pickles to try ("Granny's recipe").

Buddy joked: "We are the only state where we eat our state tree." The sabal (cabbage) palm is the state tree. The edible cabbage comes from five-year-old trees, ubiquitous in the area. Swamp cabbage has a taste and texture reminiscent of kohlrabi.

A dozen years ago, Buddy invited his friends to watch football because he had the only satellite dish in the area. He smoke-cooked meats, marinated with his homemade sauce. He had spent years fine-tuning and taste testing and fiddling around to come up with his sauce. Someone said, "You should bottle and sell this." So, a business was born: Gator Hammock Sauce. All five handmade sauces use natural ingredients and are spicier than traditional Louisiana sauces.

Buddy says his great-grandfather named the "cough-and-miss-it" town in 1923 using part of his name, Felix, and his wife's name, Ida, to come up with Felda.

The plentiful Florida Cracker food was downright sinful, including smoked steak, chicken, ribs, a special cooked swamp cabbage, salad, ranchero pinto beans and sausage. Buddy insisted after all this that we try his sour orange pie. And before we left, he insisted that we load up on what was left to take home with us. Buddy was on FoodTV on a segment filmed in Felda in 2001.

Florida Train Ride

Christmas Train/Boat Trip

Fifty people from one community boarded the Seminole Gulf Railway train at Colonial Station in Fort Myers, and filled the *Sanibel* car, for a fun trip to Punta Gorda in mid-December. The train has four 1930s-1950s vintage cars; all filled with revelers for this special trip. The aptly named other cars: *Captiva, Marco*, and *Gasparilla*. Seminole operates on 115 miles of track and also runs dinner trains with a mystery theater. Atlantic Coast Railway built the first tracks to Fort Myers in 1885 after Florida Southern had extended track from the north to Punta Gorda. The rail line claims to be the "longest running dine train with murder mystery show in the USA." We later took the murder mystery show train several times and enjoyed trying to solve the mystery. It operates five nights a week.

After a leisurely swaying, rock-and-roll journey, the train pulled into the Punta Gorda railway station, now an antique store and museum. During the train ride we were served hors d'oeuvres of crackers, cheese, and grapes, followed by split pea soup and then a salad, the first three courses of what would be a five-course dinner. Drinks were available. Passengers were seated at tables for four. White tablecloths and napkins added a top-restaurant look. Carol, our server, did an exceptional job.

After spending time browsing in the antique shop, the group boarded two buses that took us to Fisherman's Village wharf where we boarded a King Fisher tour boat. The boat toured Charlotte Harbor and up and down the canals, under a starlit sky, so we could see the red, green and white Christmas lights festooned on the homes and boats. Although somewhat chilly, warranting a jacket, the enclosed boat made viewing the lights a pleasant experience. The canals shimmered with reflected lights.

"Everything is beautiful," one among the group said. Another of the group, on her second Christmas trip said, "We especially enjoyed the candle light dinner on the way back." (The train's generator failed, so the only light we had, came from candles, which did add to the ambience.)

Choices for the main course, on the train ride home, were poached salmon, baked stuff chicken breast or prime rib. We tried the poached salmon, which was excellent. A tour member said: "Everybody at our table loved it. Several said they'd like to do it again. We heard that this was a fun trip. Now we know why, and can heartily recommend it."

The train boarded at 3 p.m. and arrived in Punta Gorda at 5:30 p.m. After the boat ride and train ride home, the train pulled in to the Fort Myers station at 9:30 p.m. The "Mystery Dinner Train" runs five nights a week, which provides entertaining and funny "whodunits" that keep you guessing. The railway also runs excursion trains, which provide views as the train crosses the Intracoastal Waterway.

If You Go.

Seminole Gulf Railway, Colonial Station off Colonial Boulevard at 4110 Centerpointe Drive, Fort Myers 33916, phone 239-275-8487 or 1-800-736-4853, www.semgulf.com.

See Chapter Fourteen for train rides in Mount Dora.

Memorable Boat Trips

We have enjoyed dozens of narrated boat excursions, all with an eco slant to them. We have found them to be fun, educational and relaxing. No matter where we travel in Florida, an entrepreneur has bought a boat and scheduled tours. The captains often turn out to be retirees who have found a new vocation as qualified boat captains with a line of patter and knowledge about their area. "This is the best job I've ever had," Captain Ralph told me. "There's always something new and different and it's fun to not only share knowledge with people, but boost conserving our natural treasures." Here are just three unique ones of the many to spark you to take a boat tour.

Sunset Soiree Champagne Cruise.

What could be more relaxing than sitting comfortably, with family and friends, in a large pontoon-boat as it lazily plies its way up the channel? Picture a beautiful evening with temperature in the 70s and the sun ready to set in a blaze of color. Two-dozen of us boarded the "Dolphin Waters," on a warm evening in January, for a lazy ride on a glassy-smooth sea. The boat, with Captain Bob in charge, pulled out of Port Sanibel Marina (behind the Lighthouse Restaurant) at 5 p.m. The boat eased along the channel at idle, mindful of the "Caution: Manatee Area" signs. The slow speed gave everyone a chance to view the expensive homes on Connie Mack Island.

John, the first mate, pointed out a modest home, which was being remodeled: "The owner paid $450,000 for that," he explained. What would a million bucks buy? Well, further along, we were looking at some homes that would go for much more than a cool million. As we picked up speed in the Back Bay, Captain Bob gave a running commentary on the Calusa Indians and historic Punta Rassa. Soon we were in sight of Bird Island, a mangrove "island" swarming with birds.

John explained, "This island is nothing but mangroves so the roosting birds feel safe because there are no predators." Captain Bob eased closer so we could get a good view, but not too close as to disturb the birds. He cut the engine so we could also hear the birds.

"What is that bird with all the red?" asked one of the grandchildren on the trip. "That's a frigatebird," John replied. "This is one place to see them."

As mentioned in earlier chapters, male frigatebirds blow up their bright scarlet gular pouches to let the female birds know where they are. The magnificent frigate birds soar on eight-foot wingspans. They avoid landing on the ground because they have such a hard time getting airborne, so they land in the mangrove trees. You don't see them flap their wings much as they just soar. The frigatebird is the original pirate, because he attacks Terns to get them to drop their prey so he can steal it!

Birds circled around over the small island, like fighters and bombers ready to land. A flock of pelicans, like a flight of kamikaze bombers, swooped in for a landing on the mangrove limbs of this mixed species rookery. There were hundreds of cormorants, anhingas, egrets, ibis, herons and pelicans along with rare birds like the frigatebird. We looked at the birds, and the birds, apparently bored by it all, stared back. A few fluttered into the air.

We left Bird Island and approached Picnic Island, with its sandy beaches and pine trees. Not a bird in sight. "If you are a sailor and looking for a place to land, look for pine trees because that indicates there's dry land." Captain Bob said. "There are also predators so the birds don't roost here."

Sunset, just after 6 p.m., sent colorful rays dancing on the waves. We had a ringside seat of the reds, oranges and purples of a Florida sunset. Mango gold colored the clouds. The one disappointment was we didn't see any dolphins, nor of course any manatees because the water temperature was 61 degrees. Manatees need 67 or more, so congregate in winter near the Florida Power and Light power plant for the warm water effluent in winter.

Circling Marco Island. We wanted a close up look at 9,000-acre Marco from the sea in a small boat. So, one day, we hired Captain Jim and his small flat-bottomed boat and with just the two of us as passengers, Captain Jim took us on a half-day boat tour. As we passed along the crescent-shaped beach, we watched brown pelicans diving for food and some dolphins playfully swimming near shore.

As we reached the south part of the island, we spotted a manatee. Captain Jim immediately shut off the engine and we drifted by the endangered manatee. Before boating past Goodland, the fishing village on the island's south tip, we saw an island formed from clamshells from the early twentieth century clam business. As we headed north, we detoured up Whiskey Creek, and maneuvered through the thick mangroves. The flat-bottomed boat, ideal for getting in and out of shallow mud flat areas, also let us get in close.

Later we slowly edged along three small islands, known locally as the A-B-C Islands, which comprise the largest mixed-species rookery in South Florida. As we approached through the shallow water, magnificent frigatebirds perched in the trees, mixed in with brown pelicans and many other birds. On this afternoon, ibises outnumbered all the other species. The wading birds like the great blue herons, snowy egrets, great egrets and ibises fly to their nighttime roost at dusk. As we lingered, thousands of birds stared at us as we looked at them. Time seemed to stand still. A few fluttered into the air but most looked bored with the non-threatening intruders. Later, thousands more birds would return from forays around Marco Island to swell the bird population to perhaps 20,000. You can use your own boat to do a tour like this, but a knowledgeable guide can point out treasures you might miss. Often people walk by, or boat by, wonders of nature and don't really see all that can be seen and appreciated. Looking carefully can reap big dividends no matter where you are, including cutting stress and relaxing tensions. A leisurely boat ride, with the salty sea breeze in your face, in an area teeming with wildlife can do that. For contrast, we also plied the canals to look at the glittering wealth of Marco waterfront homes.

"Double Sunshine." At Tin City, U.S. 41 in Naples, phone 239-263-4949. The "Double Sunshine" does a 1-1/2-hour narrated cruise to view wildlife and the beautiful homes of Port Royal. The "Captain Paul" provides ½-day fishing tours to the bay and the "Lady Brett" offers ½-day deep-sea fishing. On the other side of the river, The Naples Princess offers cruises, phone 239-649-2275, as does the Marco Island Princess from 951 Bald Eagle River, phone 239-642-5415. On one of our trips a mother and baby dolphin kept pace with our boat as we cruised down the Gordon River. The captain said there is a $2,500 fine for circling too close to them. He noted the Florida Fish and Wildlife Conservation Commission recommends a viewing distance of 50 feet. But often, as in this case, the dolphins come along. The two dolphins jumped and played alongside, and later played in the boat's wake. The Captain said, "They know us, and are familiar with the pontoon tour boats." Clearly the mother dolphin trusted the boat to let her baby play alongside. The dolphins, leaping and diving put on a show that garnered ohs and ahs from the tour boat passengers. The mother swam upside down with her ventral fin pointing out of the water. "Did you see that?"

Other Boat Cruises

Cocohatchee Eco Boat Tour. At Cocohatchee Nature Center, 12345 Tamiami Trail North (U.S. 41) in North Naples, Florida 34110, phone 239-592-1200. Four narrated tours daily wind through mangrove estuary with sightings of herons, ibis, osprey, and egrets. On one of our trips, dolphins followed along playing in the wake. The center also rents canoes and kayaks. We enjoyed a sunset cruise to watch the fiery ball sink into the horizon of the Gulf.

The Captain J.P. We had a fun trip with family members down the Caloosahatchee River on the Captain J.P. on a "River Escape Buffet Cruise." The 600-passenger Captain J.P. also has a trip on part of the 156-mile Okeechobee Intracoastal Waterway that connects the East and West coasts. The Lake Okeechobee Cruise starts with an 8 a.m. bus ride to Clewiston, then a 90-mile narrated cruise into Lake Okeechobee and 90 miles west along the Intracoastal Waterway through three sets of U.S. Army Corps of Engineers locks. The cruise, which includes breakfast, lunch and dinner, ends up in Fort Myers at 7:30 p.m. The company also has an 80-passenger *Jungle Cruise*, which cruises the Orange River during manatee season (November-April). The Captain J.P. sails from Ft. Myers yacht basin, Ft. Myers, Florida, phone 239-334-7474, www.jccruises.com. From I-75, take exit 141 and go six miles west to downtown Fort Myers area, turn right on Lee Street or Hendry Street to Edwards Drive.

Tropic Star of Pine Island Pineland Marina, 13921 Waterfront Drive, Pineland, Florida 33945, phone 239-283-0015. www.tropicstarcruises.com. Tropic Star has a full-day narrated nature cruise from their marina on Pine Island, on a 59-passenger shallow-draft boat fashioned after the *African Queen* The marina also rents canoes and kayaks.

Glass-bottom Boats. The top three for seeing the reefs and colorful fish are at Biscayne National Park (Chapter Ten), John Pennekamp Coral Reef State Park (102601 Overseas Highway, near Key Largo; phone 305-451-1621), and from Key West (Chapter Thirteen). The 65-foot, 149-passenger catamaran "Spirit of Pennekamp" goes out to the shallow reefs to see all the colorful fish and also to the sunken Naval vessel *Spiegel Grove*. The Pennekamp Park was named in honor of John D. Pennekamp (1898-1978), a long-time Miami Herald assistant editor who championed environmental conservation.

Chapter Thirteen
Key West Mini-Vacation
Adventures

If you haven't been to fun and funky Key West, then make plans now to go. If you have been to Key West, you will want to go again after reading this chapter of our adventures there. You'll add a new dimension to your next visit. We couldn't wait to return to Key West, so we could go to Fort Jefferson, a don't-miss visit to the least visited of our National Parks.

Colorful Key West, which has a warm tropical climate, is the most remote destination you can visit in the Continental United States. The Spanish named it Cayo Hueso (Island of Bones). Over time, pronunciation shifted to Key West. More than two million visitors crowd into Key West annually, in a town of just 28,000 full-time residents on an island less than two miles by four miles in size. Most visitors seem to have a clear intent of letting it all hang out and having fun. Key West's rich past of pirates, wreckers, turtlers, writers, artists and poets attracts history buffs. It is a haven for artists and writers, ever since Ernest Hemingway arrived in 1928.

Key West has a unique identity with an eclectic culture mix of quaint gingerbread houses, white picket fences, raucous bars, some bizarre behavior and dress, posh boutiques and expensive galleries, celebrations and S's: sunning, shopping, spectacular sunsets, swimming, snorkeling, sea adventures, sidewalk cafes, sunken gold, shipwrecks, salvagers and schooners.

Before Henry Flagler extended his Florida East Coast Railways in 1912 to Key West after seven years of effort to build 128 miles over two dozen islands, Key West was a mosquito-infested mangrove swamp reachable only by boat. After the devastating Labor Day 1935 hurricane wiped out the railroad, and killed more than 400 persons, the Overseas Highway was built on its roadbed and opened for traffic in 1938. If you'd like to know more about Flagler's quixotic railroad venture, and its immense engineering and construction challenges, we recommend Les Standiford's excellent book, *The Last Train to Paradise.* Also see Chapter Fifteen, which describes visiting Flagler's mansion.

In our visits to Key West, the Duval Street scene, which bustles with activity, seems unchanging in some ways. You can't keep count of the piercings, tattoos, exotic "fashions" in the anything- goes laid-back life style you see walking on the main drag. Nary a necktie in sight, nor a jacket. The streets are alive with tourists. Beach bums mix with wealthy retirees, along with some staggering victims of Duval Crawl (hit every bar on Duval). Music floats outside from the many saloons. "Let's go bar hopping" lives alongside tourists visiting attractions, taking boat tours, dive trips and going fishing. Even the locals join in with the people watching in a live-and-let-live support of diversity. As someone observed, "Everybody is somebody else's weirdo."

Some restaurants and shops we remembered from our first trip were not there on our next visit. If you took out all the T-shirt shops and the bars/cafes/restaurants there wouldn't be a lot left in Old Town! The anything-to-make-a-buck attitude shows up and down the bright tourist strip of Duval Street, which stretches from the Atlantic Ocean to the Gulf of Mexico (about 1-1/2 miles) with bars, shops, galleries and restaurants. To be fair, the better shops, upscale restaurants and galleries tend to outweigh the tacky T-shirt shops and loud bars, compared to past visits. The economy clearly thrives on tourists, but the early economy, in contrast, was based on sponges (gone), shipwrecks (gone), and cigar making (nearly gone).

What may be a festive din to some visitors may be simply loud cacophony of sound to others. Hemingway, if he were alive today, might not recognize his Sloppy Joe's Bar: loud and crass, but jammed with people who like the loud music and ambience. He would have a tough time finding a seat and who could separate him from all the impersonators. You'll see more Hemingway look-alikes in Key West than Presley imitators in Las Vegas.

With very little affordable housing, many of the people who work in Key West have to live somewhere else. The Real Estate Law of Location, Location, Location really applies here. It means big bucks for homes mostly for people with deep pockets. When you see a modest-looking old house on a small lot in Key West priced at $489,000, you can see why many who work in Key West can't afford to live there. For most of us, the cliché "This is a nice place to visit but I wouldn't want to live here" fits, if only because of the housing cost. A lot on Sunset Key, at the harbor of Key West, was advertised for $1.4 million. How about a one bedroom, one bath condo in Old Town for $310,000?

Plan Ahead and Some Tips for Saving Money.

A visit to Historic Tours eTicket Center (www.htatickets.com) can save you a bundle, especially if you will have time to visit the major attractions. For example, a Super Saver Passport that would cost $128.35 for an adult is available for $105. A best value for seeing major attractions is available for just $55, to include the Conch Train or Trolley, Aquarium, Hemingway Home, Shipwreck Historeum®, Flagler Railroad Station, Bone Island Shuttle, and shopping discounts. You can also call Key West Passports, 1-888-362-3474 for package deals.

Going in the off-season (after April 15) saves money and stress. Visit websites like Travelocity, Orbitz, Travelweb, Hotels.com and Expedia for special deals. Check out the hotel websites for special offers. Empty rooms in the off-season mean special rates! Read this chapter to pick out the things you *really* want to do and those to do if you have time left. If you're not surfing the net, then call ahead for bargains at hotels. This chapter shows phone numbers and Internet addresses. Generally, you can save 10% or so by getting tickets online.

After you arrive, take the "train" or the "trolley" first to get oriented. You can see where you want to spend some time, and you'll save time by planning the attractions you want to see. Also, pick up a map. Most of these, along with guidebooks, have money-saving coupons.

Traveling to Key West.

You have a choice of a sea ferry, with a four-hour boating trip from Fort Myers, driving, taking a bus tour or flying. The X-Press, one of the sea ferries from Ft. Myers, has taken 100,000 passengers in three years. Cost is about $110. We met many visitors from out of state who flew to Miami, then rented a car for the 100-mile drive to Key West. Cape Air flies a 9-passenger plane from Southwest Florida International. Gulfstream International flies to Key West from Orlando, Miami, Tampa, Jacksonville, and Fort Lauderdale. Naples Air flies from Naples.

Florida Keys Shuttle (1-888-765-9997) operates 15-passenger vans between Key West and Miami, and stops between, five times daily.

We talked to people who came in on the morning ferry, who planned to leave that afternoon on the ferry. We talked with people who came in on cruise ships, usually with a day in Key West. There's so much to do in Key West, a day simply won't do it to get the unique flavor of the real Key West beyond the cheap souvenirs. If you can do so, schedule more than a day. Even if you stay several days, you will still miss something. We time our visits to spring/early summer or fall, when there are fewer tourists, lower rates. We also try to avoid the major events that draw large crowds, like Fantasy Fest in late October, which draws 60,000 and fills the hotels.

On a visit in 2001, we chose to drive to Key West from Ft. Myers, a 300-mile drive. Even in off-season month of May, the last 100 miles on heavily traveled, two-lane Highway 1 takes awhile to get to Mile Zero. Helpful mile markers along the way remind you of how far you have left to get to Mile Zero. We stopped for lunch in Key Largo, after leaving at 8:30 a.m. We arrived in Key West at mid afternoon, having avoided the traffic snarls that occur during the season. Fellow guests at our bed and breakfast inn said they drove from St. Petersburg in less than eight hours. Other guests at the Inn drove from Miami "in less than three hours," they said. If you are driving from Orlando, plan on a nine-hour drive. Pensacola is nearly 800 miles from Key West.

You have time to look on the way because of so many 45 mph zones and the traffic. You look at water on both sides with the Atlantic to the east and the turquoise-hued Gulf of Mexico to the west, either from the 42 bridges (especially from Seven-Mile Bridge south of Marathon) or from narrow islands.

On a visit in June 2003, we stopped at Whale Harbor (mile marker 84) in Islamorada for lunch. Islamorada claims the title, "Sport Fishing Capital of the World." We managed the 260-mile trip from Naples to Key West in six hours, including an hour stop for lunch. Look to the west from Seven-Mile Bridge and you can see the remains of the Overseas Railway. On the way you can stop and enjoy a variety of activities and spend hours or days.

Accommodations in Key West.

More than a dozen bed & breakfast inns and hotels, including the Hyatt, 601 Front Street, Hilton, 245 Front Street, Ocean Key Resort, 0 Duval Street, Pier House Resort, Caribbean Spa, 1 Duval Street and others are near the waterfront in Old Town. Others on North and South Roosevelt Boulevard include the Sheraton Suites, Grand Key Resort, Hampton Inn, Sunrise Suites, Comfort Inn, Days Inn, Radisson Hotel, Quality Inn, Marriott Courtyard, and others. You have a wide variety of choices to stay, from casual to expensive.

Many hotels have special packages. The Fairfield Inn, for example, has one that includes a scooter. Most inns have romantic packages. Room rates drop after April 15. What was a $260 a day (plus 11.4% sales and room tax) before April 15, for example, is a $195 one after April 15. Generally, rates are higher, as you would expect, near the harbor, attractions and in Old Town. For example, a room at the Hilton on Front Street in the off-season is $200 or so versus around $100 at the Hampton on North Roosevelt. If you are not registered in a downtown hotel, the trolley likely comes by your hotel and you can get on and off at your convenience. You can ride the Bone Island Shuttle for $7 a day. It goes by most of the hotels.

Curry Mansion. 511 Caroline Street, 305-294-5349, www. currymansion.com. We chose to stay in Old Town, just a block off Duval Street, at the bed-and-breakfast Curry Mansion. Once upon a time the turn-of-the-century Curry Mansion was the home of the son of Florida's first self-made millionaire. In fact, Key West in those days was the richest town in the United States. The money came from salvagers, called "The Wreckers," who saved lives from ships on the reefs, but also recovered all the goods, thus becoming rich.

Now the mansion, home to a bed and breakfast, is also a 15-room museum open to the public for tours with antiques, Tiffany glass and objects, Audubon prints and Hemingway memorabilia. There's even a widow's walk atop the 3-story mansion. The mansion not only reflects the rags-to- riches story of Bill Curry, but also the present owner, Edith Amsterdam, who noted: "The former Milton Curry Mansion has been our home since we bought it and began it's restoration in 1974; only the piano, glass bookcase and buffet were in the house at that time." Our favorite room is the dining room, which is loaded with antique furniture and with the table elegantly set for eight.

The Curry Mansion has 22 guest rooms, including an addition at the back. It also has eight rooms in an "annex" across the street, where we stayed on our 2003 visit. Our room was all wicker furniture with canopy bed and a separate sitting room. Each evening Bill "Nine Fingers" plays the piano from 5 p.m. to 7 p.m. with "big band" tunes, during the daily cocktail party with complimentary drinks at the bar near the pool. Breakfast (8 a.m. to 10 a.m.) also came with the room. Cocktail time was a fun time to compare notes on attractions and restaurants. So, while the room cost may be more than others, so are the amenities.

On our five-day visits, we parked the car upon arrival and didn't use it again until we left. Everything we wanted to see, or do, is within walking distance of the inn. If you tire, rental bikes and golf carts are at nearly every corner. Key West can be a special, romantic place. During our last visit, people who were attending a wedding party occupied most of the rooms at the inn!

Conch Train. 201 Front Street, phone 305- 294-5161, www.conchtrain. com.

After arriving in Key West, and getting settled, we took the 90-minute Conch (pronounced konk) train tour of the small, historic island on our first visit. Don't look down your nose at the touristy train, because it worked well for us in getting oriented and selecting what we wanted to go back and see. The Conch Trains, which appear to be remodeled jeeps, pull strings of trailers made to look like passenger train cars. Drivers spew a running commentary. People crowded the walks, but "nowhere near the number of people a few weeks earlier," according to the Conch Train driver who, by the way, claimed to be a Conch (native of Key West). He views Key West as the Conch Republic, he said. We took that at face value, because his other information proved to be helpful.

Surprises.

Mapping out a general plan helps you make the most of your time, but count on Key West surprises that can cause plan A to fail. Change is a constant in nature and in Key West. Rough seas can cancel a boat tour. In summer, hurricanes threaten. Friends who came to Key West on the sea ferry, with plans to return on it the next day, were left stranded when the boat did not come down the next day (because of weather). We had planned for two months in advance of our visit to go with Florida Lighthouse Association members on a chartered Fast Cat to Ft. Jefferson. As Robert Burns said, "The best laid plans….." When we arrived for boarding at 7:30 a.m. (that's rising early in late night Key West), the captain informed us the engine had blown. The trip was off. Plan B, going on another tour boat didn't work out because it was sold out. You can fail to achieve your original plan and gain opportunities you never planned for, which is what happened with us. We visited the Truman Little White House and Aquarium, and did other things, then went to Ft. Jefferson the next day, for a memorable trip.

Attractions, Activities and Adventures.

Many of the attractions line up on Whitehead Street, which parallels Duval Street. They start at Front Street with several clustered in a small area at 1 Whitehead Street, including the Key West Shipwreck "Historeum®" and the Key West Aquarium. The Museum of Art and History in the Old Custom House (281 Front Street) and the Clinton Square Market are nearby. On the other side is Mallory Square, which comes alive toward sunset. You can pick the daytime attractions you want to see and work your way down Whitehead Street to the Southernmost Point

In between the Aquarium at one end, and the Southernmost Point at the other, we visited all the attractions up and down Whitehead Street (and on nearby side streets) during visits to Key West. We also got our walking in and we were educated while on vacation in a fun way. We would visit a few of the attractions each day and also mix in sunning, or a boat tour, or other activity

For example, we visited the Aquarium and the Shipwreck Historeum® one morning then cooled off shopping in nearby air-conditioned Clinton Square Market, and then lunched at nearby Rooftop Café. We took the two-hour Glass-Bottom Boat tour at 2 p.m. We also walked through the nearby Memorial Sculpture Garden, with the magnificent sculpture, "The Wreckers," by Artist James Mastin at the entrance. That evening, we sat on the pier to watch the spectacular sunset, then after sunset we followed the crowd to Mallory Square to watch the jugglers, acrobats, magicians with card tricks, trained cats, fortune tellers and other street entertainers.

Another day, we checked out the Key West Lighthouse and Hemingway House, then walked to the Southernmost Point. We lunched at Kelly's Caribbean Bar and Grill, and then visited nearby Mel Fisher's Museum and some of the shops. We did succumb to T-shirt bargains for family members, post cards, bought a rum cake at Tortuga Rum Cake shop, selected a blouse at Fast Buck Freddie's and picked out a Panama Jack straw hat for sun protection. Browsing in the unique small shops can be interesting.

Here, in a general order, on or just off Whitehead Street, from the Aquarium, Memorial Garden and Shipwreck Historeum® are: Audubon, Mel Fisher, Heritage House, Truman Little Whitehouse, Ernest Hemingway Home, Key West Lighthouse and Southernmost Point. Fort Zachary Taylor entrance is at Southard Street.

What are our favorites? First, if you don't have a specific interest, then the tour guide can make or break a tour. The guide at the Truman Little White House brought history alive, provided little known trivia items (source of "The Buck Stops Here") and humor to make our visit a delightful one. At the Aquarium, the woman conducting the tour did a great job, including feeding sharks by hand. She knew a great deal and clearly loved what she was doing. The naturalist/diver on the glass-bottom boat provided excellent commentary on the coral reef and fish.

Because we have long-admired Hemingway's books, a visit to his home was a must for us, and we were not disappointed. As long-time lighthouse buffs, visiting the lighthouse was a priority for every visit. Many of our favorite attractions turned out to be Historic Tours of America attractions. They hire good people and train them to enhance your tour. Our favorite adventure in Key West, however, was our trip to Fort Jefferson. Plan on a full day for this one-of-a-kind trip.

What are the most popular attractions according to locals we asked? The Conch Train and Mallory Square (sunset celebration) are number one-two. Hemingway Home, Mel Fisher's Maritime Museum, Truman Little White House, and Jimmy Buffett's Margaritaville follow as most popular. The Aquarium is very popular. "And, of course the Southernmost Point; everyone goes there to take a photo."

Here are some comments on the attractions, based on our visits, to help you pick out ones you would like to visit.

Key West Aquarium, 1 Whitehead Street, phone 305-296-205, www. keywestaquarium.com. We visited the aquarium first, on our first visit, which is appropriate because it was the first Key West attraction. Built in 1932-1934 by the depression-era WPA (Works Project Administration), and now twice the size of the original, the aquarium remains a popular place to visit. Although we have been to some much larger aquariums, we especially enjoyed this one because of the intimacy; the tanks are open and you are looking down into them. Kids love visiting here because of the touch tanks and being able to pet a shark. The touch tank is up close and personal. Daily shark and turtle feedings are at 11 a.m., 1 p.m., 3 p.m. and 4:30 p.m. so time your visit to coincide with one of these. Adult tickets are just $9, less if you get one in advance on the Internet.

Key West Shipwreck Historoeum®. 1 Whitehead Street, phone 305-292-8990, www.shipwreckhistoreum.com. Key West became the richest city in the United States from cargo salvaged from the many shipwrecks on the treacherous reefs of the Florida Keys. The salvagers made Key West rich, during their heyday 1830-1860. In addition to recreations of a wrecking schooner of the time and its crew, you can get a great view of Key West from the Lookout Tower. Besides, you can get your Stairmaster® exercise climbing the stairs! Imagine a time when "There is scarcely a day that you may not see from 100 to 150 square rigged vessels passing Key West in the Gulf of Mexico" said Stephen Mallory in 1850. What a sight that must have been, when Key West was a boisterous seaport of hardy and adventuresome seamen. It's still boisterous and a seaport, but riches don't come from salvaging wrecks. We thought the presentation a bit corny.

Key West Historic Memorial Sculpture Garden, Mallory Square. This display of bronze busts of "depicting men and women who made Key West such a vibrant and important outpost of American culture and folklore" warrants a look. It opened in 1997, with funds from engraved bricks that were sold to pave the garden. The large sculpture at the entrance provides a photo opportunity, judging from the number of people standing by it to get their picture taken!

John Audubon House. 205 Whitehead Street, phone 294-2116, www. audubonhouse.com. Captain Geiger, a wrecker and ex-pirate, with his nine children, occupied this home in the 1830s. He salvaged sunken ships in the 1820s. John James Audubon (1785-1851) visited in 1832. There are 28 original engravings along with Dorothy Dowty's collection of porcelain birds. That provides some historical interest as well as the opportunity to look at Audubon engravings, including the 18 he did while in Key West.

Mel Fisher Maritime Heritage Museum. 200 Greene Street, at Whitehead and Greene, phone 305-294-2633, www.melfisher.org. At the late Mel Fisher's museum, we looked at some of the booty he brought up from the wrecked Spanish Galleons, Nuestra Senora de Atocha and Santa Margarita, which sank in a hurricane in 1622, forty miles from Key West. We watched an interesting 18-minute film on his years of the search. Mel Fisher, who died in 1998, persisted in his 16-year quest. Efforts continue today with year-round work that has yielded additional silver and gold coins, iron cannon balls, olive jar shards and other amazing discoveries.

Heritage House & Robert Frost Cottage. 410 Caroline, between Whitehead and Duvall Streets, phone 305- 296-3573, www. heritagehousemuseum.com. Built in the 1830s, the Caribbean Colonial house reflects the lives of seven generation of Porters, with the focus on Jesse Porter, who last lived in the house. Known as Miss Jesse, she hosted celebrities, including Tennessee Williams, Thornton Wilder, Gloria Swanson, Sally Rand and others. Poet Robert Frost spent many winters in a cottage in the garden. Poets Wallace Stevens and Archibald MacLeish were guests, as was philosopher John Dewey. One of her forbearers was Bill Curry. She led the effort to restore the Audubon House in the 1950s. She was "the island's grand dame of hospitality." Jeane Porter, sixth generation, wrote a book, *Key West Conch Smiles,* which, through the lives of the Porter Family, provides an insight into 200 years of Key West culture. Jeane Porter grew up with the Hemingway boys, so combines her own stories with those of her mother. Because the house is not on Whitehead, the visitor level may not be as high as more popular attractions. If you like orchids, the garden has 200 examples of them blooming January-April. You can also hold a dinner party in the garden (40 to 80 people), the guide said; and even rent the museum for an event. The Robert Frost Festival of Poetry is held in April each year.

Harry S. Truman Little Whitehouse: Florida's Only Presidential Museum. 111 Front Street, phone 305-294-9911, www.trumanlittlewhitehouse. com. We entered from Whitehead and Caroline Streets. The surprise of a burned out engine in the chartered tour boat had scrubbed our pre-paid trip to Ft. Jefferson, so we walked over the few blocks to the Little White House, instead, not really expecting much. Were we surprised! Again!

The tour guide, a Key West resident and substitute teacher when she isn't doing guided tours for Historic Tours of America, brought history alive with a fascinating glimpse into the life of President Harry S. Truman (1884-1972) in his 11 visits of 175 days to what became the Little White House. The 10-room house, built in 1890 on the waterfront of Key West Harbor, was for the commandant of the Naval Station that surrounded it. The president first visited in 1946 for rest prescribed by his doctor.

The guide said, "The president could have a working session here without all the interruptions in Washington and he could relax. He loved to walk, sometimes in town. Obviously security was different then. At midmorning he would often go to what was then called Truman Beach for a swim."

The Navy redecorated the spartanly furnished house in 1947 to make it more comfortable for Bess Truman. The restorers put it back as it was in that era. Your tour takes you past his poker table. Poker was one of his favorite amusements. The decorators spread a royal flush in front of his favorite spot. His desk in the living room, where he worked daily, has the famous, "The Buck Stops Here" sign.

"Where did the phrase, the buck stops here, come from?" the tour guide asked. No one knew. "The buck was an item passed to the person who would deal next. Some would pass it on, not wanting to deal; thus "passing the buck." The buck stopped when a person would take the responsibility to deal, thus "the buck stops here."

Of course the museum has a reproduction of the newspaper declaring Dewey the victor in the 1948 election. A large photo upstairs of Lauren Bacall posed on a piano with Harry Truman playing catches your eye. Bess reportedly didn't like it. There are two roosters on a table in the dining room. What did they signify? Before the donkey, the rooster was the symbol of the Democratic Party!

Did Truman like it in Key West? He wrote Bess March 13, 1949..."I've a notion to move the capitol to Key West and just stay." Yes, we agree. A survey in 2001 rated President Truman the fifth best president, behind Lincoln, Washington, Franklin and Theodore Roosevelt. Personally I would rank Eisenhower in place of Franklin. But we liked Truman, if only because he was from Missouri! He told it as he saw it and made some huge decisions that took a remarkable courage.

During his tenure, among the major events were: Dropping of the Atomic bomb in 1945 to end WWII, signing the United Nations Charter in 1945, The Berlin Airlift, The Marshall Plan, the Truman Doctrine, creation of the North Atlantic Treaty Organization (NATO), the Korean War, and the firing of General Douglas MacArthur. He dedicated the Everglades National Park. He desegregated the military, so when I entered in May

1951, the army was desegregated even though in the nearby Georgia town segregation still included separate bathrooms, marked white and colored.

Thomas Edison stayed at the house in World War I in 1918 when he worked on depth charges for the U.S. Navy. President Eisenhower recuperated from a heart attack at the house in 1956. President Carter celebrated New Year's Eve there in 1996 with family and friends. Colin Powell hosted a meeting at the Little White House in 2001.

The house remained the quarters for the commandant of the Truman Naval Station until it closed in 1974. The restoration and opening of it as a museum, made it just as President Truman left it for us to get an insight into our 33rd president in an unusual way. The tour exceeded our expectations. We learned a lot we didn't know about Truman. A fellow tour member said, "I'm past 75 years old, and I learned a lot I didn't know, even though I was around when he was president."

Fort Zachary Taylor State Historic Site. Entry at Southard Street, Truman Annex Gate, phone 305- 292-6713. The Civil-War era fort, which is open for tours, was built in 1845. There are 87 acres of park with a white sand beach and picnic areas, a quiet get-away- from-it-all place for sunning and beach time. The fort played a small role in the Civil war when Union Captain Bannon came to Fort Taylor in 1861 to set up a blockade, which kept 300 Confederate ships from coming into port. The Fort is one of two National Historic Landmarks in Key West, the other being the Hemingway Home.

Ernest Hemingway Home and Museum. 907 Whitehead, phone 305-294-1575, www.hemingwayhome.com. Built in 1881, the author bought the Spanish colonial home in 1931 and owned it until his death in 1961. He added a large swimming pool in the 1930s, which cost $20,000, a princely sum in those days. We visited the study where he wrote a number of his novels, including *To Have and Have Not, The Snows of Kilimanjaro,* and *For Whom the Bell Tolls.*

Cats are everywhere, many of them six-toed descendants of Hemingway's nearly 50 cats. We asked, "Who takes care of all these cats?" A tour guide answered, "The museum is a privately owned business. The care and feeding of the cats is one of the expenses and done by caretakers of the museum. In fact, all the cats get their annual shots, too." We also learned that all the cats are named. Did you know that a group of cats is called a clawder of cats? And another piece of trivia: a group of kittens is called a Kindle of kittens. The guide added, "Most cats have five toes, but Hemingway thought 6-toed cats were good luck."

The guide explained that Hemingway would write until noon, and then go fishing. "After fishing, he went to Sloppy Joe's." The walls of his studio display some of his hunting and fishing trophies. We soaked up the feeling this home of a Nobel-prize winning author invokes. Papa Hemingway won the Nobel Prize for his powerful, style performing mastery of art of narration." This shows in his most popular book, and our favorite, the Pulitzer Prize- winning, *The Old Man and the Sea*. He certainly inspired and influenced us.

Ubiquitous Stray Chickens.

As we walked across Whitehead Street from the Lighthouse, one afternoon, to the Hemingway Home, we watched a hen and ten chicks marching across the heavily traveled street. People on the sidewalk were waving at cars to gain the driver's attention. After the chicken gained security on the sidewalk with her chicks, she started out to the street again. Tourists shooed her down the sidewalk, so she entered the grounds of the Hemingway Home along with the small chicks. With five-dozen cats prowling the grounds we aren't sure what happened to the chicks.

Chickens and roosters are indeed everywhere and a problem for Key West. With 2,000 wild fowl wandering Key West's streets, the city issued a contract in 2004 to a "chicken catcher" to bag up to 900 birds at $20 apiece.

Key West Lighthouse and Museum. 938 Whitehead Street, phone 305-294-0012.

No visit to Key West should go without a tour of the Lighthouse Museum and climbing the 88 steps of the 86-foot conical masonry tower to get a panoramic view of the island and ocean, even if you aren't a lighthouse enthusiast. You can see Hemingway's house across the street and a view up and down Whitehead Street. On one of our trips, we attended a reception held by the Florida Lighthouse Association. Where else would you hold a kick-off reception in Key West for the Florida Lighthouse Association than the Key West Lighthouse?

If you'd like more on lighthouses, check out Chapter Sixteen. A good book on Florida lighthouses is *Florida Lighthouse Trail* edited by Thomas W. Taylor.

Southernmost Point. Whitehead and South Streets Yes, we snapped a photo, like millions of other tourists, at the "photo opportunity" (a mandatory place, it seems, for everyone to go to and take a photo). At Whitehead and South Streets, you are 90 miles from Cuba and 150 miles south of Miami.

Flagler Station Railway Historeum®, 901 Caroline Street, phone 305-295-3562, www.flaglerstation.com. The station is near Historic Seaport, fishing charter boats, the tour boat to Ft. Jefferson, and Turkey Kraals. The museum celebrates the terminus of the Flagler railroad in Key West.

Flagler was a remarkable man with a grand vision, which, when completed, some called the "eighth wonder of the world." He started the Key West Extension when he was 75 years old in 1905 and rode to Key West on the train in 1912. The museum has historic photos and memorabilia, inside a Florida East Coast Railway car. The museum shows a short movie, *The Day the Train Arrived.*

Glass-Bottom Boat. 2 Duval Street, phone 305-293-0099, www. seathereef.com. We decided to snorkel without getting wet, so we took the "Pride of Key West" glass-bottom boat to view the only living coral barrier reef on the continental United States. The catamaran quickly moved to a position above the reef, which is six miles from shore. We were able to see dozens of brilliantly colored species of tropical fish in the azure waters among the coral reefs. The guide explained the majestic Elkhorn and brain coral that looks so sturdy but is very fragile, as we viewed through the plastic "windows" in the bottom of the boat to the reef just 20 to 30 feet below us. In fact, we were able to get 45 minutes of viewing you could only get by scuba diving. Some divers, in fact, were in the area. The boat passed close enough to Sand Key Lighthouse to give us a good view from the deck.

Other Attractions, Tours, Fun.

Duval Street has several attractions, including Oldest house Museum, 322 Duval Street, and Southernmost House, 1400 Duval Street. Ripley's Believe it or Not, which closed, was scheduled to re-open at 108 Duval Street. Key West Ghosts, 904 Whitehead, provides ghost tour evening walks ($15), which provide a narrated look at some bizarre aspects of the past, along with a walk in the cemetery. East Martello Museum, 3501 South Roosevelt, is in a Civil War fort.

Key West has more than two-dozen art galleries, many of them displaying the work of Key West artists. You can go parasailing, fishing, snorkeling, scuba diving, boating, sailing in the Tall Ships and skydiving. Rentals are available for Waverunners®, boats, scooters, and battery-operated golf cart-type "cars." If architecture interests you, then take a short walk down Caroline Street, from Duval Street, then turn on William Street to see a variety of architectural styles, including several Gingerbread Houses (with their elaborate, cut-out balusters, decorative trim around the eaves, scrollwork porches), century-old Victorian homes, conch-style homes with tin roofs and shady porches; and white picket fences. Several are bed and breakfast inns.

Fort Jefferson; finally, and it was worth the wait! Dry Tortugas Ferry, Yankee Freedom II. 240 Margaret Street, phone 877-634-0939, www.yankeefreedom.com and www.fortjefferson.com.

We focused our 2003 visit on visiting attractions we had not seen before, but our main reason for the visit was to go to Fort Jefferson, with fellow Florida Lighthouse Association members; and see other lighthouses in the area. We weren't able to do that trip, but our exciting trip on the Yankee Freedom made up for any disappointment. The captain went out of his way, literally, to make our trip memorable. More about that exciting event later; but first, join with us in our adventure to Fort Jefferson.

The Dry Tortugas National Park, declared a park in 1992, is not only the least visited of our national parks, but the most remote and isolated park. Ponce de Leon visited in May 1513 and named the tiny seven-island chain the Tortugas (turtles). Reportedly, he and his men caught more than 100 sea turtles in one night. Later, sailors added the word "Dry" because there was no fresh water on any of the islands. The seven islets have a total of less than 80 acres in the 64,700 acres of the park. The seven islands in the cluster: Garden Key, East Key, Loggerhead Key, Bush Key, Long Key and Middle Key which can be awash in summer. The largest is Loggerhead Key with 22 acres. The fort occupies 12 of the 15 acres of Garden Key.

John Audubon, who spent two months in 1832 in the area on the Cutter Marion, said of the Dry Tortugas: "five or six extremely low uninhabitable banks, formed of shelly sand, and are resorted to principally by that class of men called wreckers and turtlers."

Mimi, at the Yankee Freedom office, the day before our trip, reminded us to bring swimsuit, sunscreen, and towel. We brought along a camera. We wore broad brimmed straw hats, vital on a hot steamy day in the sun! If you didn't bring your snorkeling gear, "not to worry, the crew will provide you gear at no charge." The trip cost $119 with a $10 discount for seniors, military and children. Tortuga Jack, our guide, met us at the boarding ramp for safety orientation. A storehouse of information, he turned out to be a valuable resource during the day. Despite the usual forecast of a 30% chance of isolated showers, we motored out from the dock on a gorgeous day, with a bright blue sky dotted with a few puffy white clouds.

We headed west promptly at 8 a.m., and moved quickly past Christmas Tree and Sunset Keys from Historic Seaport, while enjoying breakfast. The 100-foot, all aluminum $3-million dollar catamaran sliced through the topaz water at 26 knots as we sat in air-conditioned comfort. We were finally on our way to the least-visited National Park!

The Captain said Yankee Freedom would follow the path of the reef past the Marquesas Atoll, site of the wreck of the Nuestra Senora de Atocha, then past Rebecca Shoal before reaching our destination 70 miles from Key West. Tortuga Jack provided a running commentary during the trip. "The Marquesas Key Atoll is the furthest north of any atoll," Jack explained. "An atoll is an island with water in the middle of it."

Ernest Hemingway frequently fished near the Marquesas with his group of friends he called his "Mob," which included Joe Russell, owner of Sloppy Joe's. In March 1930, he and his group were marooned at Fort Jefferson for 17 days because of storms. For the small fishing boats, the trip to Key West took 10 hours or more! We passed by the area of shallow shifting sands known as "The Quick sands."

"Land Ho!" the Captain announced. Low on the horizon, we could barely make out a blur that soon became a tower as a thin pencil toward the sky, which became Loggerhead Key lighthouse; and then the second shorter tower atop Fort Jefferson, and then the wide brick Fort Jefferson came into view. We saw, according to the guide, "the largest brick structure in the Western Hemisphere."

As we approached the dock, we could see that the channel between Bush Key and Garden Key had filled in with sand. Bush Key is the only significant nesting area for the sooty tern in North America. Amazingly, they spend the first three years of their life in flight over the ocean, rarely landing. Some fly all the way from the West Coast of Africa to nest in the Dry Tortugas. They also provide an example of unintended consequences. The gulls used to leave before the terns arrived, but humans unwittingly caused a problem by feeding the gulls. Now they stay and destroy tern eggs. "Don't feed the birds."

"During March through September, more than 100,000 nest here," Jack said. "During winter, this area is a flyover for more than 200 varieties of birds, and a birders paradise." Birds at the Dry Tortugas include boobies, brown pelicans, sooty terns, and magnificent frigatebirds. For snorkelers and divers he reminded them: "Never touch or stand on coral. Don't damage the living coral. The reef is one of the most biologically diverse marine eco-systems in the world, but very fragile." Most on board thought some tour guide comments obvious, but apparently others "didn't get it" because damage continues to the reefs.

As we approached the fort, we could see that nearly all the gun ports were broken open, leaving a ragged edge of bricks, and signs of neglect. The six bastions jut out from the pentagon shape of the crumbling rust-colored brick walls, with six sides of unequal lengths as the fort was skewed to fit an irregular island.

"Each of the gun ports had iron shutters that could be opened and closed. When these rust, they expand and push the bricks and mortar out. Salt water speeded the process," Tortuga Jack explained

195

Fort. Jefferson, named after our third president, Thomas Jefferson, was one of the nineteenth century coastal forts, and the largest, which stretched from Maine to the Dry Tortugas. Fort Jefferson's construction began in 1846, and continued for three decades, but was never finished. Sixteen million bricks were shipped to Garden Key in sailing ships for the undertaking of building a fort that was obsolete before it was finished, and plagued with problems. The guide cited one example: "The design included large cisterns for storing water, with a system to capture rainwater. Unfortunately, the foundation settled, as much as a foot, because the fort was too heavy for the sand island. Seawater came in through cracks to contaminate the fresh water."

The seven to 15-foot thick walls, designed to repel the cannon balls of the past, were no match for rifled cannon invented before the Civil War, thus the fort apparently was obsolete when built. After getting off the boat, we crossed the moat on the bridge into the sally port of the fort. Moat? Yes, the fort incongruously is surrounded by a moat. "Why a moat?" we asked. "It isn't as silly as it might look, to have a moat around a fort surrounded by the Gulf of Mexico. In this case, rather than foot soldiers, or people, the moat kept boats from getting close to the fort."

We spent 4-1/2 hours at the fort, which provides plenty of time for a 45-minute guided tour (by Tortuga Jack), a picnic lunch, a visit to the park "store" and snorkeling. The tour-boat operator brought all the food, water and drinks. No public water, food or facilities exist on Garden Key. With the toilets closed, the fort was also off limits for camping in 2003. Camping resumed in 2004.

We wandered around the parade ground to see the remains of the original lighthouse (not much to see, with only the foundation remaining). Once inside, we eagerly climbed the 50 steps in the sixth bastion directly under the lighthouse. The upper level, with steps inside the coal-black sheathed tower, is closed to the public. The lighthouse has functioned as a harbor light ever since the Dry Tortugas Lighthouse at Loggerhead Key was operational in 1858. Standing atop the fort wall, we watched several people snorkeling as they looked for colorful fish outside the moat wall. The entire park is now a protected area for bird and marine life.

We asked the woman running the visitor center about Nevada Barr's book, *Flashback.* "Yes, she visited here and we all read the book. She even used the real names of two of our people, Cliff and Linda, in the book." *Flashback* tells a story of past and present Fort Jefferson. James Fennimore Cooper used Garden Key for the setting of his 1848 novel, *Jack Tier.* Hemmingway's short story, *"After the Storm"* (1932) takes place near Garden Key.

We watched an interesting 11-minute video about Fort Jefferson in a small room adjacent to the gift shop. The fort, designed for 450 cannons on three tiers, never had more than 89 guns. The barracks for 1500 men no longer exist. During the Civil War, the fort was a Union military prison for captured deserters. It also housed Dr. Mudd, convicted of aiding and abetting John Wilkes Booth in President Lincoln's assassination. In 1867, yellow fever swept through the fort with deadly results; 38 deaths, including the fort's doctor, 270 ill out of 400 soldiers and prisoners. Dr. Mudd ministered to the sick and, for his efforts, was granted a pardon by President Andrew Johnson in 1869.

The Army abandoned the fort in 1874. Vandals trashed the place. Eventually, the fort became a wildlife refuge. In 1935, the government proclaimed it a national monument. In 1992, it became part of the Dry Tortugas National Park. We pondered the significance of this huge fort on a remote island and the vision that must have been clouded with cataracts in the same way of the vision of the designers of the Maginot Line. In the case of Fort Jefferson, however, it never fired a shot at an enemy. On the other hand, the "Park News" claims: " The fort fulfilled its intended role. It helped to protect the peace and prosperity of a young nation."

The two sea ferries do not stop at Loggerhead. There is no camping, no toilets, and no water for the public. Knowing that our "approved" visit to Loggerhead had been cancelled, the Yankee Freedom captain steered the boat the extra three miles west toward Loggerhead Key. He pulled the boat close alongshore at idle so we could get photographs of the lighthouse, farthest from land of any lighthouse in the world. The 151-foot brick conical tower has deteriorated, with rusting railings and platform, so the rangers have put climbing the 204 steps off limits, even for those approved for visiting the island. The walls are six-feet thick at the bottom. After our photo opportunity, the captain steered a course back to Garden Key and on to Key West.

Two marine biologists spent their time at Key West on our trip getting samples of ailing coral to determine what is causing patches of coral to die. We sat with them on the smooth 2-1/2 hour ride back to Key West, and gained insights into the fragile coral ecosystem. Although we had spent the day at Fort Jefferson, we were ready to visit this unique, remote fort again.

Dine Out! Oh, happy days.

Key West has more than 150 restaurants of one kind or another. Some on the waterfront offer "complimentary sunsets." Clearly, there are many other good ones in a city that claims more restaurants per capita than anywhere in the United States! Many offer yellowtail snapper caught in local waters, a favorite of Conchs (locals).

If you're looking for a place for ice-cold margaritas and Caribbean food, you don't have to look far in this lush tropical island. Jimmy Buffett's Margaritaville, of course, has margaritas. Alonzo's Oyster Bar offers a Prickly Pear Margarita. Casual open-air restaurants offer tempting appetizers, too, with conch fritters a favorite. The cultural diversity of Key West shows up in the variety of restaurants: American, Cuban, European, French, Italian, Japanese, Polish and more. Although there are chain restaurants in Key West, the usual parade of the fast-food fare you see in most towns does not exist. Chili's, Benihana, TGI Friday's, Papa John's Pizza and Hard Rock Café are scattered among the many unique restaurants like ones we tried and enjoyed.

If you want to find a good restaurant, always ask a local or fellow guests, where you are staying. Here are some of the restaurants we liked and some recommended by others during our visits.

A&B Lobster House. 700 Front Street, phone 305-294-5880. Pricey but our favorite. The stuffed lobster was a gourmet delight. The setting, inside and outside, is relaxing and social. We liked their key lime pie, too. Hedonistic indulgence.

Alonzo's Oyster House. 700 Front Street, phone 305- 294-5880. Yes, the same address with Alonzo's downstairs and A&B upstairs. Not as expensive as upstairs (entrees $5-$10 less than upstairs), but excellent. Only Oyster Bar in town.

Antonia's. 615 Duval Street, phone305- 294-6565. Curry Mansion hostess recommended as her favorite. "Lovely." Upscale Italian restaurant. A few rise above the everyday variety Italian restaurant. This is one of them.

Bagatelle. 115 Duval, phone 305-296-6009. Bagatelle is in a charming former two-story home. We dined upstairs, inside during a particularly warm humid night. Another time we dined outside on the second floor veranda and watched the Duval Street activity. Excellent food and service.

Conch Republic Seafood. 631 Greene Street, phone 305-294-4403. We sat outside, near the dock We watched the boat traffic, and moored yachts in the marina, while munching on excellent conch fritters, and sipping a glass of wine (2-for-1 happy hour, 4 p.m.–7 p.m.).

El Meson de Pepe. 410 Wall Street, phone 305- 295-2620. Cuban cuisine. "Eat the food the locals love."

Grand Café. 314 Duval, phone 305- 292-4740. We lunched inside on a sweltering day and rated the conch fritters among the best in Key West. Attentive service.

Hot Tin Roof (at Ocean Key). 0 Duval Street, 305-296.7701. Try the conch chowder and the Yellowtail Snapper. Overlooks harbor.

Kelly's Caribbean Bar and Grill. 303 Whitehead, phone 305-293-8484. Caribbean cuisine. Owned by actress Kelly McGillis. Housed in the historic Pan Am Airlines ticket office building.

Mangia Mangia. 900 Southard Street, phone 305- 294-2469. Heard at the cocktail hour: "My wife is Italian and she is picky about sauces, which is why we go to Mangia Mangia." Traditional. Dependable.

Mangoes. 700 Duval, phone 305-292-4606. Some fellow guests at the inn said Mangoes was their favorite.

Rooftop Café. 310 Front Street, phone 305-294-2042. We had a great lunch in this upstairs café; and a view.

Turtle Kraals. 231 Margaret Street at Historic Land's End Marina, phone 305-294-2640, www.turtlekraals.com. It's near the Flagler Museum. At the site of the Old Turtle Soup Cannery, it has a lively bar, blues music. The Tower bar provides good sunset view. Caribbean and Cuban menu.

Three of the Many Bars (which are also restaurants):

Here are three of the most popular bars, of several dozen! They all have in common, pub grub and large sales of their "world famous" T-shirts, along with jewelry, cups, shot glasses, posters, jackets, hats; most of it with their popular logo. How about a ParrotHead visor?

Sloppy Joe's. 201 Duval Street, phone 305- 294-5717. Loud and boisterous until 4 a.m.

Hog's Breath Saloon. 400 Front Street; at Front and Duval, phone 305- 296-4222, www.hogsbreath.com. Always a crowd when we were there.

Jimmy Buffett's Margaritaville. 500 Duval Street, phone 305-296-9089, www.margaritaville.com

Popular place, especially for Parrotheads! Cheeseburgers in paradise.

Chapter Fourteen
Nine Florida City Adventures

If you live in Florida, visits to other Florida cities offer a fun alternative to longer vacation trips up North. Just because you have been to Orlando and its theme parks, where the attractions there are well known, and Key West, which deserves a chapter by itself (Chapter Thirteen), doesn't mean you've seen all that Florida has to offer!

As a resident, you can enjoy where you live the sunshine, golfing and other recreation, and the local beaches. As a "tourist" to other destinations, you can explore and learn about Florida's colorful past, enjoy fine restaurants away from home, take nature excursions, and soak up a perspective on your adopted state. No one should be bored with so much to do so close.

With historic attractions throughout Florida, you can gain a window into yesterday and a sense of what life was like that boosts your understanding of today. There are 10 forts, two Civil War battlefields, 30 lighthouses and a variety of other historic sites scattered across the state. Florida has more than 200 museums. See www.museumstuff.com. Florida has 35 of the nearly 2,500 National Historic Landmarks in the United States. These are places where "significant historical events occurred or where prominent Americans worked or live." A click on www.cr.nps.gov/nhl will lead you to information on these.

The State of Florida has an excellent tool for you to use to select "hubs" to visit, major cities and surrounding areas. Simply go to www.flausa.com and click on the link *Travel on a Tankful*. You'll see seven major cities listed with a link to show you what attractions are in the area. The site also lists 28 other locations, with specific information for each. All you need to do is choose your start point, or select from our picks. Simply jot down the ones you want to visit, then add them to your list in Chapter Nineteen.

Order the booklet *Worth the Drive,* which describes 17 off-the-beaten-path, self-directed driving tours that will "help you explore fascinating treasures anywhere your travel may lead you throughout the Sunshine State." Even if you don't want to take the full drive, the booklet provides the key places in an area to visit. The site also will provide you six Theme Tours and 10 Scenic Road Tours. The FLAUSA web site will also supply you as a resident, upon request, a colorful and excellent book, *Great Florida Getaways.*

With all this planning help you can identify the places you want to go and add to your list of things to do. You can also download printable maps to help.

City/County "Secrets."

With the stunning growth in Florida, metropolitan areas expand and grow together, which you would expect. What tourists and many part-time residents do not realize, however, is that homeowners with a city address may not live in the city! In many cities, the population of those with a city address outside the city outnumbers those living within the city limits. Fort Myers, for example, with a population of just 49,000 is the best-known city in Lee County, but adjacent Cape Coral's population is more than twice that of Fort Myers. Cape Coral also is the largest city in square miles (116). Fort Myers, the incorporated city, has less than 10 percent of Lee County's nearly 500,000 population.

In many Florida cities, more than 10 percent of the population lives in the "city" only part-time. The *Naples Daily News* in 2004 noted that 91,000 seasonal residents call Southwest Florida home for a median five months of the year. Approximately 30 percent of the seasonal residents live here six months with 12 percent for seven months. Of the total Collier County population (2003 estimate) of approximately 292,000, the city of Naples had only 22,000. In the county, more than 230,000 had a Naples address but did not live in the city of Naples! Even Tampa, the third most populous city in the state, has only a third of Hillsborough County population. Other than signs that might tell you, you might be hard-pressed to know when you left Miami-Dade County to Broward County to West Palm County.

With the county population and area much larger than the major city, the county government becomes much more influential in the lives of residents. Using Fort Myers as an example, the Lee County government had 2,200 employees in 2004, excluding the law enforcement, and a budget of $700 million on projects and services. In recent years, both Bonita Springs and Fort Myers Beach have incorporated to exert more influence and control locally. Fierce arguments can erupt over jurisdiction, such as replacing the Sanibel Causeway (county versus Sanibel residents) and building an overpass in Naples (county versus City of Naples). In Collier County, the county government employs 3,500 (including 1,200 in the sheriff's department).

Adjacent county governments have a symbiotic relationship because of the need for cooperative efforts, but these often are with very different county attitudes: for example, uppity white collar Collier and Palm Beach with adjacent blue-collar and less expensive Lee and Martin.

Published guides, including those issued by the state tourism, often will focus on regions, or group adjacent cities: Tampa/St. Petersburg/ Clearwater, Fort Myers/Naples, and Miami/Fort Lauderdale. Southwest Florida can mean Lee (Fort Myers) and Collier (Naples); but also encompass Charlotte, Hendry and Glades Counties.

All of this may make little difference to the tourist, but the structure does matter to you if you are a resident. And having a sense of the geography and surrounding area, does impact your planning in choosing a "hub" location from which to explore the area. If you want to explore Miami, the beaches and South Beach nightlife and attractions to the north, staying in Miami may make sense. If you plan to visit the Everglades National Park and Biscayne National Park, however, the "hub" may be less-expensive motels south of Miami in Florida City or Homestead.

We recommend an "overview" trip to identify what you really want to spend time on during a mini-vacation. You can take a tour bus as we'll tell you about in going to Miami, or drive to the city and take a trolley tour (or in Key West, the conch train). The narrated trolley tours cover the spectrum and exist in most cities. Sarasota has a Scenic Trolley. You can board the Marco Trolley on Marco Island, Naples Trolley, Mount Dora Trolley, and St. Augustine Trolley; among others. Most trolley tours allow you to get off and get back on later. Even as residents of Naples, we found the trolley tour informative. Our visitors gained from going on the trolley and enjoyed the tour. Most cities also have boat tours, which provide a different perspective.

Following along on our theme of magic 3s, our top three places to go: Key West (Chapter Thirteen), Naples/Fort Myers and Orlando. Our next top three are: Sarasota, St. Augustine, and Mount Dora followed by Tallahassee, Miami, and Tampa. Each has a mix of fascinating historic attractions, fine restaurants, first-class shopping and a wide variety of things to do.

Our Top Three Places to Visit

Chapter Thirteen describes our visits to Key West, our top choice. Orlando easily out-distances all locations in the nation for visitors. That includes us, but we said at the outset that a wealth of information exists for you about Orlando and its attractions (Walt Disney World, Animal Kingdom, Disney MGM Studios, Epcot, Universal Studios Florida, Sea World, and Islands of Adventure). We enjoy going to Orlando, and the theme parks, but all the other destinations have appeal for exploring nearby state parks, refuges, lighthouses, "castles," parks and outdoor activities; which this book emphasizes. In a Top 10 Spring Getaway list, www.Citysearch.com ranked Key West as its top choice and included Miami and Orlando among the top destinations in the United States.

Naples/Fort Myers rounds out our top three, not only because of beaches, shopping, dining, but also because of so many interesting county, state and national parks nearby.

Naples/Fort Myers.

In a 2004 report by CNN/Money on the hottest getaway towns for vacation home buyers, two of the top five are in Florida: Naples and Fort Myers. The cities are not only vacation home havens, but among the top ones in Florida with home value increases. (Others include Boca Raton, Sarasota, Jupiter, Punta Gorda, and Sanibel). *U. S. Housing Markets* cited Lee County (Fort Myers) and Collier County (Naples) as one-two in the hottest housing markets in the nation.

Our top three things to do on a visit using each city as a base, and excluding the beaches and restaurants of which both Collier County (Naples) and Lee County (Fort Myers) have in abundance, follow:

Fort Myers Top Three.

1. J. N. "Ding" Darling National Wildlife Refuge (Chapter Ten).
2. Six-Mile Cypress Slough (Chapter Ten).
3. Edison-Ford Winter Estates, 2350 McGregor Boulevard, phone 239-334-3614, www.edison-ford-estate.com.

"There is only one Fort Myers, and 90 million people are going to find it." Thomas A. Edison. He also said, *"Fools call wise men fools. A wise man never calls any man a fool."*

Edison's winter home, on 13 acres along the Caloosahatchee River, attracts tourists, snowbirds and locals like us who also take the guided formal tour. Once you've done the formal tour as many times as we have, you don't go unless family and friends visit. The Estate people once urged me to volunteer as a guide. Instead of only guided groups, we suggested they have alternate self-guided tours with volunteers stationed to answer questions, a system that works well at Corkscrew Swamp. Nonetheless, everyone we have taken to the Estates has enjoyed the tour; because you not only visit the historic homes of Thomas A. Edison (1847-1931) and Henry Ford (1863-1947), but the botanical gardens, research laboratory and museum. The guide pointed out that the "lab looks about the same as when Edison conducted his last experiments in it." Check out the massive banyan tree, imported from India and given to Edison by Harvey Firestone in 1925. The circumference of the roots exceeds 400 feet. The only larger one we have seen was in Hawaii. You will also see Florida's first swimming pool and several old Ford vehicles.

We have enjoyed the Edison Light Festival Parade and Show in February, which draws large crowds. You can watch from along the streets in the traditional way of watching parades, with 175,000 others, or do what we do: watch the full parade in the high school football stadium. Board one of the more than 50 tour buses that drop you off at Fort Myers High School stadium, where you can watch from a reserved seat. While the 150-unit parade winds its way to the stadium, musical groups entertain followed by a fireworks show. The parade units enter the stadium so you see all the units as they complete the parade. The tour buses follow the parade into the stadium and line up around the track to take you home.

You can also use Fort Myers as a base to visit Koreshan National Historic Site (Chapter Twelve), Pine Island, the "forgotten" island (Chapter Five); Lovers Key (Chapter Five), Solomon's Castle (Chapter Fifteen), Manatee World (5605 Palm Beach Boulevard, Fort Myers, Florida 33905, phone 239-693-1434, www.manateeworld.com.), which has one of the largest congregation of manatees in the wild; and Babcock Wilderness, 8000 State Road 31, Punta Gorda 33982, for a 90-minute narrated swamp buggy tour. Everglades Wonder Gardens in Bonita Springs, phone 239-992-2591, has "over 2,000 species of native wildlife and plants," alligator feeding and "the world's largest American crocodile."

The CREW (Corkscrew Regional Ecosystem Watershed) Marsh has hiking trails and an observation platform that overlooks a marsh area. CREW is 18 miles east from I-75, exit 123, 4600 Corkscrew Road, Estero, Florida 33928, and phone 239-657-2253.

Check out www.fortmyers-sanibel.com for detailed information on the Fort Myers area.

Naples Top Three.

1. Corkscrew Swamp Sanctuary (Chapter Ten)
2. Everglades (Chapter Ten)

3. Caribbean Gardens. 1590 Goodlette-Frank Road, Naples, Florida, phone 239-262-5409, www.napleszoo.com.

Caribbean Gardens Zoo celebrated its fiftieth anniversary in 2004 and eighty-fifty year since its founding as a botanical garden and thirty-fifth year as a zoo, when Lawrence and Nancy Tetzlaf (Jungle Larry and Safari Jane) added animals.

The top three things to do at the 52-acre zoo: go to the open-air Safari Canyon show, watch the feeding of the alligators and take a narrated boat ride around monkey islands. Also, of course, stroll through the zoo to see the exotic animals; and don't miss the Florida panthers! The zoo supports a host of conservation projects.

You can also use Naples as a base to visit Rookery Bay National Estuarine Research Reserve with its environmental learning center, which opened on the twenty-fifth anniversary of the Reserve in 2004. The reserve has three 15-passenger tour boats to see some of the 150 species of birds and animals that thrive within the reserve. You reach the reserve, southeast of Naples, by driving south on State Road 951 from U.S. 41 to Shell Island Road, phone 239-417-6310, www.rookerybay.org.

Also you can visit Collier County Museum, 3301 East Tamiami Trail, Museum of the Everglades, 105 Broadway, Everglades City, Fakahatchee Strand Preserve State Park, take the guided Old Naples Walking Tour (Collier County Historical Society, at Historic Palm Cottage, the second oldest house in Naples, 137 12th Avenue South, phone 239-261-8164), the Teddy Bear Museum, 2511 Pine Ridge; www.teddymuseum.com. and many other activities. Interested in wolves? See them at Shy Wolf Sanctuary Education and Experience Center (by appointment only, call 239-455-1698; www.shywolfsanctuary.org). The non-profit all-volunteer sanctuary, started by Nancy Smith, provides a home for displaced animals; and includes two-dozen wolves and wolf dogs, a Jaguar-Leopard cross, a cougar, coyotes, foxes and "even a Florida Gopher Tortoise." Enjoy the 13-mile canoe trail in 6,300-acre Collier Seminole State Park, 20200 East Tamiami Trail, phone 239-394-3397. The park has one of only three original native stands of Royal Palms in Florida. Remnants of old logging rail beds now make good hiking trails within the swamp.

Collier County has 30 county parks, of which a half dozen are along the beach.

Second Top Three Places to Visit

Sarasota Sojourn Mini Vacation

We packed three major events, lunch, some shopping and a 200-mile roundtrip to elegant Sarasota. into a couple of days in August, a good time to visit without the crush of tourists and snowbirds. Sarasota, which is an hour south of Tampa, makes a good "hub" from which to visit surrounding areas. Money magazine named Sarasota the best little city in the nation. It's noted for its deep appreciation of the arts. We enjoy the contrasts; on the one hand sophisticated, on the other hand casual, large city amenities, yet friendly small-town atmosphere.

John D. MacDonald (1916-1986), prolific writer of 78 books, with 15 million in print, lived in Sarasota. He penned the popular Travis McGee series and probably spawned the current crop of Florida writers of the genre. For purposes of this book, MacDonald's book *Condominium* provides perspective and insights, but my first "discovery" of him was in 1964 with his first Travis McGee novel, *The Deep Blue Good-bye*. He followed it with 20 more books about Florida-based McGee (in his houseboat *The Busted Flush* docked in Fort Lauderdale). Every book has a color in the title.

We visited the Mote Aquarium and Laboratory, had lunch and walked around St. Armand's Circle for some window shopping, then toured the Marie Selby Botanical Gardens and, later, Historic Spanish Point near Osprey. We visited Ca d' Zan during other visits to Sarasota as described in the next chapter. It was closed for several years, including during this visit. The bayside city of Sarasota has beaches at Lido Key and Siesta Key, the 1,800-seat Van Wezel Performing Arts Center, Oscar Scherer State Park, Classic Car Museum, Sarasota Opera (historic house downtown, 61 North Pineapple Avenue) and some world-class shopping and dining.

Mote Aquarium and Laboratory. 1600 Ken Thomson Parkway, Sarasota, Florida 34236, phone 941-388-4441. Check out www.mote.org for discount coupon. William R. (Bill) Mote, founder of the aquarium bearing his name, died at age 93 in 2000. He remained active at the laboratory until his death. Mote, a remarkable man, launched not only the lab in 1965 when he retired and sold his transportation business to Southern Railways, but also world-wide excursions to explore marine life. He moved the Mote Aquarium and Laboratory to its present site in 1978. He donated another $1 million in 1988 to build the 35,000-gallon shark exhibit. He donated $1 million in 1994 to Florida State University to establish a chair for interns to serve at the lab. He made things happen. His personal story adds depth to the tour of this interesting aquarium. It is also a working laboratory. Entrance fee is $10 per person.

Although the aquarium isn't perhaps as awesome as the Florida Aquarium, the Monterey Aquarium or the Tennessee Aquarium, it has worthwhile features those don't have, which makes a visit fun. Two manatees are an attraction, for example. And the lab.

If you go, don't miss the multimedia 12-minute film on sharks. The shark tank has three species of shark: nurse, black nose and sandbar. In among them are tarpon, other fish and a 350-pound grouper. Why don't the sharks eat the other fish? The guide said, "The sharks are well fed so don't pose a risk to the fish." Shark research at the lab focuses on the fact that sharks appear immune to many diseases, including cancer. Why? The answer may provide help from these fearsome predators for humans. They may turn out to be saviors. Mote Lab is working on it.

We enjoyed touching the stingrays in the Rays Touch Tank (yes, stingers had been clipped). Sea Horses amaze me because they are the most ornate and delicate looking of the fish, even though most are less than six inches. Sea turtles, the stranded dolphin and whale hospital and snook breeding are all in a separate building. It also included during one of our visits, Hugh and Buffett, two manatees; one 12 years old, the other 16 years old and 1,400 pounds (at the time of the visit).

After an educational tour of the Mote Aquarium on Lido Key, we stopped at St. Armand's Circle nearby, which boasts more than 100 upscale specialty shops, clothing boutiques, galleries and restaurants. What was a tiny fishing village now is an upscale shopping area. Try crab cakes or amberjack at the Crab and Fin Restaurant. On another day, we ate at Marina Jack's Restaurant (on downtown bayfront at 2 Marina Plaza). We sat by a "wall of glass" and watched the boats cruise on the bay.

Marie Selby Botanical Gardens. 811 South Palm Avenue, Sarasota, Florida 34236. At the gardens, which opened more than 25 years ago, we strolled first into the display house where among scores of orchid species was the Dove (sometimes called the Holy Ghost) orchid. Entrance cost is $12 per person. Selby has 15 distinct gardens, including Banyan Grove, Wildflower, The Fernery, Live Oak Grove, Hibiscus and others on the 11 bay-front acres with 20,000 colorful plants. The gardens display thousands of orchids and bromeliads.

Garden columnist Duane Campbell called the gardens the "supernova in the constellation of botanical gardens." It's easy to agree with him. The former mansion is now the museum and store. They also sell plants. Some of these are small air plants (bromeliads), which absorb nutrients through their leaves and do not require soil. A creative way to have these indoors is to put them in a large seashell, which they can happily enjoy.

We walked by a stand of bamboo that creaked and groaned in the wind, evoking a feeling of being on an old sailing ship. We stopped at the large bo tree, sacred in the Hindu and Buddhist religions, and listened as the wind rustled the leaves like silk taffeta. The red, white and black mangroves along the shore are clearly identified and explained. We looked at the peeling red bark of the jumbo limbo tree, nicknamed the "tourist tree" (because of the bark peeling off in layers being reminiscent of peeling, sunburned vacationers).

We returned to the gardens in December to see the "Lights in Bloom," which featured the gardens in thousands of twinkling lights at every weekend. The pathways wind through nine acres lighted for the holidays. For information, call 941-366-5731, www.selby.org. To get there from interstate 75, take Exit 210 west seven miles to U.S. 41 and turn left, go three traffic lights, and then take the first right onto Palm Avenue. Parking is across the street from the entrance at the end of the block.

Spanish Point. A few miles south from the Selby Gardens, on Highway 41 near Osprey, the Historic Spanish Point sticks out into Little Sarasota Bay like a finger beckoning to "come here." The visitor center, on the National Register of Historic Buildings, once a school built in the 1920s, now houses exhibits, museum shop, ticket counter and small movie theater. Tour costs $7 per person. Before you go, print out a walking map and discount coupon at www.historicspanishpoint.org. Gulf Coast Heritage Association, Inc, a not for profit corporation, operates the point, 337 North Tamiami Trail, Osprey, Florida 34229, phone 941-966-5214.

Walk from the parking lot, into a 30-acre quiet oasis in bustling Sarasota County, for a fascinating history lesson of three eras: prehistoric, pioneer times (1867-1910) and the Palmer era (1910-1918). Bertha Palmer, widow of Chicago magnate Potter Palmer, bought a large portion of Sarasota County. Bertha developed magnificent formal gardens and lawns around pioneer dwellings, including the Sunken Garden and Pergola; which are impressive today. The Palmer family donated the site in 1980.

Point cottage, built in 1931 for Potter Palmer III and his wife, is now an educational center. We clambered up 18-foot high middens (shell mounds, and ancient "trash heaps," which provide clues to life when the Indians occupied the Point). The Cock's Footbridge provides a view of the mangrove shoreline. John Webb and five children came from New York in 1867, settled on the point and farmed 10 acres. The restored Webb packinghouse shows where the Webb's processed citrus fruit for shipment to Key West on their own schooners. The Guptill house, built in 1901, on a shell mound, by Frank and Lizzie Webb Guptill, reflects the pioneer era. Mary's Chapel, in a grove of trees, is alongside a pioneer cemetery, where the Webb family is buried. Mary's Chapel is often used for weddings these days. Palmer bought all the Webb family land and buildings in 1910.

Myakka State Park. 13207 State Road 72, Sarasota (9 miles east of Interstate 75 from exit 210), phone 941-361-6511. The largest, and one of the oldest state parks, with 45 square miles of wetlands, prairies and woodlands, and two shallow lakes, features an unusual 85-feet long suspended walkway 25 feet high between two towers. The park has 39 miles of hiking trails; fishing, camping and airboat tours. A seven-mile scenic drive winds through the park. The Civilian Conservation Corps (CCC) started working on the park in 1934. It opened in 1942. As with many other parks, early restoration efforts focused on correcting decades of fire exclusion (unintended consequences) that happened before people understood the dependency of grasslands on fires. The park has a few log cabins it rents. Airboats will take you on a scenic cruise on the Upper Myakka Lake. The park teems with interesting wildlife.

St. Augustine Anamnesis, Mini Vacation.

Rather than visit St. Augustine on our own on our first trip, we joined a group bus tour to St. Augustine in December. It seemed like a good idea at the time, but this was a trip not soon to be forgotten, but recalled (anamnesis) and talked about because of mishaps.

"We had fun anyway," said Hank, one of the tour group people. His comment echoed the feelings of his wife, Joan, and most of the people on the trip. Another couple, Sandy and Don said, "Despite the cold and problems, we had a wonderful time. The camaraderie of the people was great."

The bus had gone only a short distance in Fort Myers when a problem developed. First the driver tried to fix a problem with the step that would not fully retract. He called his office. They sent a mechanic to work on it. He gave up, so the bus parked near a Burger King to await a replacement bus. The driver transferred the bags to the new bus and we pulled away after an unscheduled hour-long "breakfast stop!"

The tour guide, Marty, a retired school principal, entertained us with stories, jokes and games on the long bus ride. Little did he know, that the bus problem was simply a prelude to further "challenges" for him. Someone said: "If you will be a traveler, have always two bags very full; one of patience and another of money." Certainly patience and humor helped.

We stopped at the Mercado Center in Orlando for lunch, where the group scattered into several restaurants. The Crab House got the highest marks. We arrived at our hotel in the historic district of St. Augustine late afternoon. The promised cookies, punch and welcome mugs failed to show. Some of the programmed "keys" didn't work. There were also some room problems, but these were taken care of by moving some people to new rooms. One couple had a room with bugs, so the people were moved. No telling what happened to the bugs.

For dinner, we boarded the bus for a short ride to a private dining room at Fiddler's Green on the bay. The restaurant, which served excellent food, is built on the former site of a casino built in 1926. Fiddler's Green is a seafaring term for sailor's paradise, "Where credit is good, and is always a lass, a glass, and a song." It lived up to the name!

St. Augustine, the nation's oldest continuously occupied city, already had a fort, a church, a hospital, a seminary and 120 houses, when the pilgrims landed at Plymouth Rock in 1620. Ponce de León had landed here in 1503, followed by Pedro Menéndez de Avilés, who founded St. Augustine September 8, 1565! St. Augustine stands as a living history of more than four centuries. That alone makes a visit worthwhile, especially if you are a history buff.

Sunday dawned cold (46 degrees) and blustery. At 9 a. m. we assembled in the lobby for the narrated trolley tour. The open-air trailers pulled by a train replica arrived on time and we boarded for a cold ride. Half way into the tour, the driver's boss called and told him to return immediately. He had the wrong group! We returned to the hotel where four-dozen frustrated people were impatiently waiting. Some were irate. Off they went in the "train."

The tour guide scrambled and made calls. The trolley that was supposed to have come, to take us on our tour, finally arrived. We rode to their start point at the old county jail. The manager profusely apologized. Apparently a driver called in sick. Whatever. We asked for a closed bus instead of the open-air trolley. The manager agreed and threw in a free tour of the county jail.

"What could happen next?" someone asked. "Don't ask!" another exclaimed. Most of the group took all this in stride and joked about the mishaps. Laughter is like changing a baby's diaper; it doesn't permanently solve any problem, but it makes things more acceptable for a while. Besides, we could compare the tour guide's chatter on the first half of the tour. The first guy was better, especially in explaining why a 600-year old tree was called "The Senator" (either because it was "shady" or because of all the "crooked" branches). We toured the old jail when we completed the tour. The tour guide at the jail, a retired corrections officer on a mission to dispel how movies portray jails, told us far more than we wanted to know about the jail, hangings and electrocutions. He had participated in nine executions, he said.

We were on our own for the afternoon. "With the temperature in the 40s, we don't have to worry about long lines," one person joked. We shopped on St. George Street, looked through startlingly realistic wax figures of famous people at Potter's Wax Museum (when Al Capone's head turns, you do a double take) and toured the Lightner Museum, which features antiques, including cut glass and the work of Louis Comfort Tiffany. Two women who toured the Fountain of Youth got locked in! We joined many others checking out the Old St. Augustine Village with nine historic houses that date back to the 1700s.

We visited the massive Castillo de San Marcos (Castle of St. Mark) Fort, which was built in the seventeenth century. We stood on the one of the four Bastions as "soldiers," in period costumes, fired two cannons. Touring the old fort is a "don't miss." It was built entirely of slabs of coquina, which consists of tiny mollusk shells cemented together by their own lime. When the British bombarded the fort in 1702, the walls, rather than shattering, simply absorbed the cannonballs. Freshwater wells in the fort are just eight feet deep. The fort never lost a battle and was never taken. Townspeople flocked to the fort during the 38-day siege of the British, who finally gave up and left.

What formerly was Henry Flagler's opulent hotel, the Ponce de Leon, now houses Flagler College. St. Augustine owes much to Henry Flagler for his remarkable vision and investments. He found a dream that only someone of immense wealth could fulfill and finance. The Florida Heritage Museum, which features the gilded age of Henry Flagler, includes a 40-foot model railroad showing development by him down the Florida East Coast to Key West. Most historians credit Flagler with developing the East Coast cities of Florida, especially St. Augustine.

Other attractions include the oldest house, oldest school, Museum of Weapons, Ripley's Believe it or Not, and Alligator Farm. We window-shopped as we wandered down narrow cobblestone streets. On a later trip we got a "scare" out of a ghost tour of the historic district at night. The tour guide kept interest alive with gripping ghost stories. We picked up a paperback copy of *Ghosts of St. Augustine* by Tom Lapham that has 24 ghost stories. In short, you have lots to see and interesting things to do!

Monday morning the temperature plunged to 35 degrees. We were scheduled for a boat tour. The blustery wind now approached a gale. "Is this Florida?" someone asked. As it turned out, the Victory III 90-foot tour boat had enclosed and open decks. Nearly everyone wisely chose the enclosed deck and enjoyed a 75-minute narrated tour of the bay area. After

212

lunch we boarded the bus for the six-hour journey home. Believe it or not, the trip home proved to be uneventful. We watched a video and napped.

Despite the problems and mishaps of this trip, the group had fun. Today, too often, everyone's fixing the blame and nobody's fixing the problem. Not on this trip. Marty, the tour guide, worked hard to get things straightened out. Tour members were resilient and part of the solution, not the problem. For the price, seeing St. Augustine this way makes sense, especially for a first visit. "The one thing we would change would be to go in a warmer month," said one tour member. "Otherwise, we had fun and enjoyed the trip." Yes, we agree! Our subsequent visits, including one focused just on touring the lighthouse, were in warmer weather and out of the peak season crowds. On our next trip, we once again "crossed over the bridge," the famous Bridge of Lions, to the lighthouse. The bridge, 77 years old in 2004, needed either repair or replacement. We would vote for repair and preservation. For more information, look at www.visitoldcity. com.

Jacksonville, home of the super bowl in 2005, an easy 45-minute drive north of St. Augustine, offers a big city atmosphere, along with nearby places to explore, including museums, Kingsley Plantation, Fort Caroline National Memorial, and Fort Clinch State Park on Amelia Island, the northernmost barrier island in Florida. The Jacksonville 20-mile coastline has some excellent beaches.

Mount Dora

Sheesh! A mountain in Florida! Hey, I have a T-shirt emblazoned with *I Climbed Mount Dora* to prove it. Well, not quite. We did trudge up from a boat ride to the full height of Mount Dora, which falls somewhat short of America's most visited mountain, Pikes Peak....by nearly 14,000 feet at 184 feet above sea level!

Joking aside, you must go to Mount Dora, a quaint little town (population 10,000) alongside a lake 35 miles northwest of Orlando. "This is what Florida used to be," one visitor noted. Mount Dora has the small-town charm of an old New England village plopped down into Florida. The Chamber of Commerce occupies the old 1903 Railway Depot, 341 N. Alexander Street.

A Mecca for collectors, Mount Dora has more antique stores per square foot than anywhere in Florida in a town with many turn of the century (no not that one but the nineteenth century) buildings. Renninger's Antique Extravaganza, held in January and February, draws thousands to its expo of 1,500 dealers arranged on 117 acres.

The antique boat show in April includes the spiffy wood 1930 Chris Craft we saw speeding across Lake Dora. With 1,400 lakes in Lake County, boats have ample room to run.

Ride the 1930 Dora Doodlebug self propelled rail car on a one-hour eight-mile trip on historic rails dating back to the 1880s. That makes for a fun nostalgia trip and diversion.

Mount Dora Doodlebug

Check out the road trolley that leaves the Lakeside Inn for a one-hour narrated tour of Mount Dora. Doing this first gives you a good overview and saves time later in pinpointing your later stops. A drive along the lakeshore offers tall pines, moss-laden oaks on one side, some palatial homes and lake views on the other.

We stayed at the 1883 Lakeside Inn, 100 North Alexander Street, Mount Dora, Florida.30757, phone 352-383-4101, which is a "traditional bed and breakfast" inn on the National Registry of Historic Places. There are also several bed and breakfast inns, a Comfort Inn and a Hampton Inn.

Mount Dora, with Eustis (population 15,000), four miles away and Tavares (population 10,000), six miles away, made up the Golden Triangle in the lake country when orange groves thrived in the area.

One of the top things to do is to hop on the Captain Doolittle, a modern (2003) 32-passenger luxury pontoon boat equipped with two environmentally friendly 90 HP motors, for either a 2-hour tour across Lake Dora and through the Dora Canal or an all-day (9 a.m. to 5 p.m.) Jungle Cruise. We tried the two-hour tour first and enjoyed it immensely particularly the time in the one-mile long Dora Canal, called the most beautiful mile in the world by famous sportswriter Grantland Rice (1880-1954), noted for immortalizing Notre Dame's *Four Horsemen*. Rice said: "A wise man makes his own decisions; an ignorant man follows public opinion."

Captains Ralph and Don expertly navigated through the narrow areas and narrated the voyage. The wildlife cooperated. We saw a family of wood ducks, a raccoon, river otter, dozens of great blue herons, and egrets in an area teeming with wildlife. The night before, on a night cruise, Captain Ralph spotted a rare black-crowned night heron, which fishes at night. Turtles poked their heads through the water surface as they swam languidly along. Anhingas perched on tree branches to dry their wings. We passed by 500-year old bald cypress trees and the remains of one reportedly 1,500 years old! Oddly, it reminded me of the tourist attraction "old crag" atop a mountain in Taiwan, because it really wasn't much to see.

The all-day Jungle Excursion winds up through Lake Dora, through the Dora Canal, Haines Creek, Lake Griffin, Ocklawaha River, through the Moss Bluff lock and through the Silver Springs area where 30 movies were made, including six of the Tarzan movies in the 1930s. You can see descendants of the monkeys used in the Tarzan movies, swinging from the branches along the banks. Lawrence "Jungle Larry" Tetzlaff (1919-1984) doubled for Johnny Weissmuller in the Tarzan movies and later brought exotic animals in 1969 to Caribbean Gardens Zoo in Naples, which is still run by his family. The producers of the old series *Sea Hunt,* which starred Lloyd Bridges, filmed 100 episodes here. With 150 natural springs at the head of the Silver River, the crystal-clear spring water could service the city of New York.

"You can travel all the way to Jacksonville by water from Lake Dora," Captain Ralph said as we dawdled in Dora Canal. Check out prices and schedule at www.captaindoolittle.com

You can headquarter in Mount Dora and visit nearby 10 state parks within less than an hour, including Blue Springs State Park, which holds a manatee festival in January and Wekiwa Springs State Park south of Mount Dora near Apopka. At Wekiwa (Timucuan Indian for "bubbling water"), the springs pump more than 40 million gallons a day into the Wekiva (flowing river) River. You can snorkel at both Blue Springs and Wekiwa Springs State Parks, which are also about one hour from Orlando. Apopka is the Timucuan Indians word for "potato-eating place."

North of Mount Dora, near Lake City (two hour drive) and White Springs are three interesting places to visit: Olustee Battlefield State Historic Site, 888-acre Stephen Foster Folk Culture Center State Park and the Nature and Heritage Tourism Center on the Suwannee River in historic White Springs. The Nature and Heritage Tourism Center (phone 386-397-4461), at Highways 136 and 41 off exit 84 from Interstate 75 showcases nature-based, cultural and historic Florida venues.

Stephen Foster's (1826-1864) song "Old Folks at Home" immortalized the Suwannee River. Since 1935, the song has been the Florida state song. The park has hiking and bicycling trails, a museum, a three-day music festival in January (140th anniversary of his death celebrated January 13,

2004) and a fiddle contest in May. For information see www.floridastateparks.org/stephenfoster. "Oh! Susanna."

The Olustee Battefield (12 miles east of Lake City), site of the largest Civil War battle in Florida, pitted 5,500 Confederate troops against an equal number of Union troops. More than 2,800 were killed or wounded February 20, 1864. Battle re-enactments occur in February. The Union troops included three regiments of blacks with the 54th made famous in the movie "Glory," which starred Denzel Washington and Morgan Freeman.

If you're up to driving further north, Big Shoals, the only stretch of major whitewater rapids in Florida, is 14 miles north of Lake City. On the way, in Cross Creek near Gainesville, is the home of Marjorie Kinnan Rawlings. A visit to the home will give you insights into frontier life in the swamps and this Pulitzer prize-winning author. She wrote, "The earth may be borrowed but not bought. It may be used but not owned."

Another Three Interesting Places to Visit

Tallahassee, Miami and Tampa.

You're Never Too Old

Tallyho Tallahassee.

Carol and Howard, inspired by some of our Florida travel stories, asked us about going to Tallahassee. They had thought about going to Tallahassee ever since they came to Florida in 1983. Finally, after nearly two decades, they planned the trip. But they had some obstacles to hurdle first. Howard had triple bypass surgery. He was mostly bedridden for a couple of months. When he felt well enough to travel, he and Carol visited up North, where he contracted bronchitis. The doctor recommended he return to Florida to recover. So this trip, which they longed to take, presented an even greater challenge than they foresaw. Six months after the heart surgery, they used a pleasant day in October to drive the 420 miles from Fort Myers to Tallahassee, registered at a motel and relaxed that evening for a tour the next day.

The morning of the day after they arrived in Tallahassee, they drove to the capitol from the motel and found, to their dismay, that all the parking lots had "employees only" signs on them. They finally found a police officer and asked about parking. He pointed down the hill. They ended up parking on the street at a four-hour parking meter, three blocks away. Determined to view the old and new state capitol buildings, they gamely trudged up the hill. They learned that the Capitol is 200 feet above sea level. Howard said, "Those who believe there are no hills in Florida can check out Tallahassee!"

The old capitol building, built in 1845 when Florida became a state, and remodeled in 1902, has been restored to turn-of-the-century splendor. It is in the shadow of the 22-story new capitol building, which was dedicated in 1978. Upon arrival at the building, they faced a daunting climb of perhaps 65 steps to get to the first floor. Once there, Howard and Carol joined a group with a tour guide. One highlight of the tour was the glassed-in twenty-second floor, which gives the visitor an unobstructed view of all of Tallahassee. "The view was positively spectacular," Carol said.

Howard's eyes sparkled when he said the knowledgeable tour guide explained the stories behind the rooms and the furniture, and about the people and lore that make up Florida's rich heritage. The old capitol has witnessed more than 155 years of political history, wars, rapid expansion and cultural upheaval. Carol said, "So many people come to Florida and know little about the history of the state. We find that learning more about the history, makes us more appreciative of what we have here.

The nearby Museum of Florida History, 500 S. Bronough Street, includes many artifacts from the early years. Long before Europeans arrived, in 1639, Tallahassee had already been the capital of the 30,000 Native Americans of the region, known as the Apalachee. Tallahassee is an Apalachee word meaning "old fields." Carol said, "There are so many rooms and so much to see, you can get lost in the museum. They even have a reconstructed steamboat." The museum also has "Herman," a skeletal prehistoric mastodon removed from Wakulla Springs.

Downtown 90-minute guided walking tours of historic Tallahassee, include the Columns, the oldest structure (1830) still standing in Tallahassee, and the magnificent homes on Calhoun Street, known as "Gold Dust Street" because so many prominent people lived there in the early nineteenth century. There are also two-hour walking and van tours, but you can choose to do-it-on-your-own as Howard and Carol did. These include walking under natural canopies of green tunnels formed by massive live oak overhanging limbs.

The 52-acre outdoor Tallahassee Museum of History and Natural Sciences, 3945 Museum Drive, features a zoo, historic buildings and a nature trail.

This was a fun trip but as Carol pointed out, there's so much to see in Tallahassee that you would need a week, not just a few days. There are plantations to see, historic churches, art galleries, the Spanish mission (San Luis de Apalachee), Ponce de Leon Park, and several museums. Florida State and Florida A&M have campuses here. Monticello is nearby.

Their never-grow-old mentality inspired others to take the trip and explore not only Tallahassee, but also the surrounding area to learn, explore and discover cultural, architectural and historic Florida.

Drive south from Tallahassee and take a walk or the jungle cruise at Wakulla Springs State Park, 550 Wakulla Park Drive, State Road 267, phone 850-224-5956. At St. Marks National Wildlife Refuge there's a lighthouse as well as trails and wildlife. At Carrabelle, see the Crooked River Lighthouse. At St. George Island State Park, 1900 E. Gulf Beach Drive, south of Apalachicola, check out the Cape St. George Lighthouse.

While in the northwest, you can also drive over to Pensacola, although the "Cradle of Naval Aviation" may warrant a separate visit. Pensacola is 200 miles west of Tallahassee, but worth a visit to see the beautiful stretch of beach, Gulf Islands National Seashore, one of the most visited national parks, the zoo, and the National Museum of Naval Aviation. You can also tour Historic Pensacola Village. The Panhandle part of the Florida birding trail, with 78 birding sites, opened in 2004 at Big Lagoon State Park. April and May are good birding months to visit Apalachicola National Forest.

Miami.

Although we had been in and out of Miami a number of times, and had visited some nearby places, we had not really "seen" Miami. We found the best way by accident when friends mentioned going on a tour bus. We went along. How else could you do all that we did in a day? We rode in a Premium Tour (phone 239-435-7997) 57-passenger "deluxe European-style motor coach" for sightseeing in South Beach, Coral Gables, Coconut Grove and the Art Deco district; a boat ride, a tour of the historic Biltmore Hotel, lunch at Bayside, shopping and dinner. The experienced tour guide professionally pointed out key facts we would not have known had we simply driven by on our own.

Miami effuses history. Hey, only in Florida would 70-year old buildings be historic, but the "Art Deco Historic District has 800 of them in pastel confetti-like colors," according to the tour guide. We passed by chic restaurants and sidewalk cafes. The bus wound its way through Miami, Miami Beach, glitzy South Beach and Coral Gables with running commentary from Harry our knowledgeable tour guide.

George E. Merrick (1886-1942) designed and built "the most famous suburb," one of the first planned communities, Coral Gables. He called it "City Beautiful." A dreamer, who could also execute his dream, Merrick envisioned in 1922 the Biltmore Hotel, Venetian Pool, a university, a grand City Hall and a Spanish-tile community of broad tree-lined boulevards. Coral Gables, just three miles from Miami International Airport, is headquarters for more than 175 major international corporations. We stopped to look at the rock swimming pool Merrick created. He designed the 820,000-gallon Venetian Pool (2701 DeSoto Boulevard).

We saw the city hall, the shops, galleries and restaurants of the Coral Gables shopping district of the Miracle Mile with elegant buildings of Mediterranean and Italianate architecture. We toured the enduring legacy of the National Historical Landmark Biltmore Hotel, including viewing the largest hotel pool in the United States, where Johnny Weissmuller (1904-1984) instructed swimming and broke a world record. He captured five gold medals in the 1924 and 1928 Olympics and made 20 Tarzan movies. He lived in Fort Lauderdale 1965-1973.

The Biltmore Hotel, a hospital from 1940-1968, sat empty until restoration started in 1983 with an opening in 1987. Colorful finches chirp in ornate cages in the lobby. "Al Capone had a suite on the first floor before World War II, when the hotel attracted celebrities like Judy Garland, Bing Crosby, Ginger Rogers and the Duke and Duchess of Windsor" our guide told us.

We lunched on chicken mango salad at Lombardi Ristoranti next to the Port of Miami. After lunch, we boarded a boat for a "scenic sightseeing cruise." Our tour boat motored past the homes of the "rich and famous" and the many man-made islands in the bay. That left time for shopping at Bayside and dinner at Bubba Gump's, before heading for home.

As you can see, the tour gave us a good introduction to Miami and pinpointed areas for future visits. We have gone to Miami for Dolphin football games, for shopping and to visit nearby attractions, such as Vizcaya and Deering Estates, and Bill Baggs State Park (with Cape Florida lighthouse).

Tampa.

Tampa makes for a great base for exploring the surrounding area. As with many of our visits, one of the first trips to Tampa was with a tour bus to Ybor City (pronounced EE-bore) to see the historic district and have lunch at the famed restaurant, Columbia, 2025 East 7th Avenue. Ybor City, named for Vincente Martinez Ybor, who established a cigar factory in 1886, is one of three National Historic Landmark Districts. Once home to more than 200 cigar factories, it now contains restaurants, boutiques, coffeehouses, and nightclubs. We visited the Ybor City Museum and took a guided walking tour.

We drove to Tampa on another occasion to visit the Lowry Park Zoo, 7530 North Boulevard, phone 813-935-8552, www.lowryparkzoo.com, with its 1,500 animals, and to tour the world-class Florida Aquarium, 701 Channelside Drive, phone 813-273-4000, www.flaquarium.org.

So, our top three for Tampa: Ybor City, Lowry Park Zoo and Florida Aquarium. Soon after a visit to Cypress Gardens, Florida's first theme park, it closed. In 2004, a buyer of the park announced plans to reopen it. Busch Gardens, however, remains a popular destination.

Rather than drive, we took a tour bus with some other couples to the enclosed Tampa Bay Devil Rays Stadium to take in a baseball game.

We stayed a week on St. Petersburg Beach and used it as a base to explore the barrier islands, boat and visit lighthouses and parks and the Salvador Dali Museum, 1000 Third Street South in St. Petersburg, phone 727-823-3761, www.salvadordalimuseum.org.

Along with friends, and members of a professional association, we visited the thriving Greek Village of Tarpon Springs 30 miles north of Clearwater. Mary caught a small-shark to win a fishing contest.

Chapter Fifteen
Florida's Gilded Age Castles

We visited each of Florida's three Gilded-Age castles on separate trips in the fall of a year, before the tide of tourists and snowbirds arrived. Trips included tours of opulent Gilded-Age Estates *Vizcaya* in Miami, *Whitehall* in Palm Springs and *Ca d' Zan* in Sarasota. These three in Florida are among the Top Ten in the United States.

In the past, we visited gilded-age castles in Newport, Rhode Island (Marble House, The Breakers, Rosecliff, and The Elms), Hearst Castle in San Simeon, California and Biltmore Estate, Asheville, N.C. Mark Twain gave the name to an age of wealth, the Gilded Age. The Roaring Twenties saw the peak. This time of unprecedented change and technological advance, made some men uncommonly wealthy. The men, wealthy beyond what most of us can imagine today, nearly a century before dot and com were introduced to each other, believed anything was possible.

In Newport, Marble House, built by William K. Vanderbilt for $11 million in the late 1800s, included $7 million spend on imported marble. Elaborate ceiling frescoes and wall coverings impressed us The Breakers, perhaps the most elaborate of the Newport mansions, has 70 rooms. Built by Cornelius Vanderbilt II on 13 acres, the estate reflects the "obscene wealth" of the era, according to one critic. Hollywood filmed *High Society* and *The Great Gatsby* (1974) at the Rosecliff mansion, called a "French palace" because it reflects the architect's inspiration of the Grand Trianon in Versailles. The palace also has the largest ballroom of all the Newport mansions (40 by 80 feet).

Other castles include Nemours, the Alfred I. duPont estate in Wilmington, Delaware; Fenway Court in Boston and the Vanderbilt mansion in Hyde Park, New York. The Nemour mansion, built in 1909 has 102 rooms. Although small in number, all these mansions have much in common: all were products of architects trained at the Ecole des Beaux-Arts, all were furnished with antiques coming from France, Spain and Italy, and all were built in a 35-year period from 1890 through 1929 and the stock market crash. Most of the owners were "captains of industry" or industrialists. Some of the owners were personally involved in the design of their "monuments" (including John and Mabel Ringling of Ca d' Zan, Hearst, and James Deering of Vizcaya).

By the 1960s most of the castles became historic museums. When we toured the castles in Rhode Island and California, we marveled at them but didn't grasp the bigger historical picture they reflected of a time in America of significance. What can we learn from the visions of the men who built the castles? When we visited the Florida castles, we did gain an understanding of the effect of these men beyond simply creating a monument. Henry Flagler created much more than a castle and impacted Florida perhaps more than any person.

Most of the castles take your breath away, but our favorite, which is not the largest, nor the most expensive, is Ca d' Zan. Our favorite individual, however, is Henry Flagler and you'll see why when you read about Whitehall and his accomplishments.

Ca d' Zan. 5401 Bayshore Road, Sarasota, Florida 34243, www. ringling.org.

The 22,000 square foot mansion built by John and Mabel Ringling, named Ca d' Zan means "House of John."

I'm standing on the large expanse of marble terrace, looking at the palatial palace from the waterfront. Warm memories transport me momentarily to times in Venice, one of our favorite places in the world. We have a sense of déjà vu, as though we are looking at the Doge's Palace and the hotel we stayed at during one of our visits, the Danieli. Were we impressed? You bet. We vow to return, but this was not to be, at least for seven years, because after our first visit, the state closed the mansion to tours for renovation. It did not re-open until 2002.

Did John Ringling (1866-1936), as he looked at his ostentatious dream home recall Venice? Yes. And so did Mabel Ringling. We later learned that Mabel wanted architectural elements of the Doge's Palace in Venice and features from her favorite Venetian hotels, the Danieli and Bauer-Grunwald. She toured Europe taking photographs of buildings and furnishings.

Ringling hired Dwight James Baum in 1921, after buying the property in 1912, to design the 200-foot long, 32-room Venetian Gothic mansion, one of the last of the Gilded Age "castles." Builders worked three years to complete it in 1926 at a cost of $1.5 million, plus another half-million dollars for furnishings and art. Ringling had the bay dredged so yachts of any size could drop anchor at the dock. Mabel moored her Venetian gondola at the dock, which you reach by walking down 13 marble steps.

The builder brought from Italy columns, doorways, balustrades, arched windows and accents all in the Venetian Renaissance style. The builder shipped in terra cotta decorative tile, glazed finishes that would withstand Florida's bright sun. Mabel personally supervised to make sure the colors were correct, and visited the kilns to be sure of color precision.

John and Mabel Ringling moved in at Christmas 1926. A 60-foot tower, which they illuminated when they were in residence, tops the mansion. As with so many grand castles, the Ringling's enjoyed the winter home only briefly. Mabel died in 1929 of diabetes at age 54, less than three years after completion of construction, but not before entertaining celebrities, including Will Rogers, Florenz Ziegfield, Billie Burke, Mayor Jimmy Walker of New York, and Rudolph Valentino.

We enjoyed touring, not only the mansion, but the Circus Museum, Art Museum and Rose Garden on the 66-acre estate. The Art Museum, which is full of masterpieces by Reubens, Van Dyck and other baroque masters, has 21 galleries. The collection includes more than 600 paintings, sculptures and 25 tapestries. The reference collection includes 60,000 volumes. We walked in the courtyard inhabited with dozens of Roman and Greek gods and goddesses, fountains and columns; experiencing again the Venetian feeling.

The last surviving brother of the five Ringling brothers who built the circus, John Ringling said: "We divided the work, but stood together." In 1929 he bought American Circus Corporation, which owned five circuses. He then owned all the major circus railroad shows. An astute businessman, he bought land and invested in St. Armand's Circle, Bird Key and Lido Key. When he died he left an endowment of $1.2 million to care for the estate. Not as astute as John Ringling, the state grew the $1.2 million only to $1.8 million in six decades. Why are you not surprised?

When he died at age 70 in 1936, Ringling left Ca d' Zan, the Art Museum and grounds to the people of Florida. In 2000, the Florida legislature appointed Florida State University guardian of the estate. The restoration, which cost $15 million, "drew on the talents of craftsmen and artisans," a docent said. He added the most difficult task was "modernizing the home's air system and fire protection." The mansion sparkles today and provides you a Venetian experience without traveling to Italy!

Tours cost $15. A private docent-led, hour-long tour of the third and fourth floors is available for $20. Call 941-358-3180 for advance tickets and for a guarantee of a tour time. First-come first-served tours start at 9:45 a.m. To get there from I-75, take exit 213 west on University Parkway to the estate. The Sarasota Scenic Loop Trolley arrives hourly during the day.

Vizcaya, 3251 South Miami Avenue, Miami, Florida 32129, phone 305-250-9133, www.vizcayamuseum.com. The Italian Renaissance style "villa" (34 rooms) built by industrialist James Deering (International Harvester) took 1,000 workers two years to complete the construction in 1916. Deering wintered at the estate until his death in 1925.

Vizcaya, along with Hearst's San Simeon and the Biltmore, were self-sufficient estates. Originally Vizcaya consisted of 140 acres with a dairy, poultry house, mule stable, and greenhouse and staff residents. Deering employed three architects: F. Burrall Hoffman designed the buildings, Diego Suarez planned the gardens, and Paul Chalfin supervised the project. Deering purchased all the furniture, lighting fixtures, doors, and other decorative elements in shopping trips throughout Europe. The mansion, filled with furnishings and arts from the fifteenth through nineteenth centuries, gives the appearance of a family living in the mansion through several generations, each adding to the furnishings. The builders could not complete the gardens until 1921 because of World War I.

The hurricane of 1926 severely damaged Vizcaya. Miami-Dade County purchased it in 1952, restored it and the remaining 50 acres to the way they appeared when Deering lived there. County commissioners granted governing authority in 1988 to the Vizcaya Museum and Gardens Trust, which is dedicated to preserving "in its historical context the legacy of a romantic Italian villa on Biscayne Bay." We appreciated our tour of the estate and their efforts. After touring the mansion, we strolled through the 10 acres of formal gardens filled with ornate garden fountains and statues. We also stopped in at the gift shop and café.

Whitehall, the lavish mansion built in 1902 in Palm Beach by Henry Morrison Flagler (1830-1913), a co-founder of Standard Oil with John D. Rockefeller, is an interesting museum not only because of this glimpse of a fascinating time, but also because of what Flagler meant to the development of Florida's East Coast. A remarkable man of vision, and especially persistent in the pursuit of his vision, he fulfilled his dream.

A few people can plan bodacious goals and visions, but not carry out the dream. A few action-oriented people can execute intricate plans. Very few can do both well. Flagler heads that exclusive list of a century ago. He hired strong people, solved challenging problems of building a railroad in swamps and erecting bridges to connect islands. He poured millions of his own money into the project. Some financiers viewed the project as unthinkable. Some engineers called the problems impossible. He came up with the plan when he was 74 years old! He turned 82 before his people completed the project.

Flagler built Florida East Coast Railway from Jacksonville to Key West. Along the way he erected luxury hotels in St. Augustine, Daytona, Palm Beach and Miami. He established tourism in Florida. In the process he bought and owned two million acres and established agriculture. Tourism and agriculture remain powerful economic forces today. He lived to see his dream of extending the rail line to Key West from Miami come true as he traveled to Key West in his luxurious private railcar in 1912. He died a year later. Flagler, a private person, once said in response to a criticism that he didn't like to talk about himself. "I prefer to let what I have done speak for me."

The New York Herald called Flagler's mansion, at Cocoanut Row and Whitehall Way, Palm Beach, Florida 33480, the "Taj Mahal of North America," phone 561-655-2833, www.flagler.org.

The numbers, 55 rooms, including 22 bathrooms and 18 servants' rooms in 60,000 square feet, impressive as they are, don't begin to reflect the elegance, opulence and grandeur; and, yes, the excessiveness of the Gilded Age. We can view it, thanks to Jean Flagler Matthews, a granddaughter who clearly inherited some of his entrepreneurial genes. The estate had been used as a hotel from 1925 until 1959 when it ran into financial difficulties. Matthews stepped in, rescued the mansion, formed a non-profit corporation, and opened it in 1960 as a museum. As a former turnaround specialist, I admire her prompt decisive action. Her grandfather would be proud.

When you walk into the Grand Hall, its ceiling depicts the "Crowning of Knowledge" with two paintings flanking the central dome depicting "Prosperity" and "Happiness." Flagler family portraits hang in the library, which also doubled as a reception area for guests. A 1,340-pipe organ dominates the music room. The Flagler's used the room not only for musicals, but also for meetings, lectures, and receptions. Many original furnishings are on display, including collections of lace, porcelains, glass and silver. History exhibits show artifacts, documents and photographs that chronicle the building of the railway. Flagler's personal railroad car No. 91, parked outside on the south lawn, displays it as it was in 1912 when he traveled to Key West after completion of the railroad. Some called it a palace on wheels.

Les Standiford's excellent book, *Last Train to Paradise,* tells the incredible story of the railway that connected Key West Island to the mainland of Florida across "a staggering 153 miles of open ocean—an engineering challenge beyond even that of the Panama Canal." Standiford writes strongly, and in a way that grips you, about how all this marvel of engineering was blown to bits in a few hellish moments of chaos by a Labor Day 1935 hurricane that today would be considered a Category 5. Man's greatest achievements pale in comparison to the power exerted by nature. The storm killed 700 persons, destroyed the railroad and countless other structures.

You'll also want to see, or stay at The Breakers, the landmark Italian Renaissance hotel "palace" Flagler built in 1896. Guests included the Rockefellers, Vanderbilts, Astors, Andrew Carnegie, J.P. Morgan who vacationed at the luxurious hotel "along with presidents and European nobility." Flagler's heirs rebuilt the hotel in 1925 after a fire. Recently the owners invested $145 million in a renovation of the landmark 569-room, eight-story five-star hotel on 140 oceanfront acres. The hotel is at One South County Road in Palm Beach; phone 1-800-784-1180.

Other "Castles"

Some other "castles" in Florida may merit a visit.

Solomon's Castle. 4533 Solomon Road, Ona, Florida 33865, phone 863-494-6077, www.solomonscastle.com. Howard Solomon, an artist, carpenter, writer and teacher has been working since the 1970s to "create" his unique castle on 55 acres, almost literally in the middle of nowhere. The shiny exterior turns out to be made of old newspaper press plates and 80 stained-glass windows. Solomon loves puns, as much as art, so both pun-filled humor and art fill the galleries. Two "men-at-arms," one clad in black, the other white (Knight and Day), stand guard at the castle doors. You can have lunch in the unique Boat in the Moat Restaurant, which indeed is a sixteenth century Spanish galleon replica in the moat around the "castle." The castle, which reportedly has been on *CNN* and in *Better Homes & Gardens* Magazine, is not open during the summer. To get there from I-75, near Bradenton, go east on SR-64 to CR 665. Turn right and go south. Make a hard left on State Highway 655 and go north approximately 100 feet to Solomon Road. Turn right and go to the castle (less than one-half mile) or check the maps on the Internet site for the twists and turns to the castle.

Coral Castle. 28655 South Federal Highway, Homestead, Florida, phone 305-238-6344, www.coralcastle.com. In 1918, Latvian immigrant Ed Leedskalnin (1887-1951) began working on a monument to his lost love.

He had left his home, Riga, Latvia, after his 16-year old sweetheart, Agnes Scuffs, called off their wedding. After living in California, he settled in Florida City.

Just five feet tall and 100 pounds, how did he move 1,100 tons of limestone used to build the castle? He said he used the secrets of ancient pyramids. The three-foot thick walls weigh a massive 125 pounds per cubic inch. Each section is four feet wide by eight feet tall and weighs 58 tons. Leedskalnin worked on his castle 28 years, and earned a living by giving tours for 10 cents.

In 1936, he bought 10 acres near Homestead and moved the castle, piece by carved stone piece, from its original location near Florida City. He continued working on it up until the time he died in 1951. A nephew inherited it upon his death, and later sold it.

We were impressed with the nine-ton gate that you can "move with one finger." This huge rock gate perhaps is Ed's most outstanding achievement. How did he do it? Experts have tried to figure it out, but apparently no one so far has an answer. Check out Ed's 5,000-pound "throne." Despite being a rock, we tried it out and found it comfortable! Called one of the "world's incredible wonders," the castle has been featured on TV, in magazines and *Ripley's Believe It or Not.* The three-and-a-half acre Coral Castle site is on the National Register of Historic Places. Rock star Billy Idol wrote his hit song, "Sweet Sixteen" about Ed's lost love. A gift shop has the usual T-shirts, thimbles, spoons, stuffed animals and postcards. Leedskalnin also wrote five pamphlets, which are available in the gift shop.

We "headquartered" at a Florida City motel to spend several days visiting Biscayne and Everglades National Parks. A stop at the easy-to-get-to Coral Castle provided an interesting interlude. The castle, open from 7 a.m. to 8 p.m. is on Highway 1, north of the intersection with the Florida Turnpike.

Charles Deering Estate. 16701 Southwest 72 Avenue, Miami, phone 305-235-1668. The 420-acre Deering Estate, bought in 1913 by Charles Deering (1852-1927) and remodeled for his winter residence, isn't a "castle," but nonetheless is worth a visit because of its site on the edge of Biscayne Bay. Fossil bones have been found that go back 50,000 years. Tequesta Indians occupied the site from early A.D. to 1700s. Deering, son of the founder of Deering Harvester Machine and International Harvester, and brother of James Deering who built Vizcaya, wintered at the home. Deering built the unusual keyhole-shaped basin in 1916-1918. Deering's descendants occupied the home until 1980. The state of Florida and Miami-Dade County bought the estate in 1985. No vehicles are allowed on the main property. The estate is popular for social events and weddings, as well as tours.

Chapter Sixteen
The Lure of Florida Lighthouses

"Nothing indicates the liberality, prosperity or intelligence of a nation more clearly than the facilities which it affords for the safe approach of the mariner to its shores." Report of the Lighthouse Board, 1868.

Introduction to Lighthouses.

Until we moved to Florida, we didn't have much interest in lighthouses. Then we read a brief article on one and decided to visit it as a day trip. We not only had a fun day, but we soaked up some fascinating Florida history. So we visited some more. And we read about them. We were hooked. You may want to visit some, so this chapter provides a brief overview of Florida's lighthouses, with comments from our visits, and the best ones for you to visit as a start.

Lighthouses have a romantic appeal to many people perhaps because of the metaphor of the light beacon symbolizing hope, or because of the dramatic history and inspiring stories of some lighthouses. For example, the fellow with the winning bid for the Dry Tortugas Lighthouse, Samuel Lincoln, set sail from Boston in August 1824 with a ship loaded with materials for his $29,847 contract. His ship sank with no survivors. He was never heard from again. His backers took over the contract and sent another ship. Only the ruins of that lighthouse inside Fort Jefferson remain.

The government built the lighthouses to aid ship navigation. The lighthouses, which were a coastal beacon point of reference, cast life-saving beams, which warned mariners away from dangerous shoals and to a safe harbor, especially on a dark stormy night. Most experts cite the oldest lighthouse in the world as the one built in 300 B.C. in Alexandria by the Egyptians. This guide to passing ships stood for more than 1,400 years. Some historians referred to it as one of the Seven Wonders of the World. The English were the first to build lighthouses on isolated rocks known to cause great danger for ships. Florida has six lighthouses built on reefs, and accessible only by boat, although some can be seen from shore.

The first U. S. lighthouse was built in 1716 in Boston Harbor. The oldest in Florida is the St. Augustine Lighthouse built in 1824. The tallest in the nation, and perhaps best known, is the Cape Hatteras Lighthouse in North Carolina. Florida's Ponce de Leon Inlet is the tallest in Florida and second tallest in the United States. The U.S. Lighthouse Board was established in 1852. The Bureau of Lighthouses succeeded the board in 1910, which was later replaced by the U.S. Coast Guard.

For many years, lighthouses were vital and important parts of seafaring, but with global positioning (GPS) few are used today. Some have deteriorated with time. Some are in remote places. Some are for sale. Others, however, have been restored to become attractions. Several have been automated and continue to operate. Lighthouse keepers started disappearing in the 1950s at the end of an era as lighthouses were either automated or abandoned. Lighthouse keepers led a rigorous, harsh and lonely life, particularly the ones on the hard-to-get-to offshore lighthouses. On the other hand, their job was a noble exciting work to keep death at bay for passing ships from treacherous rocks and shoals.

In the *Ancient Mariner*, Samuel Taylor Coleridge (1772-1834), writes:

> *Oh! Dream of joy! Is this indeed*
> *The lighthouse top I see?*
> *They stood as signals to the land*
> *Each one a lovely light.*

Many of the lighthouses are majestic structures that inspire painters. When we walked to the Sanibel Lighthouse, however, we did not get a romantic feeling about the ungainly, metal water tower-like structure. Some visitors who see the offshore lighthouses along the Florida Keys think they are oil derricks, but lighthouse lovers have a different view. The changing tides, low fog, hurricanes and the perilous reefs resulted in 200 shipwrecks, which caused Congress to appropriate funds for the first four lighthouses in May 1824. Lighthouses, of course, would warn ships away from the dangerous reefs. Each of the Florida reef lighthouses has a story. Today, most are diving and snorkeling destinations.

Many of Florida's lighthouses are in parks, wildlife refuges and recreational areas so you have more to see and do than just visit the lighthouse. Thirty lighthouses remain in Florida, although "several may be doomed to disappear in the near future" according to the Florida Lighthouse Association. A few "unofficial" or faux lighthouses also exist.

The U.S. Coast Guard, in 1999, declared six of the 30 Florida lighthouses surplus. Increasing annual maintenance costs have resulted in the lighthouses being declared excess Federal property. The six were: Amelia Island (near Jacksonville), Cape Canaveral, Crooked River, Egmont Key near Tampa, Boca Grande Entrance Rear Range Light (Gasparilla Island) and St. George Island. The new owners likely will be other Federal or state government agencies, but if no other government agency acquires them, they could be sold to private owners. The U.S. Air Force took over Cape Canaveral Lighthouse, for example. Of the six, all except the Boca Grande Entrance Rear Range Light are historic sites. Federal law guarantees public access (because of the National Historic Preservation Act of 1966). The owners of the Boca Grande Lighthouse have first priority, for example, to buy the Rear Range Light on Gasparilla Island.

In 2000, the National Historic Lighthouse Preservation Act enabled the government to transfer ownership (give away) of 300 lighthouses to state and local governments and to nonprofit organizations. The St. Augustine lighthouse was one of the first six to have its ownership transferred July 20, 2002 to a private non-profit organization. The St. Augustine lighthouse also hosted a national seminar November 2003 on lighthouse care, administration, preservation and management. U.S. Secretary of the Interior Gale Norton said the St. Augustine lighthouse could serve as a role model to other organizations aspiring to own and operate a lighthouse. Other seminars in 2004-2006 will be held in Michigan, New England and California.

Lighthouse lovers view the lighthouses not simply as scenic attractions, but important treasures to preserve. Few states have worked as hard as Florida on preserving lighthouses although six states each have more lighthouses than Florida. Nineteen states have none. Michigan leads with 118, followed by New York 68, Maine 64, Massachusetts 52, Wisconsin 36 and California 34.

"I can think of no other edifice constructed by man as altruistic as a lighthouse. They were built only to serve. They weren't built for any other purpose..." George Bernard Shaw.

The St. Joseph Point Lighthouse, which is now a private residence, is the only privately owned one of the 30 Florida lighthouses (in 2003), so there are really only 29 "public" Florida lighthouses. Just six have towers open and with museums.

The Fresnel (pronounced frA'nel) Lens.

You can get the best view of a First Order Fresnel Lens (largest) at the Key West Lighthouse Museum. There they have one you can walk inside of through a cutout to view it from the inside. The Fresnel lens, invented in 1822 by French civil engineer Augustin Fresnel (1788-1827), has hundreds of individual pieces of glass in a metal frame to focus the light. The pieces are in concentric rings, which leave a grooved appearance. The lens magnifies the light into a single beam. He solved the diffusion problem that earlier lighthouse systems had, so the beam extended for a great distance. . It has an amazing efficiency as it can throw the beam 18 miles from a 100-foot tower.

There are seven "orders," or sizes of lens with the first three orders for seacoast lights, while orders four through six were smaller for bay or harbor lights. The largest of the seven "orders" of size, is nearly 12-feet tall and six feet in diameter.

The Key West Museum also has two smaller fourth order lenses in the same room with the first- order cutaway. The museum at the Ponce de Leon Inlet Lighthouse provides excellent exhibits on the Fresnel Lens. Two first-order lenses are on display at Ponce de Leon Inlet Lighthouse.

Favorite Lighthouse Story.

In seminars I used this story about disregarding feedback to make a point about listening.

On a dark and stormy night, a huge naval ship plowed its way through tremendous waves as it sailed down the coast. Rain came down in buckets through dense fog.

Suddenly a light was spotted in the distance on a collision course. So a message was sent to the oncoming ship. "We are on a collision course. Change your heading 10 degrees north."

The return message: "Change *your* heading 10 degrees south."

"This is Rear Admiral Johnson. We are on a collision course. Change your heading 10 degrees north."

The immediate reply: "This is Seaman Fourth Class Jones. Change your heading 10 degrees south."

The third message came back: "I am standing on the bridge of the largest capital ship in the Navy, and every gun and missile is pointed directly at you. We are on a collision course. Change your heading 10 degrees north."

The final reply: "I am standing in a lighthouse. Change *your* heading!"

Lighthouse Builders.

Winslow Lewis of Boston built more lighthouses than any other contractor. Of the ten he built only Amelia Island and St. Marks towers survive. Lieutenant George Gordon Meade, later famous as the general who defeated Robert E. Lee at Gettysburg, designed, built or worked on seven lighthouses, including Jupiter Inlet and Cape Florida which are open today; and Carysfort Reef, Sand Key, Cedar Key and Sombrero Key. He also built the long-gone one at Rebecca Shoal.

Level 1. Visit a Few

If you have simply a casual interest, then make it a point to visit one or more of the six lighthouses open to the public, and that have museums and shops: Cape Florida, Jupiter Inlet, Key West, Ponce de Leon Inlet, Port Boca Grande, and St. Augustine. We have visited, and climbed all six, although Port Boca Grande does not require much climbing. Each of these six has unique appeals that make them worth a visit, but if we stay with our theme of magic 3s, then our picks would be Ponce de Leon Inlet Lighthouse, Jupiter Inlet Lighthouse and St. Augustine Lighthouse. Perhaps the best way to start is to pick one of these three nearest you. We chose to visit these first along with other lighthouses that were convenient to see during the trip.

To help you pick one or more to visit, read about our visits to them, as follows:

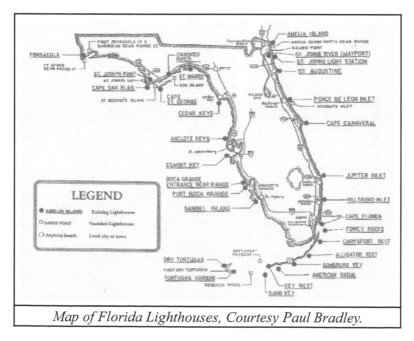

Map of Florida Lighthouses, Courtesy Paul Bradley.

Ponce de Leon Inlet Lighthouse. Near New Smyrna Beach at 4931 South Peninsula Avenue, Ponce Inlet, Florida 32127, phone 386-761-1821, www.ponceinlet.org.

This lighthouse is one of the tallest in the United States and Florida's tallest at 175 feet, the equivalent of a 10-story building. A climb to the top of this one takes an energy sapping 203 steps! The climb, however, is worth the effort because you're rewarded, along with the other 200,000 people who visit the lighthouse each year, with a magnificent view of the Florida coastline. The lighthouse is at the end of the peninsula at Ponce Inlet, which takes a scenic drive down Atlantic Avenue along the Atlantic Ocean for four miles from the bridge crossing the Halifax River. The Ponce Inlet Lighthouse, which is listed as a National Historic Landmark, is one of the few in the United States that has all the original buildings of the keeper, assistant keeper, and pump house. A major attraction, in addition to a large gift shop, is the Museum of the Sea, which has fascinating models, navigation instruments, pirates' treasure and paintings. A building built in 1995 houses "The finest collection of restored Fresnel lenses in the world." Exhibits explain the history and technology of the lenses. The display includes the first-order lens that was used in the Cape Canaveral Lighthouse from 1865-1993 and the first-order lens used at the Ponce de Leon Inlet Lighthouse from 1887-1933. We enjoyed touring the F.D. Russell, a 46-foot tugboat, built in 1938, which is in the boatyard.

The Ponce Inlet Lighthouse was the last of the tall, brick towers to be built in Florida in 1887. Author Stephen Crane (1871-1900), shipwrecked 12 miles off the Florida coast in 1897 in the *Commodore*, used the Ponce de Leon Inlet Lighthouse to lead him safely to shore. That experience worked its way into his *Open Boat,* in which he describes the harrowing adventure in "waves the hue of slate except for the tops which were foaming white."

Jupiter Inlet Lighthouse. 805 N. U.S Highway One, Jupiter, Florida 33477, phone 407-747-8380.

Open Saturday through Wednesday. Before touring the cherry-red lighthouse, we watched an excellent 15-minute video, which depicts the history of the lighthouse. Standing at the top, after climbing 37 steps on the 50-foot hill to the lighthouse, then the 105 cast iron spiral steps in the lighthouse; we looked across the bay to Jupiter Island, and Perry Como's former house. You have a gorgeous unrestricted 360-degree view from the top. A youngster exclaimed during one of our visits: "It's an awesome view!" Jupiter Island, a 17-mile long barrier island, is home to many celebrities and has a median home value of $6.5 million. The Jupiter Inlet Lighthouse, designed and built by George Meade in 1860, is Palm Beach County's oldest structure. It is on the National Register of Historic Places. The lighthouse has a first-order light with its original Fresnel lens, which may be the oldest in continuous operation in Florida. The lighthouse has a gift store. The 108-feet high tower is built on a 48-foot high ancient Indian shell mound more than 1,300 years old. The Loxahatchee River Historical Society operates tours to this lighthouse within a functioning Coast Guard station. The Loxahatchee Historical Society also operates the DuBois Pioneer Home, built in 1898, and the Loxahatchee River Historical Museum. Harry DuBois and his blind date, Susan Sanders climbed to the top of the lighthouse in February 1898, where he proposed marriage. Later that year, they built what is now the DuBois Pioneer Home. The lighthouse hosts many weddings and has a special "Toast at the Top" Valentine Day for couples.

Jupiter Lighthouse

St. Augustine Lighthouse. 81 Lighthouse Avenue, St. Augustine, Florida 32080, phone 904-829-0745, www.staugustine.com.

St. Augustine is an interesting place to visit, especially if you are a history buff. Boat tours swing past the island to give passengers a look from the sea. One of the days we visited was a cold, raw, windy day in December. Taking a ride to the lighthouse, then climbing the 219 stairs to the top of the 165-foot tower will warm you up

Our first visit to St. Augustine combined visits during several days to other St. Augustine attractions. The lighthouse was not the purpose of our trip. Our next visit, however, in better weather, focused just on touring the lighthouse. Certainly St. Augustine is steeped in fascinating history, but so is the lighthouse. The lighthouse built in 1874 "replaced" a watchtower the Spanish built 50 years earlier. The lighthouse, which is listed on the National Register of Historic Places, has a museum and gift shop. The curator said more than 130,000 visitors a year visit this venerable lighthouse.

From the lighthouse keeper's log, September 21, 1887; "Schooner Dream went on sand bar near old lighthouse at 3 a.m. Nine passengers rescued by keepers. Lost anchor, sails and small boat. Vessel floated off in damaged condition."

Our Next Three Favorite Lighthouses

Key West Lighthouse. 281 Front Street, Key West, Florida 33040, phone 305-295-6616. You can see Ernest Hemingway's house across the street, after an easy climb of 98 steps to the top of the 86-foot tower, less than half the climb of St. Augustine or Ponce de Leon. The lighthouse, rebuilt in 1847 was the beginning of the end for the Wreckers, because the beacon guided the ships to safety. The third-order lens in the tower was installed in 1858. The hurricane of 1846 had swept away the lighthouse along with fourteen of the keeper's family and staff. The lighthouse keepers would witness hurricanes in 1851, 1856, 1878 and 1894. In 1898 the keepers would have witnessed the arrival of the battleship Maine on its way to tragedy in Havana harbor.

As mentioned earlier, the museum has a Fresnel first-order lens and two smaller fourth-order lenses. The former lighthouse keeper's house at the site is a treasure trove of the heyday of the lighthouses.

We not only wanted to visit the Key West Lighthouse, but the other lighthouses in the area, to reach our goal of visiting all 30 Florida lighthouses. As we left Key West Lighthouse, we looked forward to seeing Sand Key and visiting the Dry Tortugas Lighthouse at Loggerhead Key and the Fort Jefferson Lighthouse (now a harbor light).

Port Boca Grande. Barrier Island Parks Society, P.O. Box 637, Boca Grande, Florida 33921 (Gasparilla Island), phone 941-964-0375. The restored white house-like lighthouse at the south end of Gasparilla Island, only 44 feet high, opened a museum in 1999. The lighthouse, built in 1890, which marks the entrance to Charlotte Harbor, was restored in 1986 after 20 years of disuse. The Florida Park Service, which owns the lighthouse, gave the non-profit Barrier Islands Parks Society permission to create a museum in the building, which was put on the National Register of Historic Places in 1980. We visited it and enjoyed seeing the displays. The museum does a good job in telling the history of the area in a top-notch way with pictures, artifacts and memorabilia in the four rooms. Once a major shipping port, because of the phosphate mined nearby for fertilizer, ships from more than 20 countries visited Port Boca Grande starting in 1912 and lasting until 1980. Freighters as big as 670-feet long came to the deep, wide Port of Boca Grande ("Big Mouth" in Spanish).

The lighthouse museum, now open daily accepts donations (free admission). Parking is $2. Getting to Gasparilla Island means going over a toll bridge ($3.50). The history of Gasparilla Island is a part of what makes it special and worth a visit not only to see the lighthouses, but the picture-postcard island and historic buildings. You can bicycle on wide bicycle paths. Fishermen at the jetty on the point reported good results with snook and snapper. Boca Grande Pass is famous for tarpon. After the inauguration in January 1999, Governor Jeb Bush plus President George Bush and then-governor of Texas, George W. Bush, vacationed in Boca Grande.

Cape Florida Lighthouse. Bill Baggs Cape Florida State Park, 1200 South Crandon Boulevard, Key Biscayne, Florida 33149, phone 305-361-5811. Florida Department of Parks and Recreation operates this open-to-the-public lighthouse. The lighthouse is at the south tip of Key Biscayne and at the end of Crandon Boulevard, just 15 minutes from Miami. The 95-foot tower, which opened in 1967, underwent a million dollar renovation in 1996. Hurricane Andrew damaged the tower, and devastated the park in 1992. With just 112 steps, Cape Florida is an easier climb than some of the others. Tours are at 10 a.m. and 1 p.m. with a sign up a half hour before. Open Monday-Thursday.

Level 2. Caught the Lighthouse Bug

If after visiting a few, you want to visit all the Florida lighthouses (all that can be visited), we recommend you pick from the "Trail" in *Florida Lighthouse Trail* edited by Tom Taylor. The "Trail" follows the state clockwise, starting in the northeast corner at Fernandina Beach. Taylor's book provides "comprehensive directions to the various lighthouse and historic lighthouse sites in Florida." The pamphlet, *Worth the Drive,* issued by Visit Florida (www.flausa.com) provides a five-day driving tour to take in a third of the lighthouses. We don't recommend you do that; at least all at once.

At one time we thought of traveling and experiencing all the lighthouses in one grand tour. We're happy we didn't do that. It would have been too much, too soon, like reading the classics before you've had enough life experience to appreciate them. Whenever we had a trip targeted for a lighthouse, we made it a point to take in other things. We also began with lighthouses close to home. You can visit sections of the trail at different times as we did. When we visited Jupiter, for example, we drove south to see the nearby Hillsboro Inlet Lighthouse. You also avoid being rushed, avoid arriving at a lighthouse at the wrong time and avoid missing interesting nearby "places of opportunity" to visit.

If you have more than a casual interest in the lighthouses, join the Florida Lighthouse Association (www.floridalighthouses.org.) The non-profit association, established in 1996, works "to foster the preservation and interpretation of Florida's unique lighthouse heritage." A goal is to preserve and open all the Florida lighthouses. One major advantage of being a member is being able to visit lighthouses you might not otherwise see. We went with other members, for example, to visit the Cape Canaveral Lighthouse, which is on the restricted Air Force base. To get membership information, email membership@floridalighthouses.org. Quarterly meetings occur at different lighthouses around the state, which gives you not only an opportunity to visit ones otherwise inaccessible, but you also get the benefit of knowledgeable speakers. Most of the lighthouses now also have associations, which sharply focus on one lighthouse.

To plan ahead and get directions to each lighthouse, use Tom Taylor's book. Pick an area, then visit the main lighthouse open to the public and stop by to see others in the area. Don't forget to check when the lighthouse you plan to visit is open. Jupiter, for example, is closed on Thursday and Friday.

The Florida Maritime Heritage Trail has fun locations made up into six themes of which lighthouses are one. See at www.flheritage.com/maritime. Here are some of the trips we took you may want to try. In visiting Port Boca Grande lighthouse, stop by, park and walk on the beach to see the Boca Grande Entrance Rear Range light just 10 minutes from the lighthouse. Have lunch at a café on the beach. After visiting the Jupiter Lighthouse, and lunch at The Crab House, drive south perhaps 45 minutes, to see the Hillsboro Lighthouse. You can see it from Pompano Beach's City Park. Spend several days at the Space Coast to take in Merritt National Wildlife Refuge, the Kennedy Space Center and other attractions in addition to the Cape Canaveral Lighthouse. Plan on a trip to St. Augustine and stay a few days to take in Florida heritage and living history of the city.

The Six Florida Reef Lighthouses.

You can see the six reef lighthouses on the way to Key West and by taking some boat rides, as we did. The living coral reefs stretch along the Keys 200 miles from Key Biscayne to the Dry Tortugas, with some 6,000 coral reefs, which have devastated thousands of ships. There are more than 800 keys from Miami to the Dry Tortugas.

A half-dozen skeletal iron screw-pile lighthouses stretch every 30 miles or so down the coast, each built on pilings sunk into the coral on which they stand a few miles offshore. These half-dozen screw-pile lighthouses, along with more traditional lighthouses, aided seafarers to avoid the dangerous reef and find deep-water paths. The skeletal design offers little resistance to wind and waves through the girders so they proved reasonably hurricane proof. Good design! More hurricanes reach landfall in Florida than anywhere in the world and the Keys have had their share.

This largest collection of iron-pile lighthouses in the world influenced Alexandre Gustave Eiffel to build in Paris his tower in 1889. So we could call these reef lights American Eiffel towers.

All the screw-pile lighthouses were automated in 1963. They still function, not only as beacons, but mark the location of reefs to protect coral and marine life dependent on the fragile coral's continued growth. Reef lighthouse enthusiasts formed the Florida Keys Reef Lights Foundation, Inc. with a mission to preserve and protect the reef lighthouses. See www. floridalighthouses.org/reeflights.

To see most of these "reef lights" up close, you need to charter a boat, although none of the lighthouses is open to the public. Although vandals have damaged them, these marvelous structures have lasted more than 100 years because hurricane winds simply go through them and they are anchored solidly in the reefs. Most show deterioration, especially rust and lack of paint. Each requires an estimated $2 million to renovate.

Fowey Rocks Lighthouse, built in 1878, is 125 feet tall. We boated around it on a charter boat from Biscayne National Park. We also visited beautiful Boca Chita Key and the Boca Chita Lighthouse built by industrialist Mark Honeywell when he owned the island. Fowey Rocks celebrated its 125th anniversary in 2003. The lighthouse is named for the 20-gun sloop of war HMS Fowey that joined the graveyard of ships in 1746. It's south of Miami and just six miles from the Cape Florida Lighthouse.

Carysfort Lighthouse, 112 feet tall, off Key Largo was built first in 1852, and was the model for the others. It's the oldest active reef light. You can't see this one from land, so you'll need to take a boat. Charter boats schedule diving and snorkeling trips to the site. Atlantis Dive Shop goes out regularly to the lighthouse.

Alligator Reef Lighthouse, built in 1873, stands 150 feet tall three miles offshore from Lower Matecombe Key in the aqua-green seas. You can see it from a distance from the Indian Key Fill causeway. A charter boat can be arranged at Robbie's Marina, Lower Matecombe Key (www. robbies.com).

239

Fowey Rocks Lighthouse

Sombrero Key Lighthouse, the tallest at 156 feet, can be viewed in the distance from Seven-Mile Bridge (south of Marathon), although you can see it best by boat because it is five miles offshore (seven miles from the bridge). When we saw it, the lighthouse badly needed a paint job. The "Spirit" catamaran goes out to the lighthouse from Marathon.

American Shoals Lighthouse, the last reef lighthouse to be built, is octagonal in shape, brown in color, 124-feet tall and seven miles offshore from Sugarloaf Key. You can rent a boat, or have a charter boat captain take you, from marinas at Cudjoe Key, Little Torch Key and Sugarloaf Key.

Sand Key, 132 feet tall, is nine miles offshore southwest of Key West. It was the first of the six to have a Fresnel Lens. Sand Key was on our priority list to visit during a trip to Key West. It, like many of the reef lights, is now a favorite dive and snorkel site. We were able to see it during a glass-bottom boat cruise and during a boat trip to Ft. Jefferson.

There were two other reef lighthouses: Rebecca Shoals Lighthouse, located 43 miles west of Key West in turbulent waters, remains only as a beacon atop the pilings, after the house was removed. Only the ruins remain of Northwest Passage Lighthouse, seven miles northwest of Key West.

The Other Florida Lighthouses.

Here is a brief summary of each of the other lighthouses listed by geographical areas.

Northeast Florida.

In addition to the publicly open St. Augustine lighthouse, northeast Florida has:

Amelia Island Lighthouse. Amelia Island Near Jacksonville and Fort Clinch State Park. The 64-foot lighthouse is not open to the public. It was built on a 55-foot mound, the highest above sea level of any of the lighthouses.

St. Johns River Lighthouse. Mayport. People in the area refer to it as **Mayport Lighthouse.** Near Mayport Naval Base. No longer functions.

St. Johns Light Station. Mayport. Near St. Johns River Lighthouse. It's just north of Jacksonville Beach. Not open to the public.

East Central Florida and the "Space Coast."

East Central Florida, in addition to the previously mentioned Ponce de Leon Inlet and Jupiter Lighthouses, has one in the middle of an Air Base.

Cape Canaveral Lighthouse. Cape Canaveral. During 1892-1894, the government moved the lighthouse to its present location because of nearby erosion. The move took 18 months to slowly pull the lighthouse on rails by mules, although the lighthouse was dismantled for the move. The keeper's houses near the lighthouse were removed in the 1950s. The lens was removed in 1993 and replaced with two one thousand watt searchlights. We visited the lighthouse, which is in the middle of an air base, and now maintained by the Air Force (since ownership passed from the Coast Guard in 2000), with members of the Florida Lighthouse Association. What a contrast between the old lighthouse and the rockets going into space! Although maintained by the Air Force, restoration efforts are underway by the Cape Canaveral Lighthouse Foundation, Inc., P.O. Box 1978, Cape Canaveral, Florida 32920, and phone 321-459-2531. The oil house was restored in2004.

Northwest Florida and the "Forgotten Coast."

Northwest Florida has seven lighthouses, with none open to the public, although some are open on special occasions.

Pensacola Lighthouse. Pensacola. Open only on special occasions and groups, and on weekends in May to October, this 171-foot lighthouse, within the Naval Air Station, replaced a small lighthouse in 1858. During the Civil War, Confederates stole the lens and hid it from Union soldiers. The lantern could be seen 21 miles from shore. The nearby National Museum of Naval Aviation, with Blue Angels Atrium and IMAX Theater, showcases the history of aviation. Miles of beaches on the Emerald Gulf Coast are also nearby. Locals call the pure white ground quartz sand, "barking " sand because it squeaks when you walk along.

St Joseph Point Lighthouse. Simmons Bayou, near Port St. Joe. The only privately owned lighthouse in Florida. Not open to the public because it is a private residence. It can be seen from the street.

Cape San Blas Lighthouse. Near Port St. Joe. This 90-foot lighthouse is identical to the Sanibel Lighthouse, but has a wild and wacky past. The first lighthouse, built in 1847 was blown over in 1851, rebuilt in 1859 only to be blown up by Confederates during the Civil War, then toppled over by surrounding water in 1880. The pyramidal skeleton tower, completed in 1885, was moved to its present location in 1919. The lighthouse, on a part of Eglin Air Force Base is not open. It can't be seen from the road.

Cape St. George Lighthouse. A hurricane nearly toppled this lighthouse, near Apalachicola, nine miles offshore and it is at risk now with water all around it. It has the dubious distinction of being the most endangered lighthouse in Florida.

Crooked River Lighthouse. Carrabelle. The Carrabelle Lighthouse Association, Inc., P.O. Box 373, Carrabelle, Florida 32322, has raised funds for restoration efforts. The 103-foot skeleton tower, identical to Anclote Key Lighthouse, replaced the 1838 Dog Island Lighthouse that washed away in a storm in 1873. The 1895 skeleton lighthouse, less expensive to build than the heavy brick towers, was built on the mainland. You have a hard time seeing it because it's hidden behind tall Florida pines. The Coast Guard transferred it to the city in 2001. The association is working to get it open to the public. The breathtaking view from the top of the tower includes the Gulf of Mexico, St. Georges Sound, Dog Island, St. George Island, The Crooked River, the 1,400-population city of Carrabelle, the Carrabelle River and Tates Hell State Park.

St. Marks Lighthouse. St. Marks. The 80-foot lighthouse is in the St. Marks National Wildlife Refuge, south of Tallahassee. The history of the lighthouse, like most of the Florida lighthouses, sparkles with dramatic events, including a storm in 1843 that washed away every building except the tower.

West Florida.

In addition to the publicly open Port Boca Grande Lighthouse, the others on the west coast are:

Cedar Key Lighthouse. On Seashore Key near Cedar Key. Reach only by boat, but the island is closed to visitors and open only a few times a year.

Anclote Key Lighthouse. Near Tarpon Springs on 180-acre island; north of Clearwater; at the mouth of the Anclote River (Anclote is Spanish for anchor.) The Ranger's house was restored in 2004 after restoration efforts in 2003 on the lighthouse and oil house. The 102-foot skeletal tower sits at the south end of a jewel of an island and has received support for restoration from the Tampa Bay Harbour Lights Collector Club, the

Florida Lighthouse Association and the Gulf Islands Citizens Support Organization, which raised money for the work.

Egmont Key Lighthouse. Near St. Petersburg on historic Egmont Key Island at the mouth of Tampa Bay. The island is a national wildlife refuge and state park and can be reached by boat, although the tower is not open for climbing. When built in 1848, the lighthouse was the only west coast lighthouse between St. Marks and Key West.

Boca Grande Entrance Rear Range Light. Boca Grande, Gasparilla Island. Although not open to the public, you can walk near this rear range light. When we visited, we parked within a few feet of the range light and the beach at Florida Parks Service parking lot. The beach appears to be more of an attraction than the old lighthouse (built 1881 in Delaware, then discontinued in 1918 and shipped to Florida and re-erected in 1927).

Sanibel Lighthouse. Sanibel Island. When you reach Periwinkle Drive, turn left to drive to the southern end and beach. Limited parking exists near the beach. The Sanibel Lighthouse is just a short walk down the beach, and a great area for shelling. The skeletal copper- colored iron-pile lighthouse rises from the beach amidst two white clapboard keeper's houses. The Sanibel Lighthouse is the last one on the Gulf Coast until the Dry Tortugas 134 miles south. We have visited the beach (and lighthouse) many times, but more for the sunning and shelling than the lighthouse!

South Florida.

In addition to the six Reef Lighthouses Cape Florida and Key West, south Florida has the following lighthouses:

Hillsboro Lighthouse. Hillsboro. South of Boca Raton. Although the lighthouse is closed to the public, you can view it, as we did, from Pompano Beach's City Park. Further, guided tours are held four times each year by the Hillsboro Lighthouse Preservation Society, P.O. Box 6062, Pompano Beach, Florida 33060, phone 954-942-2102. Check out www. hillsborolighthouse.org for information about the colorful history of this lighthouse. Hillsboro was the site of the U.S. Postal "barefoot" service of one round trip a week with 28 miles by small boat and 40 mile on foot on the beach. A statue of Ed Hamilton, by sculptor Frank Varga, was moved to the lighthouse grounds in 2003. Hamilton, U.S. mail carrier lost his life in 1887. An annual Boy Scout Mailman hike along the beach keeps the history alive.

Garden Key Lighthouse. The Dry Torugas. Right on the beach but not open to the public. At Fort Jefferson National Monument, a park operated by the National Park Service. It's a three-hour ferry ride from Key West.

Loggerhead Key Lighthouse. The Dry Tortugas. Small island seventy miles west of Key West. Marks the entrance to the Gulf of Mexico. Near Garden Key and Fort Jefferson.

Faux Lighthouses.

Several lighthouses have been built privately that were never Coast Guard approved, but have interesting stories. You'll see lighthouse replicas all over Florida, especially along canals and attached to restaurants.

Mount Dora Lighthouse. Mount Dora, Florida. This 35-foot tall stucco lighthouse, built in 1988 with contributions from the citizens, is the only inland freshwater lighthouse in Florida. It's at the tip of a 2,000-foot long peninsula, Granthan Point that sticks out into Lake Dora like a finger pointing across the five-mile lake. The blue flashing light generates jokes as well as light for a "private aid to navigation." Chapter Fourteen describes our visit to Mount Dora.

Boca Chita Lighthouse. On 32-acre Boca Chita Key, a secret treasure of Biscayne National Park, in Biscayne Bay, south of Miami, and near Fowey Rocks Lighthouse. Don't miss visiting the island. See Chapter Ten for our visit to Boca Chita.

Faro Blanco. Marathon, Florida (at mile marker 48 on U.S. 1). This privately built and owned octagonal pyramidal white lighthouse with a red band, is part of Faro Blanco's Marine Resort.

Level 3. Collector

To step up to the next level, you need to be a passionate lighthouse addict, who digs into the history of the lighthouses, obtains a lighthouse passport and checks off the visits, supports the restoration of lighthouses and attends the meetings.

The U.S. Lighthouse Society sponsors the National Lighthouse Passport. These are available for $7.50 (plus $1 shipping) from Wayne Wheeler at lighthousesoc@aol.com. The passport covers 160 lighthouses that have a passport stamp. You can donate money during the visit to the lighthouse to get your passport stamped. You have an official record of your visits (a collection if you will) and at the same time help promote restoration efforts. Participants send the Passport in when filled out and receive an embroidered patch that says, *"I've Seen the Light"*.

Ceramic Lighthouses.

Lighthouse visitors also seem to be avid collectors of limited edition ceramic lighthouses. **Harbour Lights,** 1000 North Johnson Avenue, El Cajon, CA 92020, for example, not only markets ceramic lighthouses, but participates in many of the restoration projects and seminars. They co-sponsored the national seminars on lighthouse operation and restoration. Harbour Lights has modeled most of the Florida lighthouses. Some are remarkable in their detail and depict the lighthouses and keeper's house as they were years ago. Harbour Lights can be reached at 800-365-1219 or www.HarbourLights.com.

Lighthouse Depot. Box 427, Wells, Maine 04090, phone 1-800-758-1444 www.lighthousedepot.com

Lighthouse Depot claims to be the world's largest lighthouse gift store with thousands of lighthouse gifts and collectibles; "The Most Complete Selection of Lighthouse Memorabilia Ever Assembled." If you love lighthouses, their store in Wells, Maine is a unique place to visit.

Videos.

Several videos have been produced about lighthouses, including the following:

Legendary Lighthouses. Six one-hour segments on PBS, produced by Driftwood Products, Inc. and WPSX-TV Penn State. Narrated by Richard Crenna.

Lighthouses. Guardians of the Night. Janson Video. 52 minutes. 1988. The video focuses on the early lighthouses and lighthouse keepers and their families in France, Britain, Canada and the U.S.

Ponce de Leon Inlet Lighthouse: A Heritage Revisited. Video. 44 minutes. 1996. Available at the gift shop at the Ponce de Leon Inlet Lighthouse Museum.

Chapter Seventeen
Quest for Florida's Best Grouper Sandwich

"Eat Grouper, Live Longer"

Grouper Sandwiches in Paradise.

You may not even like grouper, but you'll still have fun with this chapter because all the restaurants mentioned serve other good food and offer a unique experience. And, if you live in Florida you really ought to try grouper! I was not a fan of eating fish at all, but grouper changed my eating habits. Besides, you are better off eating fish and reducing your red meat intake!

Along with grouper sandwiches, we'll also talk about key lime pie, gator bites, and conch fritters. This is, after all, a book about living in Florida.

Are these sophisticated restaurants? No, but they are unique, casual and comfortable. They aren't cookie cutter restaurants. They have great grouper sandwiches. Many have an old Florida feel about them or are simply fun to get to, away from the large restaurant chains and Wal-Martization of America. Most are "cafes" or "grills." Some open only for breakfast and lunch. Others open for lunch and dinner. If lunch and grouper sandwiches are good, then so is dinner!

Grouper.

The popularity of red grouper, a brownish red fish with blotches on its side, has caused over fishing with demands from some to limit commercial and recreational fishing. Grouper live in the near shore reefs for their first six years or so then move offshore to deeper waters. They live to be 25

247

years old. They are commonly caught at 25 pounds but some are caught up to 40 pounds. One effect of limiting the fishing will be an increase in the price of this delicacy.

Is it fresh grouper? Like any fish, it needs to be fresh to be good. Is it red, black or scamp grouper? Some claim black and scamp grouper are best but most restaurants serve the more common red grouper. Properly prepared, grouper is nothing short of sublime.

Red grouper is tender, mild, firm and with a pleasant flavor and denseness of flake; and the most common grouper available. Black grouper is similar but they swim in colder deeper water, which allows for a more vibrant flavor and crisper texture also found in the scamp, the king of the grouper. In the fish market, in 2004, red grouper was $11.95 a pound, while black grouper was $14.95, to illustrate the difference.

Although a forgiving fish to prepare, the quality key is the restaurant obtaining the grouper from reliable sources. Imported pre-cut filets can be a problem. So can "dumb groupers" (with ciguatera, which causes the fish to swim sideways and drunkenly). Both can give grouper a bad rap.

One small step below grouper for a fish sandwich is mahi-mahi (dolphin). For dinner, we also like pompano and snapper. Grouper is best. In Key West, you would be hard pressed to beat yellowtail snapper caught in the local waters. Why grouper? The simple answers: we like it and it's good for you. We said to a waitress, when ordering our "usual" grouper sandwich: "I guess we're in a rut." She replied: "If you're in a rut you like, I say stay in it!"

Restaurants.

Let's start with a warning: Even the best restaurants can have an off day. A new waitress, just learning, doesn't perform like the ones you are used to who have provided fast, friendly service. Perhaps there's a new cook, or the chef didn't show up that day. Whatever the reason, we have left favorite restaurants disappointed when the food or service didn't live up to past experience. Even worse, some of our favorite restaurants have gone out of business. Others have changed hands, with a loss in quality. Some restaurants that are great on one visit can't seem to maintain that level consistently.

On one visit to a favorite restaurant during a month-long moratorium on commercial fishing for grouper because of "over fishing," the waitress suggested we try mahi mahi (dolphin) instead of grouper. "The grouper can be a little tough if you want it blackened. It fries up real well if you want it fried." Because of lack of availability of Florida waters grouper, their grouper temporarily came from elsewhere. Letting us know about the grouper source says a lot about the restaurant. By the way, the mahi sandwiches were excellent.

Our advice to restaurants is the same as to any business: status quo is never good enough, even if changes are painful. The best way to improve is to get some mystery diners to rate the service and food. Use the results of ratings to make needed changes. Try some extra touches to enhance the meal and boost customer care:

- At Matanzas Restaurant the waitress brought a half-carafe of ice tea along with the two glasses of tea we had ordered. At another restaurant, ice tea comes with a wedge of lemon, and a mint leaf.

- At Sunrise Café the waiter brought water with a wedge of lemon in it, without being asked. Orange juice comes in a frosted mug, with an orange slice on the mug's lip.

- Learn frequent diner's names and call them by name. Treat each diner as though he or she was the mystery diner rating you and your restaurant. After all, word of mouth and good reviews are the best advertisements.

All of us have our picky-picky ideas about food and drink. One of ours is ice tea.

Ice Tea. Being an ice tea person and purist—no sugar, no froufrou flavors, no artificial sweetener—we find the brews often too weak. Some lose color from dilution from melting ice. Others were weak to start. We like a strong, dark color ice tea the color of mangrove water. Studies suggest green tea can work as an antioxidant and may strengthen the immune system, reduce heart disease, help high cholesterol and prevent some cancers.

Cole Slaw. Cole slaw should be cold and crunchy with a light, slightly sweet zesty dressing. Cole slaw, however, comes in a wide variety in restaurants from limp, warm and inedible to a delectable dish to accompany a grouper sandwich.

Two Starters and a Dessert.

Conch Fritters. Conch are chewy mollusks which are tenderized and used in salads, spicy red chowder, and which are also chopped, breaded and fried as conch fritters. The best ones are crunchy on the outside, moist on the inside and *not* greasy. We enjoyed conch fritters at Mantanzas in Ft. Myers Beach and at Little Bar Restaurant in Goodland but the fritters had a special taste in Key West at the Grand Café, 314 Duvall Street; phone 305-292-4816, and at the Conch Republic Seafood Restaurant (see below).

Gator Bites. Taste like chicken. Try some. The best gator bites we have had were at Gatorama, 6180 U.S. Highway 27, Palmdale, Florida 33944 and at Everglades Seafood Depot Restaurant in Everglades City, Florida. Gatorama, however, is not a restaurant but an alligator farm with hundreds of alligators. Who better to know how to do gator bites than an alligator "farmer?"

Key Lime Pie. Key Lime pie is the dessert of choice in Florida; and light mellow yellow, not lime color. Tiny key limes have a tarter taste than limes. The key lime filling texture needs to be creamy. We liked the key lime pie at the A&B Lobster House in Key West and at other restaurants there. Several of our favorite places headline their own homemade key lime pie, including Randy's, but there are more recipes for key lime pie than stews. Key lime pie may be topped with meringue, or a little whipped cream or as we like it, without topping.

Here's Randy's *"Famous Homemade Key Lime Pie"* recipe:

One-9-inch graham cracker piecrust

One-14-ounce can sweetened condensed milk

6 ounces dairy topping

½-cup *Randy's Famous Homemade Key Lime Pie Juice* (shipped nationwide)

Mix condensed milk with dairy topping at medium speed until blended. Add *Randy's Famous Homemade Key Lime Juice* to mixture. Blend well. Pour into graham cracker piecrust. Refrigerate 3 hours before serving. Top with a dollop of whipped cream.

If you don't want to fool with doing a pie, Randy's pie, made by his "pie guy" and friend of more than 30 years, Bo Barclay, is a bargain at $10!

Sour Orange Pie. A unique pie, similar to key lime pie, is sour orange pie. Buddy Taylor, of Taylor Grocery, Highway 29, Felda, Florida 33930, phone 863-675-0687, provided us a recipe. Taylor also produces sauces, seasonings and pickles under the Gator Hammock brand. Buddy was featured on Food Network: *"Food Finds: Foods of the Everglades."*

Sour Orange Pie (makes two pies)

Two nine-inch graham cracker pie shells

Two cans sweetened Condensed Milk

Two eight-ounce container of Cool Whip

One 12-ounce fresh sour orange juice, or if not available use 12-ounce can of frozen orange juice and one cup of key lime juice

One teaspoon orange extract

One eight-ounce softened cream cheese

Mix together until lumps are smooth. Pour into crumb crust and refrigerate. Freeze for best results. Pies can be frozen for two weeks, but any longer than that the ingredients break down and the crust gets mushy. Let thaw for 20 to 30 minutes before serving. (We like it frozen!)

Salad. One way to spare the carbohydrates in a sandwich bun is to have blackened grouper Caesar salad instead. Our vote for the best is Chrissy's (more later about the restaurant). For a salmon Caesar salad, with a light well-balanced dressing, you can't beat Sam Snead's Tavern, 2460 Vanderbilt Beach Road, Naples, Florida, and phone 239-592-9999.

Rankings

Blackened Grouper Sandwich. To hit a top score, the blackened grouper needs to be good-sized (6-8 ounces), to fit or exceed the bun, spicy outside and moist fresh fish inside. It's best if thick (3/8-inch). The bun should be toasted slightly on the grill, so it doesn't become soggy.

Atmosphere. A unique décor adds to special ambience but nothing beats waterfront on a beautiful, balmy day, so we've listed the best grouper sandwiches at landlocked restaurants and the best at waterside.

Service. Smiling, attentive, friendly with good timing. Lively.

The Landlocked Restaurants: Best Grouper Sandwiches

Our top three: Randy's, Chrissy's and Rode's.

Randy's Fish Market Restaurant. 10395 Tamiami Trail N.(U.S. 41 N) Naples, Florida 34108, phone 239-593-5555. Randy Essig, who has owned other restaurants, opened this one in 2003. Thick, fresh grouper fillets for the sandwiches come from his on-site fish market. What turned out to be a delectable filet came perched atop a ciabatta bun supplied by La Maison du Pain. We asked for potato salad rather than French fries and were pleasantly surprised with a large scoop of homemade potato salad, made with redskins just as we like it, and light mayonnaise. Randy's offers choice of toppings, but typically sandwiches come with tomato and lettuce, along with a dish of coleslaw and a pickle. Their homemade key lime pie rates among the best as we mentioned. Service was outstanding. Glass display cases, filled with catches of the day, front into the restaurant. The galvanized steel-topped tables, island-style artwork, high ceiling with open rafters with a couple dozen of woven baskets hanging from them and faux flamingos nesting on them, along with whimsical colorful faux fish and shorebirds on walls and dividers, combine to give the place a relaxed and funky look. Each table has a hook for women's purses. For soup, try

Randy's seafood gumbo, which is packed with seafood, tomatoes, bell peppers, rice and Cajun spices.

Chrissy's Wildside Café. 5026 Airport Pulling Road, Naples, Florida 34105, phone 239-649-0059. Chrissy's is a cut above the ubiquitous strip mall restaurants. It's wedged in next to retail stores in the carillon center, and not a "seafood restaurant," but you'll be hard-pressed to find a better blackened-grouper sandwich. Stuffed zebras, monkeys and other animals rest on the dividers in the restaurant and African artwork adorns the walls to give the eccentric décor a "Wildside" look. Chrissy Bianchi has had a restaurant in Naples since 1989. She's a hands-on visible owner, which translates to consistency. We also like Chrissy's blackened grouper Caesar salad; with a generous nearly half-pound grouper steak perched atop the Caesar salad. A blackened grouper sandwich with stir-fry vegetables (instead of potato) was a healthy treat. Yes, you can also cut the carbs by skipping the bun!

Rode's. 3756 Bonita Beach Road, Bonita Springs, Florida 34134, phone 239-992-4040 or 1-800-786-0450. Rode's houses a bar, restaurant, fish market and fruit/vegetable market in a building that has been expanded a couple of times. High ceilings, exposed beams, ceiling fans and faux palm trees provide the décor in a restaurant crowded during the season. Rode's "Famous Grouper Sandwich," a 7-ounce grouper impeccably fresh filet steak, cooked to perfection comes with tomato, lettuce, coleslaw and fresh fruit with a choice of French fries, potato or rice and beans. We opt for the healthier rice and beans. Rode's offers their homemade key lime pie, not only in the restaurant, but "shipped next day anywhere in the Continental U.S.A."

Gulfcoast Grouper and Chips. 338 Ninth Street North (Tamiami Trail), Naples, Florida 34102, phone 239-643-4577. Calling this small café cozy is like calling a phone booth small. Inside this cramped strip-mall restaurant are just eight tables with six of them seating two patrons! The small size, and perky waitresses, guarantee fast service. After all, the waitress has only a few steps to go from the kitchen! The kitschy décor includes black and white photos of Elvis, Humphrey and Marilyn, celebrities from the past easily identifiable by one name. Their blackened grouper sandwich comes, with pickle, tomato slice, lettuce, Cole slaw, in a plastic basket. The waitress refilled our ice tea glasses frequently and looked as though she genuinely liked what she was doing. What a difference that makes!

Buffalo Chips. 26620 Old 41 Road, Bonita Springs, Florida 34135, phone 239-947-1000. Although perhaps more famous for chicken wings ("Bonita's best chicken wings"), this funky restaurant also features a grouper sandwich. On January 26, 2003 they claim to have set a one-day record of selling 16,482 chicken wings. If you have a hankering for sizzling hot chicken wings, you've come to the right place! This easy-on-the-purse casual restaurant, with its eccentric décor, makes you wonder if you should have stopped in. The grouper sandwich will tell you that stopping in was a good idea. Buffalo Chips specialty grouper sandwich is lightly breaded and fried. If you like it fried, then Buffalo Chips rates high with a generous-size sandwich. Have a beer in the frosted Mason jar mug.

Paradise By-the-Water......and Also Great Grouper Sandwiches

Are you also fond of dining outside by the water? If so, choices abound for doing this in Florida and, no surprise; the grouper sandwiches often are the specialty. Getting to some of these places is more than half the fun. Further, there's something about the fresh, salty air, balmy breezes and watching the boats and dolphins that makes food taste better. For that reason, restaurants on the water probably have margin for error. We have included only those we enjoyed.

Matanzas Inn and Restaurant. 416 Crescent Street, Fort Myers Beach, Florida 33931, phone 239-463-9258, www.matanzasrestaurant.com. We enjoy a visit for lunch or dinner at this waterfront restaurant on Estero Bay. The deck overlooks Matanzas Pass and the high span bridge built in 1979 to connect Ft. Myers Beach and the mainland. The first bridge built in 1921 was destroyed by the devastating 1926 hurricane. Dining on the deck, we not only watched the boat traffic, but some bottlenose dolphins frolicking nearby along with egrets and pelicans. "Pete", a pet white egret, strolled around the deck. The waiters and waitresses wear white shirts with epaulettes, to strike a nautical look. The dock master, who has a busy job directing boats into a place on the dock, wears not only the epaulettes, but also a jaunty sailor's cap. We sat so close to the edge of the deck that if we had been any closer we would need a life preserver. The six-ounce grouper steak comes on an egg hamburger bun with tomato, lettuce and fries. Coleslaw is an alternative to fries. Rode's, Randy's and others include the coleslaw and add a piece of fruit.

If you go for dinner, try our dinner favorite there, delectable stuffed grouper (seafood stuffing and provolone cheese). It will fulfill its visual promise. Key West-style conch fritters are good. Rather than ask if you want dessert, the wait staff ask, "would you like a piece of Key Lime Pie?" It's worth saying yes.

Did you know? As late as 1948, the entire island north of the bridge (approximately 110 acres) was purchased for only $125,000.

Snook Inn, 1215 Bald Eagle Drive, Marco Island, Florida 34145, phone 239-394-3313. This all-out casual waterfront restaurant, built on shells from a former clam factory, overlooks the Marco River. It has a spacious deck and patio area. Great views. We sat outside under a chickee hut, and enjoyed blackened grouper sandwiches in a relaxed atmosphere. The reasonable ten-dollar price includes the salad bar. The Snook Inn cuts three grouper steaks per pound for sandwiches. Service was prompt and attentive without being obtrusive, so we could relax and enjoy the view.

The Waterfront Restaurant. 2131 Oleander Street. St. James City, Florida 33966, phone 239-283-0592. The Waterfront Restaurant on Pine Island has a unique ambience in a nearly century old building on the water at an ancient site full of history of the Calusa Indians, Seminole Indian Wars, Ponce de Leon, and Civil War blockade runners. Teddy Roosevelt fished the area, hauling in the world record for a manta ray (13 feet). The restaurant, in a former schoolhouse, moved to the present site in the 1940s. Ah, what about their grouper sandwich? It's a half-pound of fresh local fish! In addition to blackened, they offer fried, broiled, Jamaican jerk, bronzed, sautéed, and teriyaki-garlic. Even on a hot summer day, we chose to sit outside and watch the boat traffic. The busy waitress kept our tea glasses full, and brought the sandwiches in baskets. They serve the sandwich with tomato, lettuce and French fries.

Whale Harbor Inn and Marina. 83.5 Oceanside, Islamorada, Florida 33036, phone 305-664-4959. A faux shell encrusted lighthouse beckons you to Whale Harbor. As mentioned in Chapter Thirteen, we sat at the back on a second-floor deck looking out at the ocean; watching birds soaring and heavy fishing boat "traffic". The balmy sea breeze cooled the warm humid air. Great lunch of conch fritters and blackened dolphin, expertly cooked with Caesar salad. Nice sea breeze. Islamorada, called the sport fishing capital of the world, has year-round fishing that attracts fisherman who try to outsmart the fish: sailfish, snapper, barracuda, grouper, marlin; and in shallow water tarpon, bonefish, and redfish.

The Crab House. 1065 North A1A, Jupiter, Florida, phone 561-744-1300. The Manatee Queen tour boat operates from docks at the restaurant into the most treacherous inlet on the Eastern Seaboard. Sipping ice tea, watching the boat traffic on the river and then looking at the Jupiter Lighthouse towering from a mound across the river, we relaxed on the spacious outside deck of The Crab House. We watched the water change color. Why is part of the water blue and relatively clear and part brown? The tide coming into the estuary causes the phenomenon. We watched boats bobbing in the Loxahatchee River with three-dozen Pelicans pushing for the best perch on a nearby pier.

Next door to the restaurant is the Square Grouper Bar, a tropical-themed Tiki bar with a bar made of material from Perry Como's house when it was renovated. The friendly waitress kept our tea glasses full, and brought us a spicy grouper sandwich and a Cajun tilapia sandwich. We never felt rushed but she appeared at opportune moments to fill the ice tea glass. As befits its name, The Crab House prides itself on succulent lump crab cakes with roasted red potato. Their key lime pie is sweet, tart and light. Unlike most of the restaurants in this chapter, The Crab House is part of a chain with half a dozen restaurants in Florida.

Conch Republic Seafood Company. 631 Greene Street, Key West, Florida 33040, phone 305-294-4403. Sitting outside you can take in the scene of boat traffic and moored yachts. Blackened grouper or dolphin sandwiches are excellent. So are the conch fritters.

Nav-A-Gator Grille, 9700 SW Riverview, Arcadia, FL 34269, phone 1-800-308-7506 or 941-627-3474, www.Nav-A-Gator.com. The Nav-A-Gator Grille (their creative spelling) is an off-the-beaten-path old Florida fish camp restaurant near the De Soto Marina. "Come by boat, or seaplane."

To get there, take exit 170 from I-75, east 3 miles on Kings Highway to the Nav-A-Gator sign and turn right. Go to the end of the road, 1.5 miles, at the Peace River. The outside looks like a fish camp or an old-time hideaway. Don't be alarmed because inside we found friendly staff, willing to please, and an eclectic décor, which includes model airplanes, fishnets, and lots of photos, stuffed animals and fish. One fellow at the bar had a T-shirt emblazoned with his poetic philosophy: *"No longer lean, no longer mean, still a marine."*

In addition to the super grouper sandwich, for which they are at least locally famous, they also offer the usual dinner fare along with gator bites, conch fritters, and swamp cabbage (called by Northerners, heart of palm). The outside doesn't look any better from the back on the Peace River side, but the food is good. As they say, "Y'all come on down." As we sat by a window, drinking ice tea, we could look out at the reproduction of an early pioneer settlement with trading post, arts and crafts and Indian artifacts. A museum of Peace River fossils, canoe, boat and kayak rentals, and vacation rental cottages are also on the property. They conduct Peace River tours on their 44-passenger boat. When dinner arrived, the waitress slid plates in front of us, with huge grouper filets in sub-sandwich size buns. Super grouper, indeed! Although the blackened spices contained a little more salt than to our taste, the sandwiches were delicious.

Lee's Crab Trap II. 4815 17th St. E., Ellenton, Florida 34222, phone 941-729-7777. (Exit 224 on I-75.) We stopped in for lunch on one of our trips, not knowing what to expect. Perched alongside the water, Lee's Crab Trap is a large, exposed wood-beam, wood columns restaurant with large windows overlooking the water and a décor of stuffed birds that are for sale. We had clam chowder and excellent grouper sandwiches. Lee's also has Crab Trap I at Palmetto, Florida.

Chapter Eighteen
55 Cost and Time Saving Tips

Before reviewing the cost and time saving tips, let's sharpen focus and mental alertness with the following puzzle called **Florida Had It:**

> Luke had it before.
> Paul had it behind.
> Matthew never had it at all.
> All girls have it once;
> Boys cannot have it.
> Old Mr. Mulligan had it,
> twice in succession.
> Dr. Lowell had it once before
> and behind; he had it twice as
> bad behind as before.

So what is *it*? *See at end of chapter for answer.

Remember that little steps lead to big savings.

1. Save as much as $400, or more, on your property tax by obtaining Homestead Exemption, which also caps your property assessments and protects your property against creditors. The two features of cap on property assessments and property protection against creditors have huge potential value. Burt Reynolds, for example, declared bankruptcy in 1996 citing $8 million in debts, yet he kept his $2.5 million home.

257

2. Save thousands of dollars by avoiding a 50 percent IRS penalty at age 70-1/2 by withdrawing properly from your IRA. Check with your tax adviser.

3. Deduct your moving expenses from your taxes and save hundreds, or thousands of tax dollars (if you qualify). As an employee, your new job location must be more than 50 miles farther from your old home, and you must work 39 weeks during the 52 weeks following the residence change. If you are self-employed, you'll need 78 weeks full-time in the two years after the move. If your employer reimbursed you for your moving expenses, you don't have a tax deduction (unless actual costs exceeded the reimbursement). As with item two, you should review with your tax adviser.

4. Residents sometimes forget to pick up the tourist travel guides, which contain coupons that save money. They work for residents, too.

5. Buy an Entertainment Book. Savings of 2 for 1 cut dinner costs in half although most restaurants don't accept the coupons January 15-April 15. Tip on what the full amount would have been.

6. Being a Florida resident saves money in many ways. If you own more than one house and spend the winter in Florida, then you need to carefully review your official residency while you enjoy the cool summer up North. Check out Chapter Three again, especially about decoupling northern state estate and income taxes. You need to be a Florida resident to do so.

7. Before visiting a Florida location or attraction, check out the web sites in this book for valuable discount coupons that will save you money on admission tickets.

8. If you're going to be gone long from home, unplug the water heater.

9. If you have an outside water shutoff valve, turn it off if you plan to be gone. If you have a valve at the street, turn it off. That will prevent your home being flooded from a water line break or other leak. You are liable for water from the main connection to the house, so if a leak occurs while you are away, you could end up with a huge water bill.

10. Unplug electrical and electronic devices, especially if you are away during the hurricane/lightning season. Florida Power & Light offers insurance on computer and appliances to protect against lightning and power surge problems. The

$2,000 coverage typically is the deductible on homeowner's insurance so is good "gap" protection for about $5 a month.

11. Before going to any park, preserve, refuge or attraction, check with them about designated times when admission prices are reduced.

12. Cool your home at 78 degrees, or warmer. For additional savings, raise the thermostat to 82 degrees as we do when we are away from home.

13. Although heat is not often used, set the thermostat on 68 degrees with the thermostat fan switch on "auto." Lower the thermostat at night or if away for more savings.

14. Install a programmable thermostat to adjust temperature automatically. Include a humidistat.

15. Clean or replace your air conditioner's filter every month. This not only saves cooling costs, but also helps your unit run more efficiently.

16. Turn off ceiling fans when you leave the room. Ceiling fans don't cool the room; they cool people in the room. A fan that runs constantly costs approximately $7 a month!

17. Avoid pre-rinsing dishes before putting in dishwasher. This can save up to $70 a year. Fill both cups with detergent.

18. Limit the time you run your pool pump. We cut our run time to six hours; and turned the heater off in summer. In winter, we adjust the time for heater to maintain water temperature.

19. If you have a swimming pool, use a "solar blanket." It extends the pool season, cuts nighttime heat loss, cuts evaporation and chemical loss and increases water temperature. A good one with a warranty costs only $100 or so; good investment.

20. Adjust the water level on your washing machine to match the load size, especially when using hot water. Use a cold water rinse.

21. Clean the lint filter in your dryer before every load to dry your clothes faster and save money. Clean the filter exhaust stack. A plugged stack, adds cost by lengthening dryer operation; and it could be a fire hazard.

22. Use the auto sensor function on your dryer, if you have one, to conserve energy by not over-drying your clothes.

23. In addition to looking for dining out coupons in newspapers and pamphlets, check out web site restaurant locations for coupons you can print out that will save you money; including two for one dinner offers.

24. Consider buying a home sooner rather than later. If homes continue to increase in value at six percent a year, a $200,000 home will cost $400,000 in less than 10 years. If you pay 20 percent down on a $200,000 home (or $40,000), the appreciation at six percent a year can double your down payment in just over three years. Yes, it can go down, too.

25. Consider buying a non-golf community home. You'll not only get more home value but lower fees.

26. Rent before buying a boat.

27. Rent for a while, to get a full appreciation for the area, before buying a home.

28. Buy your home in the off-season; May-September.

29. Know which upgrades on a new home purchase you can have done later for less money.

30. Buying a "spec" home, or "inventory" home will usually save you money, if you can accept less customizing.

31. Check on whether a developer will offer a discount for payment of cash. Some developers will discount one or two percent.

32. Buying a home not in a flood zone will save $2,000 or more in annual insurance.

33. Add an extra garage when your home is built to save on future outside storage cost.

34. In buying a new home, make sure you have enough outlets for ceiling fans, TV cable, phones, and electrical. Go overboard, because these can cost more if done later. Don't overlook outlets and hose bibs on the lanai.

35. Unplug electrical and electronic devices while you are away to avoid lightning damage.

36. Don't buy a new car in another state within six months of relocating to Florida unless the sales tax is the same (six percent). If the sales tax is less in the state where you bought the car, you will owe the difference in Florida if the car is less than six months old.

37. Review your assets in terms of Florida's Intangible Tax. Shift some to tax exempt assets.

38. Use a pest control service to protect against termites and bad bugs.

39. If it seems too good to be true, it probably is, as the saying goes. Protect yourself against scams (examples in Chapter Six). Ask questions and listen!

40. Use mulch.

41. Make your lawn more Florida friendly, which will save you money. See Chapter Seven.

42. Take a trolley tour to gain familiarity with a city. You'll save time and money by doing so.

43. Check out the Internet for lower-cost tickets in advance (for example, www.htatickets.com).

44. Go during the off-season to Key West (and other Florida locations and attractions).

45. Obtain the Florida resident discount for tickets to Disney World and other attractions.

46. Get your mortgage pre-approved then shop for a home.

47. The off-season means empty rooms at motels and hotels. We have saved by calling the motel directly (rather than the national 800 number) and mentioning we lived in Florida.

48. Don't forget to ask for your discount on motels/hotels for AARP and AAA.

49. If you bought, or sold a house, you are entitled to deduct your share of pro-rated property taxes (see your closing statement).

50. When you prepare your taxes, don't overlook the tax deduction for loan fees ("points") if you purchased a home. The loan fee qualifies as an itemized interest deduction in the year of the home purchase.

51. Moving time is a great time to de-clutter. Remember, Florida homes don't have basements. Sell your extra stuff through classified ads, garage sale, at a consignment store or online.

52. It pays to die in Florida. You may not care, but your heirs will. For example, if you have a $1.5 million estate, and have a Wisconsin residency (where we once lived), your estate would owe more than $60,000! If you were a Florida resident, no state estate tax would be due; a savings of more than $60,000. Where is your residency?

53. Check to see if your county issues free beach parking permits. These save you parking fees when going to the beach.

54. If you, or your children, plan to go to college, residency can save you $10,000 in tuition at state universities (versus non-resident tuition).

55. If you don't have one, install a rain sensor on your sprinkler system, which will save water.

*Letter "L"

Chapter Nineteen
Your List of 99 Things to Do

If you're one of the people who have read this book all the way through to this final chapter, congratulations. You are certain to save thousands of dollars. You can also enhance your first five years in Florida, by developing your list of things to do, places to see, and dollars to save, based on what you have read in this book and your personal desires.

Top 33.

First, your assignment—should you choose to accept—is to list everything you would like to do from reading this book, in the next five years, whether it's saving money, buying a home, joining a club, visiting a lighthouse or a park, golfing, boating or whatever! What do you want to do? Have? Learn? Check out Chapter Eighteen for a review of cost and time savers. Which of the beaches, 157 state parks, 35 historic places, 30 lighthouses, 10 forts, 36 state forests or three national parks will you select? How many can be combined with a trip that accomplishes other goals? Why list 33 to start? We have found that a shorter list and step-at-a-time actions make for a doable way to proceed. Review all our top three picks to help you do your list.

Second, put the list in priority order. You'll find the easy way to do this is to pick the top three first, as we have throughout this book. Next do the rest of the top 10. As you move down the list, priority slotting the items becomes tougher.

Third, put a time goal on each one. A goal not quantified with a date or an amount simply remains a dream.

Fourth, after doing the first 33, start on another list of 33, then a final list of 33. Repeat the process for each group of 33. As you accomplish one of the goals, and find you'd like to do it again, then start a new list of

263

places to re-visit. Visits will also surface other things you'll find to add to a list. It's easy to do. It works!

So, let's get started. Here's an example: *stroll the boardwalk at Corkscrew Swamp Sanctuary.* Here's another one: *Buy new home in Florida in June through September and save thousands of dollars. Join an aerobics class. Buy a boat.* You may want to add entertainment venues that we did not describe in the book, such as Disney World, Busch Gardens, Sea World, or your local orchestra or sports teams. *Join a Church. Take in a spring training baseball game. Go see the Dolphins play (the bottlenose ones in the Gulf and the football ones in Miami).*

Develop a budget (Quicken® provides an easy way to do this. Use the ideas in Chapter Four so you have enough money to do the things you want to do and don't run out!)

If you still work and are in business, *The Power of Focus* by Jack Canfield, Mark Hansen and Les Hewitt provides a comprehensive way to implement strategies for improvement. The book inspired our ideas of Top Threes for living in Florida.

Description	Date to Do By	Comments
1.		
2.		
3.		
4.		
5.		
6.		
7.		
8.		
9.		
10.		

Resource Guide

The following recommended books offer specific information on topics in this book and will enhance your understanding of Florida. All of the references previously mentioned in the book are included. (*See asterisks*)

Recommended Reading.

America's Atlantic Coast Lighthouses: A Traveler's Guide. Kenneth G. Kochel. Kenneth Kochel Publishing. Clearwater, FL. 1998

America's Lighthouses: An Illustrated History by Francis Ross Holland. Dover Publications. 1988 (1972) 226pp. Written by historian Holland (of National Park Service), this carefully researched book provides a full-scale history of America's lighthouses. 100 photos.

Bansemer's Book of Florida Lighthouses by Roger Bansemer. Pineapple Pres, Inc., Sarasota, FL. 1999 $29.95 144pp. This book has more than 200 paintings and sketches along with informative text, all by the author. He visited each of the thirty Florida lighthouses

Choose Florida for Retirement. James F. Gollahscheck. The Globe Pequot Press. Old Saybrook, CT. 1999

*Condominium. John D. MacDonald. A Fawcett Crest Book. N.Y. 1977. Mix sloppy building construction, condominium rules and regulations, a hurricane, characters and crisp writing and you have a recipe for an interesting novel that at the same time provides insights into Florida living as valid today as when written.

Favorite Birds of Florida. Dick Schinkel and David Mohrhardt. Thunder Bay Press, Holt, MI. 1995. The book has a full page of text and a full-page color illustration of each of 125 bird species.

*50 Fabulous Places to Retire in America by Lee Rosenberg and Saralee H. Rosenberg. Career Press, Hawthourne, N.J. 1991. Of their top 50, nine are in Florida!

*"Flashback" by Nevada Barr. G.P. Putnam & Sons. New York. 2003. 387pp. $24.95. *Flashback* is Barr's eleventh Anna Pigeon mystery, all set in National Parks. Barr has been a park ranger. Anna, in *Flashback*, is a temporary supervisory ranger on Garden Key in the Dry Tortugas National Park. Although fiction, Barr provides some fascinating descriptions of both life today in the fort and life in the fort more than 130 years ago.

Florida by Chelle Koster Walton. Compass American Guides, 1745 Broadway, New York, N.Y. 10019. 2003 (Second Edition). 340 pp. With some beautiful photography by Ton Arruza, this book provides a dazzling picture of Florida, including a brief history and well-written descriptions of all the regions, with their attractions. Excellent overview guidebook

Florida's Fabulous Flowers by Winston Williams. World Publishing, Tampa, FL 33623. 1999. Fabulous color photographs.

Florida's Fabulous Trees by Winston Williams. World Publishing, Tampa, Fl 33623. 2000. Fabulous color photographs.

Florida's Hurricane History by Jay Barnes. The University of North Carolina Press, Chapel Hill, N.C. 1998

Florida Hurricanes and Tropical Storms, 1871-2001, by John M. Williams and Iver W. Duedall. University Press of Florida, Gainesville, Fl. 2002

*Florida Landscape Plants by professor John V. Watkins and Thomas Sheehan. The University Presses of Florida. Gainesville, Florida 32611. 1986

*Florida Lighthouse Trail by Thomas Taylor (editor, Florida Lighthouse Association). Pineapple Press, Sarasota, Florida. 2001. 191pp $12.95. Top-notch descriptions of all of Florida's lighthouses and how to get to them.

A Gardener's Guide to Florida's Native Plants by Rufino Osorio. University Press of Florida. Gainesville, Florida 32611. 2001.

Ghosts of St. Augustine by David Lapham (illustrations, Tom Lapham). Pineapple Press, Inc. Sarasota, Florida. 1998. $8.95.This 168-page book includes 24 ghost stories of St. Augustine.

Guide to Florida Lighthouses by Elinor De Wire. Pineapple Press, Inc. Sarasota, Florida. 1987. 96pp. This slim, but beautiful book, briefly traces the story of each of the lighthouses, accompanied by photographs of most of the lighthouses; some in color. The cover shows the restored Boca Grande Lighthouse.

Guide to the Great Florida Birding Trail. Edited by Julie A. Brashears and Susan Cerulean. Illustrations by Nancy Meyer. The University Press of Florida. Gainesville, Florida 32611. 188pp. 2002

Irresistible Overnights. A Guide to the 203 Most Delightfully Different Places to Stay in Florida by Bob Rafferty and Loys Reynolds. Rutledge Hill Press, Nashville, TN 37214. 2000. 287 pp. The husband-wife team selected their personal favorite 203 hotels, motels and inns from more than five thousand in Florida. They list the particulars of each inn in eight vacation regions in Florida, which makes it easy to select a spot in the region you are visiting.

Key West Conch Smiles: A Native's Collection of Legends, Stories, Memories by Jeane Porter. Mancorp Publishing. 1998. 344pp $20. Packed with family vignettes of raunchy pirates, politicians, eloquent poets, fan dancers and film stars. On sale at the Heritage House Museum. Breezily written with dashes of humor makes this a readable book.

Last Train to Paradise by Les Standiford. Crown Publishers. New York. 2002. 272 pp. $24.00. This is not only a gripping true account of an engineering marvel, Henry Flagler's Florida East Coast Railway, but a tribute to a remarkable visionary, leader and businessman who did the "impossible."

"Lighthouses of the Dry Tortugas" by Neil E. Hurley. Historic Lighthouse Publishers, Aiea, Hawaii. 1994. Third printing 2002. 80pp $12,95 Hurley, a Coast Guard officer, carefully researched this illustrated history of the Dry Tortugas lighthouses. He has included many old photographs; along with drawings.

Motorist's Guide to Everglades National Park. Florida National Parks and Monuments Association, Inc., 10 Parachute Key #51, Homestead, Florida 33034. $3.95. Handy pamphlet briefly covers key points of interest with color photographs. Includes pages on Fort Jefferson at Dry Tortugas National Park.

Sibley Guide to Birds by David Allen Sibley. Alfred A. Knoft, New York. 2000. $35 Sibley not only wrote the book but also did the illustrations.

Sibley Guide to Birds of Eastern North America. Alfred A. Knoft, New York. 2003. $19.95. 432 pp.

Taylor's Guide to Orchids by Judy White. Houghton Miflin Co. 1996. This book has more than 300 stunning photos of orchids.

The Florida Keys, Volume 3, The Wreckers, by John Viele. Pineapple Press, Inc. Sarasota, FL 2001.

The New History of Florida by Michael Gannon. University Press of Florida, Gainesville, FL. 1996.

The Orchid Thief by Susan Orlean. Ballantine Books, New York. 1998. Interesting insights and history in the Fakahatchee Strand.

The Power of Focus by Jack Canfield, Mark Victor Hansen and Les Hewitt. Deerfield Beach, Florida: Health Communications, Inc., 2000. Provides the idea for making lists and setting priorities. "Your ability to focus will determine your future."

What Every Homeowner Needs to Know About Mold by Vicki Lankarge. McGraw-Hill, New York. 2003. This slim (134 pages) book does a good job in telling what you should know about household mold and what you can do about it.

Wild Orchids of Florida by Paul Martin Brown. University Presss of Florida, Gainesville, FL. 2002. Florida orchid fanciers say this book, with drawings by Stan Folsom, is the best reference guide on orchids. The author thoroughly covers the 118 species and varieties of Florida orchids.

Yankee's Guide to Florida Gardening by Hank and Marlene Bruce. Winner Enterprises. 1995

Index

About the Author

Stan Farnham has been a U.S. Forest Service fire fighter, a U.S. Army paratroop officer, a technical writer, a company CEO, president of condominium associations and president of two national associations. This is his second book.

He led five manufacturing companies, as a turnaround CEO, from dire straits to profitability during the 1990s. Stan and wife Mary moved to Florida after he completed his fifth successful turnaround.

A graduate of Drake University, Stan and Mary have six grown children. She participated in the adventures described in the book. She

also has been active in homeowner associations, and conducts a water aerobics class three days a week.

To get in touch with the author, visit the web site http:// soyouwanttomovetoflorida. com.